Assassinations Anthology

Assassinations Anthology

Plots and Murders That Would Have Changed
the Course of WW2

Edited and Introduced by
John Grehan

Frontline Books

ASSASSINATIONS ANTHOLOGY
Plots and Murders That Would Have Changed the Course of WW2

First published in 2017 by Frontline Books,
an imprint of Pen & Sword Books Ltd,
47 Church Street, Barnsley, S. Yorkshire, S70 2AS.

ISBN: 978-1-84832-697-2

For more information on our books, please visit
www.frontline-books.com
email info@frontline-books.com
or write to us at the above address.

Printed and bound by CPI Group (UK) Ltd, Croydon, CR0 4YY
Typeset in 10.5/12.5 point Palatino

Contents

Introduction

Political assassination as a means of regime change, long pre-dates the likes of Caesar and Cassius and Hamlet and Polonius. Indeed, the fact that Shakespeare could present such scenes to a largely illiterate audience demonstrates that the planned murder of rivals for personal or political reasons was a perfectly understandable method of effecting change. It has often been the case that under dictatorial regimes, which have generally been the norm throughout history, assassination was the only course of action available to the oppressed populace.

The instability and economic decline across Europe following the First World War (which itself had been triggered by the assassination of Archduke Ferdinand), ushered in a period of intense political assassination – in Germany alone, by 1923, there were more than 370 political assassinations. This, consequentially, led to the emergence of powerful leaders who were prepared to eliminate all opposition as a means of restoring order. Such opposition as remained could not therefore use legal means of achieving its aims, for there was none available. This left opponents of the regime with only one means by which they could effect change – assassination.

It is hardly surprising, then, that Adolf Hitler was the subject of numerous assassination attempts throughout the 1920s, 30s and 40s. Many of these came remarkably close to success, and often the Führer survived by a matter of minutes or millimetres. The infamous 'Valkyrie' assassination attempt on him on 20 July 1944 failed simply because von Stauffenberg's briefcase containing the explosives was moved just a few inches away from where it had been placed, to behind one of the stout wooden supports of the conference table, resulting in the blast being deflected away from Hitler.

It was a very close call, and has led to endless speculation about what might have happened if that briefcase had been left untouched or moved to another side. Had that or any other of the other attempts on Hitler's life succeeded, then the history of the twentieth century might have taken an entirely different course.

The question that has been asked many times is, if Hitler had died at any stage in the Second World War, would Germany have immediately sued for peace, or would the generals have taken over and fought a far more militarily-practical war than the obdurate Führer?

Equally intriguing is the possible failed assassination attempt on General de Gaulle on British soil. Who, one wonders, was behind that scheme, and how would Anglo-French relations have developed if he had been killed? Had the aircraft he was to fly on set off just a few minutes earlier it would have crashed to the ground.

Would the troubled region of the Balkan's have known a more settled future if the German plan to eliminate Josip Tito had succeeded in 1944? Would the Allies have had to invade Japan if the revolt by officers had prevented Emperor Hirohito from surrendering in August 1945?

The number of considered or actual assassination attempts during the war might be surprising to many. This includes one suspicious incident which has not found its way into this anthology. In November 1943, President Roosevelt was sailing to North Africa to attend the Cairo and Tehran conferences on the battleship USS *Iowa*, with a strong US Navy escort. On the 14th of the month, the *Iowa* demonstrated its anti-aircraft capability whilst the escorting destroyers simulated a torpedo attack on the battleship. Somehow, something went wrong and the destroyer *William D. Porter* actually launched an armed torpedo at *Iowa*. Because the escorts had been told to maintain radio silence for fear of alerting German submarines, they attempted to communicate the impending disaster by signal lamp.

In the ensuing panic, *William D. Porter* sent an incorrect message, adding further to the rapidly-mounting anxiety aboard the destroyer. With visions of being responsible for killing the President, the captain of *William D. Porter* broke radio silence. Upon hearing that a torpedo was heading towards *Iowa*, Roosevelt asked to be pushed out in his wheelchair onto the deck to watch the approaching missile.

Iowa immediately took avoiding action and the torpedo exploded in the battleship's wake some 3,000 yards astern of the battleship. It is said that the crew of *Iowa*, believing that an assassination attempt had been made upon the President, trained its 16-inch guns on the destroyer, until it was accepted that the incident, which lasted for only four minutes, was a genuine mistake. While errors do indeed occur and the torpedo was almost certainly fired by mistake, there remains an element of doubt – because a torpedo cannot be *armed* by accident.

In *Assassination Anthology* a number of well-known authors and historians have looked at past events where key individuals were involved in either attempts on their lives, or strange incidents occurred which, had they led to their deaths, might have radically affected the outcome of the war.

The possible consequences for the world had Stalin and Jan Smuts been murdered are investigated, as are the assassination attempts on Gandhi and Mussolini. Also investigated are the peculiar circumstances relating to the theft of a valuable Gainsborough painting in 1940. Just how great a role did the Government's Chief Whip, David Margesson, play in persuading British MPs to accept the unpopular Winston Churchill as Prime Minister, and what would have happened if Margesson had been killed when the Gainsborough disappeared? Equally intriguing is how the war in the Pacific would have developed if the Japanese puppet, President Garcia of the Philippines, had died when he was shot whilst playing golf? It is fascinating stuff.

Grounded in actual events, the various scenarios portrayed in this collection, examine the likely chain of events that would have followed if the assassination attempts had succeeded. A few inches, a few moments – that was all the difference between life and death, and between the past that we know and one that we can only imagine.

John Grehan,
Storrington, West Sussex,
January 2017.

The Contributors

ADRIAN GILBERT has written extensively on military history in the twentieth century. His books include the award-winning *Imperial War Museum Book of the Desert War*; *Germany's Lightning War*; *POW: Allied Prisoners of War 1939-1945*; and *Challenge of Battle: the Real Story of the British Army in 1914*. Adrian's special interests include the First World War, the development of sniping, and alternative military histories, the latter leading to the publication of *Britain Invaded*, a fictional account of the German conquest of Britain in 1940 based on actual archival sources.

JOHN GREHAN has written, edited or contributed more than 300 books and magazine articles covering a wide span of military history from the Iron Age to the wars of the twentieth century. John has also appeared on local and national radio and television to advise on military history topics. He was employed as the Assistant Editor of *Britain at War Magazine* from its inception until 2014. John now devotes his time to writing and editing books.

JAMES LUTO has been researching the war in the Far East for nearly thirty years. His interest in this theatre was inspired by his grandfather, a veteran of the Fourteenth Army. As well as having compiled *Fighting with the Fourteenth Army in Burma*, James has also penned numerous magazine articles relating to the events of the Second World War. James, who lives in West Sussex, is also an avid collector of artefacts and memorabilia relating to the fighting in the Far East.

MARTIN MACE has been involved in writing and publishing military history for more than twenty-five years. He began his career with local history, writing a book on the Second World War anti-invasion defences and stop lines in West Sussex. In 2006 he began working on the idea for *Britain at War Magazine*, the first issue of which went on sale in May 2007. Martin continues to be involved in the publishing of military history.

DAN MILLS served for twenty-four years in the British Army, reaching the rank of Warrant Officer Class 2. During his long military career he served on operations in Northern Ireland, Bosnia, Kosovo, Iraq and Afghanistan, receiving a Mention in Despatches for his actions during the Iraq War. Since leaving the Army in 2010, he has forged a career as a writer and security consultant. His first book was the best-seller, *Sniper One*.

ROBERT MITCHELL has been involved in military history for many years. He has written for numerous magazines and is a regular reviewer of military history publications.

ALEXANDER NICOLL is a frequent contributor to military history publications such as *Britain at War Magazine*, his particular interest being the events of the First and Second world wars.

ANDY SAUNDERS is a military historian, author and researcher specializing in military aviation history with particular emphasis on the Battle of Britain and the air war over north-West Europe in the Second World War. The author of numerous books and titles on such subjects, Andy is currently the editor of *Britain at War Magazine*, the UK's best-selling military history monthly.

PETER TSOURAS was an analyst at the U.S. Army's Intelligence and Threat Centre in Washington DC, specialising in twentieth-century European history and its interpretation. A respected and renowned military historian, Peter is the author of such publications as *The Great Patriotic War, Disaster at D-Day, Hitler Victorious, Gettysburg: An Alternate History, Third Reich Victorious, Cold War Hot* and *Disaster at Stalingrad*.

NIGEL WEST is an intelligence expert and critically-acclaimed author. Such is his depth of knowledge in these fields that *The Sunday Times* noted that, 'His information is often so precise that many people believe he is the unofficial historian of the secret services. His books are peppered with deliberate clues to potential front-page stories.' In 1989 Nigel was voted 'The Experts' Expert' by the *Observer*.

Chapter 1

Killing The Red Tsar
The Assassination of Joseph Stalin, 1937

By Peter G. Tsouras

It was late 1936. The NKVD[1] official sat back in his chair aghast, his eyes as big as saucers. I.L. Shtern was no ordinary member of the Soviet secret police. He was working on a mission directly from the General Secretary of the Communist Party of the Soviet Union, the GENSEC himself, Josef Stalin. Shtern's chief, the People's Commissar for Internal Affairs and head of the NKVD, Genrikh G. Yagoda, had given him the orders himself.

Stalin's special target had been for two years now the old Bolshevik elite that had carried the Party from revolution through civil war to the victory of the establishment of Soviet power. No one but Stalin must be left to claim the legacy of Lenin. Stalin had mentioned to Yagoda that evidence of collusion with the Tsar's secret police, the Okhrana, might be found to bring his enemies down. So it was that Shtern was looking through the old files of the Okhrana in the NKVD's main headquarters on Lubyanka Square in Moscow.

What Shtern had found had terrified him to the core of his being. And he had every reason to be terrified. The Great Terror was already unfolding in waves of arrest in 1936. Already hundreds of thousands had been arrested, half of them shot, and the rest sent to a short life in the camps of the growing concentration camp system, the GULAG[2]. Russia had not known such terror since the paranoid madness of Ivan the Terrible had nearly destroyed the Russian state. The sight of NKVD men with their telltale green collar tabs was enough to terrify anyone. He ought to know for he was one of them.

Now there it was in the files, the object of his fear, the name of Iosif V. Dzhugashvilli. That was Stalin's own Georgian name (Stalin was his revolutionary *nom de guerre*), and it was not there as an object of surveillance. He was a double agent for the Okhrana working to betray his own revolutionary colleagues. And his reports were there in his own handwriting with which Shtern was intimately familiar. '*Shto delo?*' ('What to do?') he asked himself. It was more than a profound question; it was a mortal question at a time when the least suspicion, or none at all, could lead to a sudden arrest, brutal torture, and a bullet in the back of the head in a white-tiled NKVD execution room. Such a fate would be ensured if he showed the papers to Yagoda.[3]

Instead Shtern took the paper to his old boss, Vsevolod A. Balitsky, the head of the NKVD in the Ukraine. In turn, Balitsky informed his deputy, Zinovy Katsnelson, who was also a member of the Central Committee of the CPSU. They subjected the papers to a rigorous examination, even calling in a handwriting expert. When they were satisfied, Balitsky sought out the Red Army's commander of the Ukraine Military District, in whom he had implicit trust.[4]

Army Commander 1st Rank, Iona Emmanuilovich Yakir, was one of the most distinguished heroes of the Civil War and three-time winner of the Order of the Red Banner.[5] Since 1925 he had transformed the foremost military district in the country into a test bed for the rapid and innovative development of the Red Army. For two years (1928-1929) he had studied at the German higher military academy and earned the praise of the German president and former field marshal, Paul von Hindenburg, as one of the most talented commanders of the post-war era. Returning to his military district, he was a moving force in the creation of the first large armoured and air force formations in the world, working closely to mould these formations to execute the concept of deep operations, the brainchild of the First Vice-Commissar of Defence, Marshal of the Soviet Union Mikhail Nikolayevich Tukhachevsky. He earned Stalin's spite for inviting Tukhachevsky to teach a special course on the theory of deep operations to senior officers. He did it despite knowing of Stalin's dislike of Tukhachevsky. In retaliation Stalin cut the Ukraine Military District into two to limit Yakir's power and excluded him from higher bodies to which his efforts had earned him a place.

By 1935 Tukhachevsky, hero of the Russian Civil War, was acknowledged as a combat commander of genius, an original theorist, and a superb organizer. Under his guidance, the Red Army blossomed into the most innovative armed force in the world and was promoted to the newly created rank of Marshal of the Soviet Union, one of only five. Thanks to Stalin's industrialization of the Soviet Union, tanks and aircraft of the latest designs and in huge numbers poured from the new factories to the Red Army. Its large armoured and air formations and its development of airborne forces were ongoing creative experiments on a scale that dwarfed the timid steps of the rest of the world's armies. At a time when the brilliant British military reformer, Major General J.F.C. Fuller, sold perhaps five hundred copies in the UK of his seminal work on the principles of war and mechanized operations, Tukhachevsky had it translated and a copy given to every one of the Red Army's several hundred thousand strong officer corps. Alas, for Fuller, the Soviet Union had not signed the international copyright convention. Tukhachevsky was doing what the theorists of modern war in the West, Fuller and Liddell Hart in Britain and De Gaulle in France, could only dream of. Only Heinz Guderian in Germany came close. After Hitler watched a panzer demonstration and exclaimed, 'That's what I want!' did Germany begin to pour the resources into building the modern, mechanized army that Tukhachevsky had already fashioned.[6]

Who was this remarkable man? This hero of the Red Army of Workers and Peasants, to it give its full title, had been a scion of the Russian Empire's hereditary nobility. The Tukhachevsky name appeared prominently in the Velvet Book of the Russian aristocracy. Even as a Marshal of the Soviet Union, he was proud to say that the ring on his finger had been worn by an ancestor who had fought Napoleon at Borodino in 1812.[7] After graduating from a military academy in 1914 at the age of twenty-one, he had joined the Semenovkiy Guards Regiment, the second most prestigious regiment in the imperial army. He was nothing but confident of his abilities and wrote. 'I am convinced that all that is needed in order to achieve what I want is bravery and self-confidence. I certainly have enough self-confidence … I told myself that I shall either be a general at thirty, or that I shall not be alive by then.'·As a young officer he idealized the military exploits of Napoleon.

Captured during the great retreat of 1915 in the First World War, he escaped four times from the Germans but was recaptured each time and finally sent to a camp for incorrigibles at Ingolstadt in Bavaria from which his fifth attempt was successful. He made his way back to Russia just in time for the 1917 Revolution, threw in his lot with the Reds, and never looked back. He became a committed communist, and his military talents were so evident that he rose like a star in the ranks of the Red Army, beating his prediction by becoming a general at the age of twenty-five when the founder of the Red Army, Leon Trotsky, gave him command of the defence of Moscow. By 1919 he was commanding an army and defeated the forces of the White Admiral Kolchak in Siberia. The next year he took the lead in defeating the White forces of General Denikin, and in 1921 he crushed the revolt of the sailors at Kronstadt who had had the audacity to demand that the Bolsheviks actually live up to their human rights and economic promises. The following year he crushed the Tambov Republic. In all this, he was 'as ruthless as any Bolshevik' resorting without hesitation to the shooting of hostages and using poison gas on the peasants of Tambov.[8]

Tukhachevsky's only defeat occurred during the Red Army's invasion of Poland in 1920. Despite that defeat, the Polish Marshal Pilsudski had the highest praise for him. 'Tukhachevsky inspired his subordinates by virtue of his energetic and purposeful work. This fine quality of leadership stamps him forever as a general with daring ideas and the gift of putting them into vigorous execution. ... Tukhachevsky handled his troops very skillfully, and anyone can easily discern the signs of a general of the first order in his daring but logically correct march on Warsaw.'[9]

That defeat was largely due to the insubordination of his commanders, and in Stalin's case, to outright sabotage. The future marshal had not held his tongue to say who was at fault. The two had already come into conflict in the fighting at Tsaritsyn on the Volga, the city that Stalin would later name for himself. The intervening years had done nothing to lessen the bad blood between the two, though outwardly they were on cordial terms.

Tukhachevsky had nevertheless stood aside, as good Party member, as Stalin cemented his power and began to kill on a level that no tsar, burdened with a religious conscious, would have dared to. The created famine, now known as the Holodomor (Murder by Hunger) of 1932-33 starved from seven to ten million Ukrainians to death. The German consul (Weimar Republic) in Kiev was reporting that the NKVD was periodically rounding up hordes of orphan children to shoot them in the woods and that people were dropping dead in the streets. A million Kazaks also died that winter, and the homeland of the Cossacks in the Kuban directly to the east of the Ukraine was so depopulated that one observer noted it would have to be recolonized.[10] Yes, in turning his back on this horror, Tukhachevsky was a good son of the Communist Party of the Soviet Union (CPSU). He was also a dead man.

Tukhachevsky's death warrant had already been determined by the GENSEC in 1936. Stalin hated, and when he hated, he feared, and when he feared, he killed. Tukhachevsky had disregarded the advice that

4

when you clash with a Georgian, such as Stalin, you either defeat or conciliate him. Otherwise he will nurse his grudge and see his opponent repaid with terrible interest. Georgians were famous for their patience in serving up stone cold revenge. At a dinner party Stalin attended in the 1920s, he was asked what gave him the most pleasure, and he had no hesitated to reply, 'Taking revenge upon my enemies'.[11]

Already in 1930 he had taken aim at Tukhachevsky, whose brilliance not only as a field commander but as an innovator was becoming more apparent. Yet Stalin's hold on power had not achieved enough traction to take him down. Too many of the Bolshevik old guard, loyal subordinates of Lenin, were still around. He would have to bide his time to strike at the man he snidely referred to as Napoleonchik (Little Napoleon).

THE COILS OF DECEIT
By 1934 Stalin was ready to begin moving against his enemies. He orchestrated the assassination of Sergei Kirov, the popular head of the party apparatus in Leningrad. Kirov had been seen as the focal point of resistance to Stalin's growing power and his ruthless exercise of it. In the voting for the CPSU's Central Committee that same year, Kirov had received three negative votes to 292 for Stalin. That vote of support reflected his leadership to those who wanted to moderate the brutality of so much of Stalin's industrialization campaign.[12] That Tukhachevsky had become a close friend of Kirov's was added to Stalin's list of damnable animosities. Another of Stalin's enemies scheduled for destruction was Nikolai Bukharin, the author of the New Economic Policy (NEP) that introduced free enterprise in light industry, agriculture, and the retail trade which revived the war-ruined economy after the ruinous Civil War. He was the idealist of the Party and was appalled by the mass deaths caused by the collectivization of the land and by Stalin's increasingly brutal policies, referring to his old Bolshevik comrade as Genghis Khan. He wrote the 1936 Soviet constitution that was filled with guarantees of human rights and was a strong advocate of proletarian humanism.

Stalin never struck directly at his greatest enemies. Like a powerful snake, he would first silently wrap them in great coils of deceit and protestations of support. Only when they could not escape did he squeeze, and then it was sudden and remorseless. There was no escape. So with Tukhachevsky. He would use the marshal's own strategic vision against him. The rise of Hitler had convinced Tukhachevsky that Nazi

Germany was a mortal enemy and that a preventative war was necessary before it became too strong. Tukhachevsky, with Stalin's tacit approval, began to sound out through military channels the armed forces of Poland, Czechoslovakia, Britain, and France on common ground to face the Nazi threat. Such tacit approval could disappear as if it had never happened leaving Tukhachevsky to face serious charges of Bonapartism. The web grew even more complex as he directed Yagoda to send agents throughout Europe to talk of a Red Army plot headed by Tukhachevsky to depose him. These then filtered back to him as official intelligence findings.

The most bizarre result was to encourage the Germans to get in on the act through the most unlikely agent, the White émigré, General Nickolai Skoblin, living in Paris. Skoblin's ambition was to gain control of the leading émigré organization in France and from that position manipulate the great powers to destroy the Bolshevik regime. He had already contacted Reinhard Heydrich, the number two man in Hitler's SS, providing information that Tukhachevsky was encouraging a preventative war against the Third Reich. Skoblin added a special dollop of poison by stating that not only did Tukhachevsky have Jewish blood but also that of being a 23rd Degree Mason. The NKVD then approached him offering to help him assume leadership of the émigrés by murdering the incumbent if Skoblin would be the source of damaging information on Tukhachevsky funneled through the Czechs. They even encouraged him to keep working with the Germans as long as he passed on to the NKVD what he learned. That fitted in beautifully with Skoblin's desire to harm the Soviets as much as possible by manipulating Stalin to destroy the leadership of the Red Army. On his next visit to Heydrich, he proposed the forging of documents proving that Tukhachevsky was a German agent. Heydrich was overjoyed and with Hitler's enthusiastic encouragement gave full support to the plan. The coils were tightening ever so quietly around Tukhachevsky and the rest of the Red Army's leadership as well.

Yet Tukhachevsky remained convinced that he faced little risk. He was warned in 1936 by Corps Commander Robert Petrovich Eideman. 'Watch out, Mikhail. You're on shaky ground.'[13]

'Watch out for what? Why shaky?'

'Because the chief won't appreciate your initiative. Don't forget you're vulnerable to attack and slander.'

'I'm not forgetting anything; I know the whole list of my 'crimes'. What's more, I know he doesn't like me. He never did. You remember the plight we were in Poland, before Warsaw in 1920? The southwest army wasn't far way, with Yegorov, Budenny, Voroshilov, and Stalin. I asked for help. Stalin refused. I implored him. He didn't give way. Trotsky had to threaten them with a court-martial. Five days too late they moved, but we were already in retreat.'[14]

Eideman had to remind him that it was not Stalin's dislike but his suspicion that was the danger fed by Tukhachevsky's frequent tactless references to the incident. He seemed to shrug it off by saying he had had no real contact with Stalin and that, 'Anyhow, I'm fully safeguarded as regards the Party and the country ... I've not the slightest intention of fighting him. Sectarian struggles are a veritable morass anyway.' He made a point of saying that he had not said a word when Stalin had expelled his great rival Trotsky or when he began arresting the Bolshevik old guard. In any case he said that his anti-German feelings were supported by the Commissar for Defence, Marshal Klement E. Voroshilov, who he believed was reporting everything to the Politburo. 'There I'm safe and supported to the hilt.' He insisted that Voroshilov and he saw eye to eye on this issue and were loyal to each other.

Eideman commented, 'I don't share your confidence in Klim, a nonentity inflated by the necessity of the times.'[15]

Voroshilov had indeed been keeping Stalin and the Politburo informed of Tukhachevsky's activities. He was more sound than men gave him credit. But in Stalin's presence, his strength of character disappeared after a certain point. Stalin had been noncommittal, but he had not squashed the efforts either. Instead he was pocketing them to use later against Tukhachevsky. He was determined not to move down the path of a preventative war against Germany. No, the Soviet Union was not ready. Instead he was looking for an accommodation that would give time for the continued build-up of the Red Army to give it a decisive edge, but that would be years away. Hitler did not plan to give him those years.

DEAD MEN
The plot against Tukhachevsky was in the hands of a new chief of the NKVD, Nikolai Invanovich Yezhov, described as the malignant dwarf, a man as ruthless as he was sadistic.[16] Into his hands fell the manipulating of the different strands of the plot. Running parallel was the plan to decimate the upper ranks of the NKVD, the men who had risen under the tutelage of Yagoda. Had Stalin learned of the existence

of his Okhrana files in the hands of the Ukrainian NKVD and the leadership of the Red Army, all his carefully arranged plots would have been tossed aside in the face of a real plot.

That plot was now unfolding as Yakir brought others into the knowledge of the Okhrana file in early January1937. He first approached Stanislas Kosior, the First Party Secretary of the Communist Party of the Ukraine. Kosior had supervised the Holodomor and been awarded the Order of Lenin for 'achievements in agriculture'. Although genocide in the pursuit of communism's radiant future did not faze him, Stalin's betrayal of the party was shocking indeed. As it was to Tukhachevsky.

He arrived at the red brick building on Vozdviyenka Street that housed the general staff of the Red Army looking forward to seeing his old friend Yakir. Now he sat back in his chair, a look of incredulity on his face as he passed the file to Yan (Yacob) Borisovitch, Deputy Commissar of Defence and head of the Red Army's Political Administration. Gamarnik read it and asked Yakir, 'Is this the only copy?'

'No, Yan Borisovitch, we have made a number of copies to be able to distribute them to those who can be trusted.'

'That was a great mistake. You have multiplied geometrically the chances it will be betrayed. Recall all the copies immediately.'

Yakir looked surprised, 'You mean to bury this? I cannot believe you would ...'

Tukhachevsky stood up. All the bile he had swallowed as a good Party man came up. 'No, one or two copies is all we need, Iona Emmanuilovich. That is all that is necessary to remove this traitor to the Party.'

Gamarnik said, 'Not remove but kill. There is an old saying that if you strike at a king, you must kill him. And remember this king is a Georgian. We dare not let him live, or we are all dead men.'

'Easy to say but harder to do,' Tukhachevsky added. 'We must plan this carefully.' The political officer could tell he was loath to commit to immediate action.

Gamarnik said to both of them, 'Tell no one else of this file until we are ready to commit ourselves.'[17]

There matters might have stood had Balitsky not picked up hints within the NKVD of Yezhov's reoccupation with finding damaging information on Tukhachevsky and other leaders of the Red Army. The marshal needed to know, but that was easier said than done. Balitsky knew enough of his own organization that Tukhachevsky was being watched closely by Yezhov and any direct communication with other members of the NKVD would be instantly known. He had to proceed by indirection. Shtern made his way to Moscow on innocuous business in the middle of January, to inform Yezhov that the review of Okhrana files was not yielding any information, but that Balitsky was redoubling his efforts in a proper Stakonovite spirit. He took a few days leave and made sure to find Eideman walking his daughter in the park. He paused to ask for a light and whispered as he drew in a puff, 'Balitsky says that Yezhov is sniffing around Tukhachevsky. It can only mean his fate is sealed. He must act quickly, or he is a dead man.' The look on Eideman's face was priceless.

Eideman immediately took his daughter home and rushed off to find Tukhachevsky and found him outside Moscow observing the training of the 1st Mechanized Corps. This formation and three others in the Western Soviet Union were the concrete expression of deep operations, the very first large tank and motorized formations in the world. Each corps consisted of four brigades of three tank battalions and one motorized infantry battalion and supporting arms. The corps was truly a powerful mobile, combined arms, fist. The power behind the fist, was the 13.9-ton BT7 tank with its 45mm gun. Nicknamed Betka, this tank's mobility surpassed any other foreign design. A variant mounting a 76mm gun was just coming into the corps to provide mobile artillery support. He was there to see it perform.

The marshal was surprised to see Eideman striding from his car to him. Before he could say anything, Eideman took him by the arm and said loud enough for those around to hear, 'I thought I'd find you out here, Mikhail Nikolayevich. It is so good to actually get back into the real army, I couldn't miss the chance. Training school children and civilian volunteers is important, I know, but I miss being around troops.'

Tukhachevsky picked up on the cue, and walked towards one of the tank battalions a few hundred metres away with Eideman in tow. 'Come, then, let's smell hot steel and mud together. We should be in time for something hot from the mess, too.'

Tukhachevsky did not need another warning after Eideman repeated Shtern's words. He was now filled with the same implacable resolve that had brought him so many victories on the battlefield. Under the cover of preparing for the Plenum of the Central Committee of the Red Army to run from February into March, he arranged to have the trusted men he would need come to Moscow. They included Army

Commander 1st Rank, Ieronim Petrovich Uberovich, commander of the Belorussian Military District; Corps Commander Boris Mironovich Feld'man, head of personnel of the People's Commissariat of Defense and deputy commander of the Moscow Military District; Corps Commander Vitali Markovich Primakov, deputy commander of the Leningrad Military District. These men could not have been better chosen; along with Yakir, they controlled the critical Kiev, Belorussian, Moscow, and Leningrad Military Districts.

Gamarnik already controlled the Party apparatus in the Red Army, and Feld'man controlled personnel and was able to vet those to be included in the plot. He was also able to transfer unreliable officers from Moscow and reassign reliable officers to replace them. Army Commander 2nd Rank, Avgust Ivanovich Kork, was the head of the Frunze Military Academy, equivalent to the U.S. Army's Command and General Staff College at Fort Leavenworth and the British Army's Staff College, Camberley. The several hundred captains and majors in attendance were the best and brightest of the Red Army, chosen on merit, and protégés of Tukhachevsky and the other reformers. They could be depended upon.

Not the least of those brought in was Army Commander 2nd Rank Jan Karlovich Berzin, head of the GRU, the Red Army's intelligence arm. Berzin had created the finest such organization in the world. The relationship between Tukhachevsky and Berzin had grown from the former's commissioning of a major study which the GRU completed in 1928, *The Future War*,which was a superb piece of predictive analysis that formed much of the basis for Tukhachevsky's development of deep operations.[18]

Tukhachevsky quickly concluded that the upcoming Plenum, which would bring Stalin himself and the rest of the Politburo into the General Staff building, was both the perfect time and place to seize the General Secretary. That would deprive him of the protection of the NKVD Special Purpose Battalion housed within the Kremlin in the old Arsenal building. As soon as Stalin entered the General Staff building, the Red Army garrison of Moscow would seal off the city, seize the Kremlin and communication centers, and disarm the 1st NKVD Division whose mission was regime protection.[19]

Tukhachevsky assembled his officers in his office to present them with his plan. Before he had started, however, Berzin made a point of saying that they should all listen to the latest broadcast of the General Secretary's speech and turned on the radio, loud enough, he said, so they would not miss a single word. With Stalin's heavily Georgian-accented Russian droning on, it was sure to confuse any listening devices, the discussion began.

'Our objective is to kill Stalin,' Tukhachevsky announced. He could hear the breath being sucked out of the room.

Berzin chimed in, 'And let's not forget Yezhov.'

Tukhachevsky replied, 'Yes, indeed. So, comrades, we have three weeks before the Plenum. Everything must be ready by then. Here are your orders.'[20]

One man they most definitely kept in the dark was Marshal Voroshilov. That was easier than expected. As Commissar of Defence he gladly extended the army's invitation to Stalin and the Politburo to attend the Plenum in the General Staff building. He was not one to meddle in the day-to-day operations of the army. He had been supportive of Tukhachevsky's reforms but had never been a member of that rising tide of talent beholden to the younger marshal. There were none of his protégés, likely to put loyalty to him ahead of anything else, that would be included in the plot.

One by one the carefully vetted commanders from the 1st Mechanized Corps were brought into the General Staff buildings on routine business and shown the Okhrana file. Tukhachevsky's appraisal of character had been shrewd. The half dozen men immediately threw in their lot with him. At the same time, Feld'man was busy transferring the most obvious Stalinist toadies from Moscow or sending them off on sudden inspection tours of very remote areas. He gave Eideman the mission to work out the details of the plan with contingencies if Stalin had to be taken other than at the Plenum. Gamarnik and Berzin were also busy making sure that every other copy of the Okhrana file had been recovered. So many copies had been made by Balitsky that they could not be sure that all had been accounted for.

Unfortunately, it was Yezhov who collected one of the stray copies. It was found in the apartment of a senior NKVD officer, one of Yagoda's men who had been arrested and shot as part of Yezhov's housecleaning, and turned over to Karl Pauker, the chief of the NKVD Operations Department. A man of limited intelligence and a drinking companion of Stalin's, Pauker was on his way to take it directly to Stalin when Yezhov intercepted it.[21] He immediately arrested Pauker and those officers who had taken part in the search. He could have kicked himself that the officer in whose apartment it had been found had been so hurriedly shot. Now he could not be questioned as to who had provided it to him.

It occurred to him, though, that the Okhrana file was poisonous to whomever touched it, including himself. He would have to think about it – but not for too long.

He had other important projects to worry about, especially that one the GENSEC himself was spinning in such a complex web – the downfall of Tukhachevsky. Yezhov had to admire how patient and relentless Stalin was in the pursuit of the destruction of his enemies. The German angle was coming along nicely according to Skoblin's reports. Heydrich was gleefully at work plotting the destruction of the marshal. That would be very useful in pulling down everyone around Tukhachevsky. Skoblin was also being very helpful in planting the stories with the Czechs that Tukhachevsky was plotting the return of Trotsky, and, of course, President Benes was making sure Stalin heard of it immediately. Yes, Tukhachevsky was doomed. And with him any hint of a preventative war against Germany. It would not be until at least May that it would all come together.

Two days before the Plenum, Stalin invited Pauker and a few of his other cronies over to polish off a few bottles of vodka. That presented Yezhov with a life or death dilemma. How could he explain that someone as dog loyal as Pauker had betrayed Stalin? It was easier to just send him over with the file. He apologized to the man and said his arrest had been to protect him from the dark forces that would have immediately killed him had they known of this obvious forgery. It was now time for Pauker to inform Stalin of the file in person. 'Now, Karl Yakubovich, you should be the one to tell the GENSEC of this nasty matter. He will be eternally grateful. You deserved it, and I don't want to steal your thunder, so don't mention me at all.'

Yezhov just shook his head as Pauker did just that. And like clockwork, Stalin called and asked him if he knew what Pauker had discussed. Feigning complete ignorance, he referred to Stalin's party invitation. There was a pause on the phone. Then Stalin said, 'Arrest him, isolate him, and see personally to his execution.' Yezhov marvelled how close the angel of death had come to him. Stalin inquired after the NKVD officers who had found the document and ordered their death as well. No wonder, thought Yezhov. If I had received a file like that on myself, I would want to kill everyone who had knowledge of it or even possibly had knowledge.

Yezhov was still not out of danger. He could tell Stalin's web spinning when he inquired next of the circle of friends and colleagues of the NKVD officer who originally had possession of the file. It did not take long for the trail to lead back to Balitsky. Yezhov then had the most terrifying interview with Stalin.

'Tell me, Comrade Yezhov, how it is that this Trotskyite forgery originated within your own NKVD? Do you not have complete control of your own organization?'

Yezhov could only stammer, 'I will see to this traitor myself, Comrade Secretary.'

Stalin just stared at him with those malevolent soulless eyes, leaned over, and said, 'I would expect nothing less. Inform me of it immediately. I don't mind being interrupted at the Plenum tomorrow.'

Yezhov was on a plane that very night to Kiev with a hand-picked detachment of bodyguards. That morning he strode into Balitsky's office and arrested him. It was convenient because the building had its own interrogation room. He personally supervised Balitsky's interrogation with a sadism that even took his own team aback. The blood spray flew across the room to coat the white-tiled walls.

As Balitsky was being broken, Yakir had already been informed. The plan had been compromised. He rang Tukhachevsky immediately. 'Mikhail Nikolayevich, Yezhov will know soon, if he doesn't already, and then the Georgian will know. You must act now. I will keep Yezhov here in Kiev.'[22]

Tukhachevsky had barely put down the receiver when he issued the order to immediately execute the plan variant where Stalin remained in the Kremlin. He then called in Gamarnik. 'Yan Borisovitch, the time has come. Arm yourself.' He strode out of the building and drove to the headquarters of the 1st Mechanized Corps.

At the same time Stalin was listening to Yezhov's almost frantic report. 'It's Kosior and Yakir, too. The whole Ukraine is rotten. And Tukhachevsky. Tukhachevsky! He and all the traitors around him have plotted against you, Comrade Stalin. They are to seize you at the Plenum today. I have already given orders for NKVD units to surround the Kremlin for your protection. The special purpose battalion should be able to defend the Kremlin until help arrives.' Stalin immediately began making his own calls to Red Army commanders he knew to be loyal. To his fury almost everyone was absent from Moscow. Then the line went dead. He put down the phone as the sound of gunfire washed over the Kremlin's high brick walls.[23]

The 1st Mechanized Brigade was moving down Ilynka Street past the giant GUM department store and into Red Square with the high red brick walls of the Kremlin looming on the other side. At the same time the trucks of an NKVD battalion also entered the square from the south heading for the Kremlin's St. Nicholas Tower gate at the northwest end of the square. It was the only element of the NKVD 1st Division that had not been surrounded in their barracks by Eideman's troops. The columns were converging at the Place of Execution, where the young Peter the Great had conducted the mass execution of the disloyal Strelsy Regiment in 1699. Tukhachevsky was riding with the brigade commander and ordered him to engage immediately. The 45mm guns of the BT7s riddled the NKVD trucks and then sped forward to crush the remnants under their tracks. The Red Army infantry dismounted its own trucks and followed the tanks making sure no prisoners were taken. The men with the green collar tabs were too hated to be shown mercy. For the second time in history it was a place of execution.

The NKVD Special Purpose Battalion by now was manning its defensive positions along the Kremlin walls and in its huge brick towers and firing down at the tanks and infantry in Red Square. All the gates of the Kremlin had been shut just moments before the tanks had entered the square. The platoon of 76mm-armed BT tanks blew the St. Nicholas Tower gate to pieces as heavy machine-guns raked the parapets of the high brick wall.

Just inside the shattered gate were the two key objectives, The Senate and Arsenal Buildings. Tukhachevsky ordered the brigade commander to now concentrate his fire on both structures. The man hesitated. His guns were already shelling the Arsenal Building where the Special Purpose Battalion was defending its own barracks. 'But Comrade Marshal, the Senate Building is where Lenin had his offices, and it is filled with great treasures.'

'And Lenin would be the first one to give this order to save the Revolution. Can we do less? As to the treasures, my family put a lot of them in there, Comrade Brigade Commander. Fire on the building.' Within minutes the building's yellow and white walls were gushing flames and smoke through great rents as fire began to lick up through the roof.

But Stalin was already gone. With an NKVD guard around him, he had fled the building through one of the underground tunnels that carried the heating pipes for the Kremlin, to find a bolt hole out of another gate, but each one was either smashed in with Red Army tanks clanking through, or blocked from the outside.[24]

They found him in one of the tunnels late that night, cornered in a utility room. Most of his guards had found a way to slip away. The few that were left looked at one another after they were told that Stalin had been deposed and declared a traitor to the Party and an enemy of the people. The thought crossed their minds to drag him out to save themselves. Dread still hung about the man, though. Stalin shot the first one to bolt for the door. The Georgian bank robber still had a snarl in him.

Tukhachevsky, Gamarnik, and Eideman had just arrived outside in the tunnel to hear the gun shot from inside the utility room. He called out, 'You, I.V. Dzhugashvilli!' By calling him by his Georgian name, he had stripped him of the name of Revolutionary fame and used the betrayer's name in his Okhrana file. 'The game is up, traitor. Surrender in the name of the people.' A full minute passed in silence.

Inside the remaining two guards were facing the door and did not see the look on Stalin's face. It was pure trapped hate. Perhaps Tukhachevsky was fool enough to accept a surrender and let him live, he thought. Yezhov was crushing the traitors in the Ukraine and sending more NKVD divisions to Moscow surely. As long as he was alive, the tables could still be turned. Then they would all pay. He would have his revenge such that even Ivan the Terrible would envy.

'Alright, Comrades, we are coming out,' he yelled.

The two guards stumbled out first and were hustled down the tunnel. Then Stalin emerged, a smile on his face. 'Comrades, there has been a terrible misunderstanding. Real traitors have set us at odds. We must ...' Gamarnik stepped forward and shot him in the forehead. Blood sprayed out the back of his head to coat the tunnel wall. There was dead silence as Gamarnik stood over the body of the man that had terrorized their vast country and looked at Tukhachevsky. 'Remember, Mikhail Nikolayevich, when you strike at a king you must kill him.'[25]

EPILOGUE

Stalin's hope of rescue by Yezhov was cut short by Yakir's decisive action. He stormed the NKVD headquarters in Kiev and killed him. With that, the NKVD was paralyzed and fell in behind the fait accompli of the coup.[26] The rest of the country was equally stunned. Increasingly relentless propaganda for the last eight years had done nothing but sing Stalin's praises and so conditioned the people to his leadership. However, the purges he had initiated had also conditioned the people to not question the unmasking of traitors. They too fell in line and only over time realized that they could breathe a lot easier.

Tukhachevsky left much of the reorganization of the government and Party to Gamarnik but remained the power behind the Party. Bukharin was elected as General Secretary of the Party with an overwhelming majority in an emergency Party congress. The old Politburo was completely replaced as well with Voroshilov and Budenny hustled into honored retirement.[27]

Tukhachevsky was confirmed as Commissar of Defence and from that position strongly pushed for the creation of anti-Nazi coalition which was much hastened by Hitler's *Anschluss* with Austria. The Czechs, who saw themselves next on Hitler's list, quickly signed an alliance with the Soviet Union and with that backing were successfully able to defy Hitler's demands for the Sudetenland. Eventually Poland, with great hesitation, joined the coalition. Tukhachevsky's boldness also stiffened the spine of the British and French who joined coalition talks with the Soviet Union.

All the time, the Red Army continued to grow and improve itself, fielding larger and larger mechanized forces supported by an increasingly powerful Red Air Force which every major power strove to catch up with. Eventually, Tukhachevsky's policies hemmed in Germany to the point where Hitler's own generals removed him, thus relieving the threat of another war that many predicted would dwarf the Great War of 1914-1918.[28]

The war that did occur was at the opposite end of the Eurasian landmass where Tukhachevsky's deep battle crushed the Japanese Army in Manchuria and drove its remnants out of China in the Second Russo-Japanese War of 1941-42.[29] That defeat so chastised the Japanese that they abandoned their plans to drive south for the oil, rubber, and metals of the Philippines, French Indochina, Malaya, and the Dutch East Indies. With the Japanese adventure in China ended, the United States and Japan found themselves without serious strategic friction and entered a long period of economic partnership.

These events allowed the United States to remain an isolationist power. Contributing to this was the dampening of the fires of world revolution as the Soviet Union under Bukharin's brief but important leadership concentrated on domestic reforms such as the decollectivization of the land, the reintroduction of the economic policies of the NEP, and enforcing the human rights elements of the 1936 constitution he had written.[30] Eventually, with the economic changes initiated by Bukharin, the Soviet Union crept slowly back into the ranks of the capitalist world over the next sixty years without abandoning the leading role of the CPSU, which became little more than a nationalist oligarchy. Little remained of Marxism-Leninism but legend.

Tukhachevsky died suddenly of a heart attack on 13 December, 1955. He was awarded a massive state funeral. A towering statue of him stands to this day outside the Kremlin.

THE REALITY

Events in reality followed this story until the notification of Tukhachevsky of the Okhrana file and his conclusion that Stalin had to be removed. Unfortunately, for the Soviet people and the rest of the world, Tukhachevsky and the others did not move with any alacrity and determination. Stalin's complex plot against the marshal was tossed aside in reality when Pauker brought him the Okhrana file found in an NKVD officer's apartment. Pulling on that string led him to the realization that Tukhachevsky also had the file and that a plot was underway. He struck first. Tukhachevsky and the others were arrested in early May under the charges of terrorism and military conspiracy, tortured into confessions that they were both German agents and Trotskyite saboteurs, and convicted in a show trial. They were shot on 11 June 1937.

Stalin went on to purge the senior officer corps of anyone that had been associated with the plotters or had benefited from their patronage, in other words, the best and brightest. Fully 30,000 officers were shot or sent to the camps, including ninety percent of the generals and eighty percent of the colonels. Most of the careful work in creating a talented and forward looking officer corps in the previous fifteen years was undone. A very frightened general said to his old friend, Marshal Budenny, a crony of Stalin, that they were taking everyone. Budenny told him not to worry because, 'They are taking only the smart ones.' That purge convinced Hitler that the Red Army was a hollow shell that could be easily defeated. He came within an ace of doing just that when he invaded the Soviet Union on 22 June 1941. Only the backs-to-the-wall heroism of the Russian people, and the release from the camps of the survivors of the purge gave the Red Army the margin to survive. It was Tukhachevsky's concepts of deep operations that was employed to beat the Wehrmacht to death on the Eastern Front.

Ironically, Heydrich took the credit for the purge with his forged documents, but they were never used by Stalin who had discovered the real plot. Nevertheless, it was the slaughter of the officer corps and the subsequent miserable performance of the Red Army in the Winter War against Finland that led Hitler to the conclusion that he could destroy the Soviet Union.

In late October 1941, the Germans had torn open the front in front of Moscow taking almost 700,000 prisoners in a vast encirclement that left only a handful of divisions to defend the capital. The Germans resumed their attack only to find that these divisions were offering the most determined and skilled resistance. A wounded division commander was captured, and under interrogation revealed that he and others had been just released from the camps and put in command of these divisions. He stated that they were determined to prove that they were not traitors and that they were worthy of Tukhachevsky. The German interrogation report commented that it appeared that Marshal Tukhachevsky commanded outside Moscow, a fitting tribute to the ghost that saved Russia.

NOTES:

1. Narodnyy Komissariat Vnutrennikh Del (NKVD) or The People's Commissariat for Internal Affairs.
2. GULAG is an acronym for the Soviet bureaucratic institution, Glavnoe Upravlenie ispravitel'no-trudovykh LAGerei (Main Administration of Corrective Labor Camps).
3. Roy Aleksandrovich Medvedev, George Shriver, *Let History Judge: The Origin and Consequences of Stalinism* (New York, Columbia University Press, 1989), p.574.
4. Vadim Rogovin, *1937: Stalin's Year of Terror* (Mehring Books, 1998), p.473.
5. At this time the Red Army did not use traditional ranks, rather identifying an officer by his position, e.g., army commander or corps commander, etc. The rank of Marshal of the Soviet Union had been introduced in 1935.
6. Sally W. Stoekcer, *Forging Stalin's Army: Marshal Tukhachevsky and the Politics of Military Innovation* (Boulder, Co, Westview Press, 1980), p.89: 'The Soviets formed their mechanized corps in the fall of 1932, three years before Germany created its first Panzer division.'
7. Victor Alexandrov, *The Tukhachevsky Affair* (Englewood Cliffs, NJ, Prentice-Hall Inc., 1964), p.43.
8. Simon Sebag Montefiore, *Stalin: Court of the Red Tsar* (New York, Vintage Books, 2005) pp.222 and 252.
9. Erich Wollenberg's 'The Red Army, Part Seven, The Red Army In the Years of Peace', Chapter Six; http://www.marxistsfr.org/history/ussr/government/red-army/1937/wollenberg-red-army/ch07.htm, accessed 4 October 2011.
10. It passeth all understanding that the Holodomor, which killed more innocents in one year than Hitler killed in the six years of the Holocaust, is almost unknown in the West. Perhaps, it might be explained by the Communist Party slogan used in the United States in the 1930s: 'There are no enemies on the Left.' The famine was created by Stalin for two reasons: (1) to break the back of growing Ukrainian nationalism, and (2) to essentially confiscate the grain harvest to sell on the international market for hard currency to buy the equipment necessary for rapid industrialization. The internal borders of the Ukraine were sealed; its outer border was already sealed. No food was allowed in and no refugees were allowed out. Communist activists from the cities raided even the pantries in the villages. Because little boys starve faster than little girls because females have an extra layer of body fat, the disproportion between males and females even into the 1980s was greater in Ukraine than any other country in the world, such was the echo of the Holodomor. Stalin suppressed the 1938 census and had the demographers shot to hide the demographic losses of the Holodomor.

11. This quotation is taken from a documentary on Stalin's family shown on Ukrainian television in July 1992 which the author watched on a visit to that country. The author of the party game was Nikolai Bukharin who stated his own greatest pleasure was to raise the living condition of the workers.

12. Robert C. Tucker, *Stalin in Power: The Revolution From Above, 1928-1941* (New York, W.W. Norton & Co., 1962), pp.240-1.

13. Eideman commanded the OSOAVIAKHIM (*Union of Societies of Assistance to Defence and Aviation-Chemical Construction of the USSR*), the vast organization which taught military skills such as radio operation, marksmanship, flying, parachuting etc., to school children as young as fourteen and to volunteers to provide a reserve of skills for the armed forces.

14. Alexandrov, p.46.

15. ibid, pp.46-7.

16. Yezhov was appointed by Stalin to head the NKVD in September 1936, replacing Yagoda. The latter retained his position as People's Commissar for Internal Affairs though he had no control over Yezhov who clearly terrified him.

17. Dmitri Volkoganov, *To Strike at a King: The Plot Against Stalin* (Suvorov Military Publishers, 1982), pp.37-9.

18. Silvio Pons, Andrea Romano, Fondazione Giangiacomo Feltrinelli, *Russia in the Age of Wars, 1914-1945* (Feltrinelli Editore, 2000), pp.189-90.

19. The guard was originally establishedas a special purpose battalion in 1935 and increased to a regiment in April 1936.

20. Volkoganov, *To Strike at a King*, pp.187-8.

21. Roman Brackman, *The Secret File of Joseph Stalin: A Hidden Life* (New York, Taylor & Francis, 2003), p.240.

22. V. Katsnelson, *Decision in Kiev: Yakir and Yezhov* (Kiev, Trident Publishers, 1952), p.229.

23. Alexander Solzhenitzyn, *Death in the Tunnels: Stalin on the Last Day* (Leningrad, Piotr Veliky Publishers, 1960), p.211.

24. Uri I. Strelnikov, *Storming the Kremlin* (Moscow, Rodina Publishers, 1952), pp.355-7

25. Yan Gamarnik, *To the Rescue of the Nation: The Red Army and the Dzhugashvilli Affair* (Moscow, Planeta Publishers, 1944), pp.344-6.

26. Walter Krivitsky, *The Last Purge: The Elimination of the NKVD as an Agent of Repression* (New York, International Events Press, 1949), pp.219-22. Tukhachevsky after the coup moved to eliminate the NKVD's numerous military formations and incorporated many of them into the Red Army. Bukharin ensured that the NKVD cadres, especially those that taken part in the Holodomor and other acts of illegality, were purged en mass. Those that were guilty of crimes were prosecuted, but most were simply dismissed. The NKVD was renamed the Central Intelligence Committee whose functions became largely foreign intelligence.

27. Guy Burgess, *Back on the Right Track: The Soviet Union After Stalin* (London, Blackfriars Publishers, 1945), pp.239-41.

28. Sergei Akhromeev, *M.N. Tuckhachevsky and the Creation of the Anti-Hitlerite Coalition* (Moscow: Progress Publishers, 1979), p.393.

29. Dmitri Volkoganov, *Tukhachevsky's Revolution in Military Affairs and the Destruction of Japanese Militarism* (Moscow, Red Army Press, 1988), pp.319-22.

30. Jay Lovestone, *Nikolai Bukharin: The Life of a Proletarian Humanist* (New York, Erstwhile Press, 1950), pp.320-32.

Chapter 2

The Shooting of
The Chief Whip
The Death of David Margesson, May 1940

By Nigel West

Set in one of the most beautiful parts of Kent, in an area known for its natural beauty and often called 'the garden of England', Leeds Castle traces its history back to the twelfth century and is located about five miles southeast of Maidstone making it within easy reach from London. During the reign of Henry VIII, the King had chosen the moated royal dower fortress as the principal home of his first wife, Catherine of Aragon.

In May 1940, it had been owned by Olive, Lady Baillie, for the past fourteen years, and the American heiress, who had inherited a substantial part of the huge Whitney fortune upon her mother's death in 1916, had spared no expense in restoring the dilapidated property which, when she had bought it with her second husband Arthur Wilson Filmer, had been unoccupied for several years and had fallen into disrepair.

Olive, then aged forty, and regarded still as quite a beauty, was a very remarkable woman. As a descendant of the Paget family, originally from Yorkshire, she had come over to England during the Great War to work as a nurse, and had married her first husband, the Hon. Charles Winn, soon after the end of the conflict. Their marriage lasted only five years, but the combination of New York money and the second son of a Conservative peer was enough to establish Olive as one of the great socialites and hostesses of the era.

As she ploughed vast sums into improving the relatively modern main house, which had been rebuilt with a great hall in the Tudor style by the Fairfax family in 1823, and making the slightly smaller Maiden's Tower habitable, Olive developed the concept of the political house-party, providing a venue on which she could generously entertain her very wide circle of friends who were drawn largely from the Conservative Party. She herself had no political ambitions, but not so her husband, Sir Adrian Baillie, the sixth baronet, whom she had married in November 1931. He had been the Member of Parliament for Linlithgowshire until 1935, but his defeat at the General Election in November of that year had not ended his service to the House of Commons. Conveniently, the death from influenza of Herbert Spencer-Clay three months later occasioned a by-election at Tonbridge, a geographically rather closer, safe Tory seat for which Sir Adrian was selected, and then elected, without much opposition.

Adrian had succeeded to his brother's baronetcy in September 1914 at the age of sixteen while still at Eton, and after graduating from Sandhurst had joined the cavalry, the 2nd Dragoons, Scots Greys, to fight on the Western Front in France. After the war he had joined the Foreign Office to be posted to the embassy at Washington, DC, and while on leave had been invited to fight his local constituency's by-election in April 1928, only to be beaten by Manny Shinwell. However, two years later he would be elected the Unionist MP, trouncing Shinwell by 3,000 votes.

Although much liked on both sides of the chamber, Adrian was not destined for high office, and held no ministerial posts. Childless, but a stepfather to his wife's two daughters, he devoted himself to his constituents and to campaigning for improved conditions for agricultural workers. He would also absent himself from many of the house-parties organized by Olive who became a central figure in London's social scene where her friends included Charlie Chaplin, Errol Flynn, and Douglas Fairbanks from the entertainment world, and Geoffrey Lloyd, Anthony Eden and Alfred Beit from the Commons.

The surroundings were relaxed, but not opulent, and provided a congenial environment in which those with no particular interest in country sports or the London season could be sure of a loyal and discreet staff to ensure her ladyship's weekend visitors were made entirely welcome and comfortable. The hospitality was generous but not lavish, tasteful but never vulgar, and intended to be the epitome of English country house style.

The Baillies had purchased Leeds when it was uninhabitable, empty of possessions and furniture, and devoid of serviceable plumbing.

Within months of her arrival in Kent, living temporarily at Mote Park, a rented property near Maidstone, she had commissioned designers, decorators and craftsmen to transform some of the medieval interiors from gloomy chambers into panelled reception rooms and what was left of the chapel into a music room.

More controversially, at the height of the abdication crisis in 1936, Olive's guests would find the King there with Wallis Simpson, and the newly-appointed German ambassador, Joachim von Ribbentrop. Although modern-day conspiracy theorists would be the first to seize on these discreet weekends as evidence of a secret, parallel government plotting to reach an accommodation with the Nazis, the gatherings were entirely private, social affairs at which men and women from very diverse backgrounds and ages could meet informally, engage in candid conversation and enjoy each other's company. There were no agendas, no cabals, and no orgies in this *demi-monde*, but there was some considerable louche behavior involving gambling and drug-taking.

At that time there was a thriving, semi-legal trade in morphia, marijuana and cocaine, whereas roulette and games of chance were prohibited, even in membership-only clubs, leaving the field wide open for entrepreneurs, such as enterprising Wing Commander John Hallett, to organize gaming tables run by experienced croupiers.

In London's West End during the so-called Phoney War, life for the upper crust continued largely unchanged, although there were plenty more uniforms to be seen. The nightclubs that had made Soho famous, such as the Nuthouse, Le Conga, Le Boeuf sur le Toit and the Miramar enjoyed great trade, and some prewar establishments, including the Studio Club in the King's Road, Pastori's, Frisco's, and the Cotton Club, gained a certain notoriety as venues where money and the right connections could buy women, narcotics, abortions, hard-to-find liquor and black-market delicacies. Other commodities were also available, through cautious intermediaries, at a price.

For most of the population, the very existence of this effete world was unimagined, and almost no word of it leaked as the media was equally implicated, with the complicity of some newspaper proprietors, and the frequent attendance of Sir Roderick Jones, the chairman of Reuter's news agency. This sphere, to the extent that it was even known about within officialdom, was regarded as off-limits by Scotland Yard, the Criminal Investigation Department working closely with the police at Vine Street, Bow Street and the newly-built West End Central to perpetuate a mutually lucrative symbiotic co-existence. As for Special Branch and MI5, both organizations were aware that Lady Baillie's set included the insurance broker Ian Menzies and his elder brother Stewart who, in November 1939, had been appointed Chief of the Secret Intelligence Service, MI6. Ian's wife Giselle had actually been a nightclub performer, appearing almost naked in a tableau of Botticelli's *The Birth of Venus*. Polite society did not demur.

Olive's largesse was certainly extravagant by wartime standards, but by no means unique. The Savoy Hotel and the equally famous Park Lane establishments may have conformed to rationing and standard meal pricing, but the countryside was hardly affected and the management of individual estates on the scale of Leeds Castle, supported by 3,500 acres of farmland, continued life behind closed gates as though unaware of the inconveniences of world war.

Unlike the Astors at Cliveden who pursued a political objective and were actively engaged in promoting appeasement with Germany, there was no equivalent at Leeds. The regular houseguests were not preoccupied with the affairs of state, although several were, or had been, senior members of Neville Chamberlain's government. Leeds did not represent a movement or any special objective, but was a *galere* comprising the rich, the famous and the decadent where one of more Duchesses of Westminster might engage in some unconventional nocturnal activities without fear of scandal. Whereas Cliveden would be discredited for their association with the Anglo-German Fellowship and activists who came to be considered Nazi sympathizers, Leeds evaded any adverse publicity and would end the conflict as initially a hospital, firstly for survivors of the Dunkirk evacuation, and later as a convalescent home for burned airmen whose lives had been saved by the celebrated plastic surgeon Archie McIndoe at East Grinstead.

Olive's commitment to Leeds would last for decades, and even after the outbreak of war she had continued her quest for furniture and art, and as her appearance in any saleroom inevitably would force up auction prices, she employed numerous experts to act on her behalf, and one such antiques dealer was Nathan Metheun, the owner of a fashionable gallery in the Old Brompton Road. He was but one of a network of people in the trade who acted on commission to offer Olive first refusal on any suitable pictures.

Just such an occasion occurred in April 1940 when Metheun acquired a fine portrait, *Anne Thistlewaite, the Countess of Chesterfield* by Thomas Gainsborough, commissioned from the artist by her husband Philip

Stanhope, the fifth earl. Metheun had taken the large painting, roughly eight foot tall and five wide, down to Leeds on Sunday, 4 May in a van driven by his employee, George McMahon. The dealer had arranged an afternoon appointment with Olive in the Maiden's Tower at three o'clock, a time that had been agreed which accommodated the limited period that McMahon would be in possession of the Gainsborough, having been loaned it for just two days, and Olive's wish to have one of her lunch guests, David Margesson, examine it before he departed for London.

Although not widely acknowledged as an expert on Gainsborough, Margesson was one of Adrian's contemporaries in the Commons, a colleague eight years older whose career path had been quite similar. He had been elected at the 1922 General Election, but had lost his seat the following year, only to find the rock-solid Rugby constituency in 1924. Educated at Harrow and Magdalene College, Cambridge, and commissioned into a cavalry regiment, the 11th Hussars, to serve in France and be decorated with the Military Cross, he had joined the Whips' office and in November 1931, had been appointed Chief Whip in Ramsay MacDonald's National Government, and was confirmed in the post when Stanley Baldwin became Prime Minister in June 1935, and again when Neville Chamberlain succeeded him in May 1937. By May 1940, Margesson had been the occupant of his official residence, 12 Downing Street, for a record nine years, a period during which he had attended Cabinet, as an *ex officio* member, chaired by three prime ministers.

Separated from his wife Frances, whom he had married while on leave in 1916, the pipe-smoking Margesson's two closest friends were a fellow MP, Geoffrey Lloyd, and Olive. Not quite his contemporary at Harrow and Cambridge, Lloyd had entered the Commons in 1931, and served as Baldwin's Parliamentary Private Secretary until he was appointed a junior minister in the Home Office in 1935, and then promoted in April 1939 as Secretary for Mines in the Board of Trade under Oliver Stanley. Although Lloyd was respected on all the benches, and well-liked within the Conservative Party, he was unmarried and relatively unknown to the general public. However, as a bachelor he was wedded to a Parliamentary life, and for much of his political life had acted as Baldwin's eyes and ears in that den of intrigue, the Members' Tea Room.

Olive's friendship with Lloyd and Margesson had lasted though both her marriages, to the extent that they seemed to others to be semipermanent fixtures at Leeds, two spare men straight from the hanky-drawer.

Margesson was anxious to return to London that same Sunday afternoon, but had complied with Olive's request that he delay his departure until after lunch so he would cast his eye over the Gainsborough, to be placed on a stand erected in the drawing-room, and offer his advice. He felt he had the time to spare because he had now made a crucial decision, following a brief meeting at tea-time on Saturday afternoon with Winston Churchill, who had motored the short distance from Chartwell. The very informal chat had been intended as an attempt to sound out the First Lord of the Admiralty on the strength of his support for the government in the following week's two-day debate on the disastrous Norwegian campaign.

The issue was of critical importance as the Admiralty would have to shoulder its share of the blame for the debacle, and Winston might need to be reminded of his responsibilities, both departmental, being in charge of the Royal Navy, and constitutionally collective, as a loyal member of the Cabinet. Margesson had already taken soundings and learned that Eddie Wood, as Lord Halifax, intended to seize the opportunity to depose Chamberlain, and all agreed that, to avoid uncertainty and the danger of inadvertently giving comfort to the King's enemies, the transition should be swift and executed with the support of the current War Cabinet.

In this task, Margesson was in his element, the unseen power broker who, in the silent purdah imposed on the Whips' office had not spoken on the floor of the House since 1924. Margesson was the quintessential Chief Whip, the government's most senior business manager who had achieved the impossible by holding the National Coalition together, and then seeing off Winston and his fellow rebels over the 1933 Indian home rule bill. Always pragmatic, despite his reputation as a stern disciplinarian, Margesson was the conduit for dissent on the backbenches, and there was nobody more skilled at taking the troops' temperature and delivering wise counsel in private to the Prime Minister, or to him in front of the Cabinet, if invited to do so.

The Chief's exercise of influence was often mistaken by outsiders as a role requiring a talent for cajolery, bullying and occasionally bribery, by the promise of dispensing patronage, but the reality was rather different. Margesson had always chosen to listen, not hector, and over the years had acquired a reputation as an *emimance grise*, his unseen hand directing Chamberlain's decision to appoint a reduced, inner

Cabinet to manage the war, and in only the previous months to replace Leslie Hore-Belisha at the War Office with Oliver Stanley, and to move Sam Hoare to the Air Ministry. His other co-conspirator was equally obscure to the electorate, for Maurice Hankey, for twenty-six years the country's most senior civil servant, had never been elected to any position, ever. After his retirement as longest-serving Cabinet Secretary in 1938, he had accepted Chamberlain's invitation, brokered by Margesson, to become Minister without Portfolio, and he too exercised power behind the scenes, albeit outside the Palace of Westminster.

Margesson's position was bolstered by what was termed 'the usual channels', meaning his continuous contact with his counterpart in the Labour Party, Charles Edwards. Since his appointment, also in 1931, the two men had developed a working relationship based on trust and mutual respect. Elected for Bedwellty in 1916 when he was already aged forty-nine, Edwards came from the most humble of Welsh farming backgrounds in Llanynllo and had his finger on the pulse of his parliamentary party. He had endured the divisive period of Ramsay MacDonald's premiership, and had already discussed the possibility of a wartime coalition before setting off to the party's Whitsun conference at the Highcliff Hotel in Bournemouth.

In their encounter on Saturday, Winston had explained to Margesson that he intended to scupper Halifax if he made a bid for the succession, and appealed to his patriotism to ensure a quick but effective coup. From his private conversations with Edwards, Margesson learned that the Opposition would demand a confidence vote at the end of the debate on Wednesday evening. He also knew that the Labour leadership would not cooperate with Chamberlain or his Chancellor, Sir John Simon, and thought it doubtful that Halifax, handicapped with a speech impediment and a commitment to Roman Catholicism, would be able to head the government from the House of Lords. Aside from these potentially disqualifying disadvantages, Halifax was the obvious successor, and infinitely more attractive to colleagues than any other contender, and especially Winston, who was so distrusted. Under normal circumstances the Conservative Commons majority of 280 would be unassailable, but in the fetid atmosphere of the Narvik disaster not even party loyalty could be relied upon to deliver the required level of support. A major rebellion, or even large abstentions, would be enough to undermine Chamberlain, and ensure his resignation. Much, of course, would depend on the reaction of the

Labour Party, and he was aware that some senior figures, such as Hugh Dalton, were already scheming with disaffected Tories to plan a new government.

As Margesson emerged from luncheon, accompanied by Olive, he contemplated his unexpected role as king-maker. Although he could not guarantee how the Parliamentary Labour Party would react four nights' hence, he sensed that history was being made before his eyes, and he was in the extraordinary position of being both ringmaster and spectator in a change of government that would determine the future of his country, and perhaps Europe too.

It was at this moment that Margesson entered the drawing-room on the ground floor of the Maiden's Tower to be introduced by Olive to Metheun, while McMahon stood aside, as though he was guarding the portrait. The picture was truly magnificent, and appeared to dominate the room, with its huge windows commanding a spectacular view over the lake and the park beyond. Even in these exquisite surroundings, the Gainsborough, completed in 1777, was the natural focus of attention, and Olive and her house-guest were enchanted with the wonderful canvass showing the Countess, in all her aristocratic splendour, sitting beside a tree, with the rolling hills of her estate in the background. Wearing a blue, low-cut gown, with her long hair gathered high, and a shawl over her arms, she is gazing across from her home, Bretby Hall, in Derbyshire.

The pair seemed almost transfixed by the impact of the picture's bright colours, and the rather superior but thoughtful air adopted by the subject. It was a classic Gainsborough, and a very fine example of his work.

'This is a truly wonderful portrait,' murmured Margesson as he stepped closer and bent down to examine the ornate gilt caption on the frame.

'A great picture by a great artist,' agreed Metheun. 'A rare opportunity to possess one of the masters, your ladyship'.

Olive nodded her head in approval, her decision having been made. 'I will have the estate office telephone you in the morning', she said, not registering the look of disapproval that had clouded Margesson's face.

'Who is selling?' he asked.

'Ah,' replied Metheun, his voice acquiring a confidential tone. 'That is a matter of some delicacy. I am not presently at liberty to divulge the identity of the present owner, but of course that information may be forthcoming after the sale.'

'I should hope so,' remarked Margesson drily. 'The last time I saw the Countess was at Witley Park in Surrey. Perhaps you know Sir John Legh?'

A look of desperation appeared in Metheun's eyes. 'I may have met the gentleman, but obviously that is not for me to say.'

Margesson straightened his back, and turned to address Olive. 'Unless I am very much mistaken, this was sold by the Canarvons, quite a few years ago, to John Legh.'

'The newspaper and property man?' asked Olive.

Margesson nodded. 'It was part of the Highclere collection sold to pay for all those Egyptian archeological digs. It's a family portrait. One of the Stanhopes married a Canarvon.'

'Well, we won't have to worry about the *provenance*, then,' observed Olive.

'You can't touch it,' declared Margesson, with finality. '*The Countess* was taken from Witley in burglary not so long ago. Legh was absolutely bereft. This is stolen.'

As Olive turned to confront the indignant Metheun, who seemed lost for words and on the point of protesting, McMahon stepped forward, drawing a revolver from his pocket and muttering something incomprehensible in a strong Irish accent. Olive screamed, Metheun turned for the door, and the weapon fired, causing Margesson to drop to his knees, a bullet having passed through his chest. With a momentary gasp, the Chief Whip fell forward onto the carpet, fatally wounded.

The death of David Margesson was widely misreported in the press as an armed robbery that went disastrously wrong, but its impact would be profound. As Margesson had anticipated, the Opposition forced a vote of no confidence on Wednesday, 8 May. When the Whips announced the result of the division, which cut the government majority to eighty-one, it meant that more than a hundred colleagues had abstained or voted against Chamberlain, despite his passionate plea for support from his friends, and Churchill's eloquence on his behalf.

This humiliation led the Prime Minister to confide in Churchill later the same evening that he could not continue, and would consult the Labour Party the following day, after he had been to the Palace to explain the crisis to the King, who was entirely sympathetic to his First Lord of the Treasury's predicament. The King expressed the view that he considered Chamberlain to have been treated abominably by his party.

For much of the night the telephone lines across Westminster were red hot as the various participants in the drama declared their allegiance to Chamberlain or threw their weight in favour of an alternative leader. The absent voice in this choreography was Margesson's, his role having been taken on temporarily by his deputy, the rather aloof James Stuart, a Scottish Unionist MP and member of the whips' office since 1935, a promotion that had taken twelve years of toil on the backbenches. The youngest son of the 17th Earl of Moray, Stuart cut a somewhat remote figure, wholly unsuited to the task of horse-trading with his political opponents. Accordingly, no such back-channel conversations took place, leaving the transition at Number Ten to be anything but smooth, and to exclude Winston from serious consideration. For staunch Tories such as Stuart, Churchill had shown himself to be a disloyal, a floor-crosser to and from the Liberals, and on occasion a troublesome rebel.

On the next morning Halifax was summoned from the Foreign Office, and Churchill strolled over from Admiralty House, to attend Chamberlain in the Cabinet Room, where the trio was joined by Clement Attlee and his deputy, Arthur Greenwood, to discuss the possibility of a coalition government. The Labour leader opined that a coalition might be possible under a new prime minister, but he would have to consult his party, then assembled in Bournemouth. Consequently, Attlee and Greenwood caught a train to Dorset, and telephoned in the middle of the next afternoon with the news that the National Executive Committee had voted to join a coalition on condition it was not led by Chamberlain. Fully expecting this reply, and in the absence of counsel from Margesson, the Prime Minister went to the Palace to resign and, at Churchill's suggestion, recommend Halifax as his successor.

Once Prime Minister, Halifax was the statesman most eminently qualified to cope with the crisis that confronted him. As a former Viceroy of India and Foreign Secretary, Halifax had vast, unrivalled experience at dealing with complex policy issues, and certainly had the measure of Hermann Göring and Adolf Hitler, whom he had met personally and negotiated with. He had not been unsympathetic to Germany's expansion into the Rhineland, Austria and the Sudetenland, earning him a reputation among Winston's supporters as an appeaser, However, like so many of his generation who had served in France during the Great War, and he had fought with his cavalry regiment, the Queens Own Yorkshire Dragoons before being transferred to a staff post, he felt a deep moral responsibility to avoid another global conflict, and to prevent Japan and Italy from joining a tripartite.

Halifax's only common ground with Mussolini, whom he had met in Rome over three days in January 1939, and Hitler, was their shared perception of the Communist threat, and this would become the basis of an accommodation reached the weekend that Nazi troops entered Belgium, Holland and the Netherlands. The alternative to peace was quite unthinkable: another world war.

The subsequent police investigation into the murder at Leeds Castle, conducted jointly by the Kent County Constabulary and the Metropolitan Police, identified Margesson's assailant as George McMahon, recently released from prison, who had served a sentence for an attempt to assassinate King Edward VIII. Metheun had been apprehended in London outside his home address in Westbourne Grove later the same evening, but no charges were brought against him after he was judged to be mentally unstable.

THE REALITY

On the morning of 16 July 1936, during a mounted parade outside Buckingham Palace George Andrew Campbell McMahon had approached the King with a loaded revolver when Special Constable Anthony Dick had intervened to disarm him. During the scuffle that had ensued, the gun had fallen to the ground, hitting the hind quarters of the King's horse. McMahon was taken into custody at Hyde Park Police Station by Chief Inspector Sands who searched him and found two rounds of ammunition and a picture postcard of the King.

Special Branch enquiries established that McMahon had been born in Dublin as Jerome Bannigan. At his trial at the Old Bailey in September 1936 he claimed that he had been paid £150 by a foreign power to assassinate the King, and asserted in his defence that he had deliberately bungled the attack. His statement was rejected and he was sentenced to a term of hard labour.

McMahon continued his subversive activities after his release, claiming to have had direct contact with leading Nazi Julius Streicher and communicated with Oswald Moseley. He continued to be monitored by the Security Services, but it was concluded that 'he is the sort of man who is perpetually thinking out magnificent schemes but who has very little ability to execute them.' He stood in a council by-election in Marylebone as an independent far-right candidate, but only received 197 votes. He died in Dublin in 1970.

The Metropolitan Police file on McMahon can be found at the National Archives, under the reference MEPO 3/1713, and the Security Service files on him are filed under KV 2/1506.

Chapter 3

The Mussolini Murder, May 1940

The Death of Il Duce, May 1940

By Robert Mitchell

Before there was Hitler, there was Benito Mussolini. Like Hitler, Mussolini's politics were shaped by the First World War, in which he had served in the Royal Italian Army before being wounded and discharged. Initially a prominent member of the Italian Socialist Party he turned against it when the socialists opposed the war, and was thrown out of the Party. This pushed Mussolini to the far right. He believed that socialism as a doctrine had failed, and had failed the Italian people.

After the war the Italian economy was in poor shape. The lira was devalued (in 1913 the exchange rate of the lira was twenty-five to one pound sterling, by 1925 it was 121 lira to the pound) and high inflation caused considerable hardship, the country continuing to function only through loans from Britain and the United States. However, the famed economist John Maynard Keynes advised the British Government not to advance any more money, calling Italy 'a hopeless case'. With the very rapid decline in post-war industrial output, unemployment rose sharply and riots over food rationing were widespread. What the country needed, Mussolini believed, was a man 'ruthless and energetic enough to make a clean sweep' to revive the Italian nation

On 23 March 1919, Mussolini reformed the small Italian fascist party as the *Fasci Italiani di Combattimento* (Italian Combat Squad), consisting of just 200 members, in Milan. Mussolini sought to make Italy strong again, offering supporters visions of a return to the glory days of Rome.

In this respect, he envisaged what he defined as the *pazio vitale* or vital space, analogous to Hitler's later *Lebensraum*, which would see the expansion of Italy into the countries along the Mediterranean which historically had been associated with the Roman Empire.

There were many features of Mussolini's philosophies which were mirrored by the Nazi Party, racial superiority being one of the most notable. He considered that the Slavs to the east and the Africans to the south were racially inferior and that following the principles of Darwin, it was only 'natural' that the stronger people would dominate the inferior ones. He declared, in a speech on 20 September 1920 that: 'The Italian border should run across the Brenner Pass, Monte Nevoso and the Dinaric Alps … I would say we can easily sacrifice 500,000 barbaric Slavs [of Yugoslavia] for 50,000 Italians.'

His words appealed widely to all classes, offering the prospect of a strong Italy that would stand amongst the foremost nations of the world, spreading its empire across the Mediterranean and North Africa.

THE MAD IRISHWOMAN

By 1921 the Fascists had become a serious political force. Mussolini received support from business leaders as he used his paramilitary wing, his Blackshirts, to suppress trade unions, and the Army backed his bid to make Italy a strong military nation. On 22 October 1922, Mussolini led the famous March on Rome at the head of 30,000 followers. Fearing civil war, King Victor Emmanuel III accepted Prime Minister Luigi Facta's resignation and handed power to Mussolini.

Mussolini gradually turned Italy into a one-party state, but received popular support for his strong government. Of course, there were many who hated and feared Mussolini and on 7 April 1926, an attempt was made to assassinate him – by an insane Irish woman.

The Honourable Violet Albina Gibson was born in Dublin on 31 August 1876. Her father was lawyer and politician Edward Gibson. He was made 1st Baron Ashbourne ten years later, and from 1885 to 1905 served as Lord High Chancellor of Ireland. According to reports in the Irish press, during her forties, Violet grew evermore obsessed with religion and began fixating on martyrdom and 'mortification', which, in Violet's mind, meant 'putting to death'.[1] In 1922, she suffered a nervous breakdown, was declared insane and committed to a mental institution. Two years later, Violet was released and travelled to Rome, where she lived in a convent. By this stage, she had become convinced that God wanted her to kill someone – even if it was herself. Somehow, she acquired a gun and shot herself in the chest. Violet survived only to turn her attention to the most prominent man in Italy – Benito Mussolini.

That spring day in 1926, the Italian Prime Minister was giving a speech at the Palazzo del Littorio. Violet went to the event, carrying a revolver and a rock. The latter was in case she needed to smash the windscreen of Mussolini's car before shooting him. As it happened, Mussolini was on foot, and he walked through the adoring crowd right in front of Violet. She pulled the trigger of her revolver just as Mussolini moved his head and the bullet only grazed his nose. She tried again, but the gun misfired.

The crowd leapt upon the Irish woman who was badly beaten before she was rescued by the police. It was quickly evident that Violet was insane, being diagnosed as a 'chronic paranoiac'. The poor women was allowed to return to the UK and taken into the care of St Andrew's Hospital, London.

Six months later, almost to the day, Mussolini survived another assassination attempt. This time it was a fifteen-year-old boy. Anteo Zamboni was the son of an anarchist typographer, Mammolo Zamboni of Bolgona. He had evidently been heavily influenced by his father's beliefs and had, no doubt, sought to gain his approval by carrying out an extreme anarchical act – to kill the country's foremost individual. This was no rash act on Anteo's part. He joined the Fascist youth movement, the Avantguardisti, in the expectation that this would give him a better chance of being able to get close to Mussolini if he was wearing Avantguardisti uniform.

Anteo's chance came when Mussolini visited Bologna on 30 and 31 October 1926. Accompanied by his wife Rachele and his sixteen-year-old daughter, Edda, and his brother Arnaldo, Mussolini spent the day of the 30th, inspecting public buildings in the city and taking the salute at Fascist demonstrations. In the evening, he set off to the train station to join the rest of his family who had been taken there earlier. With him in the car were Count Dino Grandi and the Mayor of Bologna.

The streets were lined with adoring crowds as the car drove slowly to the station. Wearing his Avantguardisti uniform, Anteo was able to pass through the police cordon and into the zone reserved for Party members. He pushed himself to the front of the gathering on the Via dell'Indipendenza. The previous evening, he had written what he must have known was likely to be his last words: 'To kill a tyrant who tortures a nation is not a crime, it is justice. To die for the cause of liberty is beautiful and sacred.'[2]

As Mussolini's car passed him, the young anarchist fired at the Prime Minister. His bullet missed Mussolini, only tearing the Mayor's uniform. Mussolini's driver raced onto the station as Anteo was set upon by the crowd, and lynched on the spot. His body was beaten, stabbed and shot, and then, quite literally, torn to pieces, his arms and legs being carried around the city in triumph by the Fascists.

After that torrid year for Mussolini, apart from a planned assassination by another anarchist called Michele Schirru, who was executed in 1931, he was able to consolidate his position, making himself President of Italy. The rise of the Nazi Party in Germany and the Falangists in Spain saw a shift towards nationalism across much of Europe, which many believed would inevitably lead to conflict. With Europe still recovering from the terrible slaughter of the First World War (Italy suffered in excess of 2,000,000 casualties of which more than 500,000 had died), many left-wing and moderate groups sought to prevent Italy being drawn into another global conflict.

With tension mounting following Hitler's annexation of Austria and his occupation of Czechoslovakia, fears grew in Italy that Mussolini would support Germany if war broke out. In 1936 the two countries had signed a treaty of mutual interest, which Mussolini saw as the creation of a Berlin-Rome Axis, and ties between the two Fascist leaders had strengthened over the subsequent years.

Communist leaders had to plan in secret, as the Italian Communist Party (Partito Comunista Italiano) had been outlawed. They saw only one solution; Mussolini would have to die to save Italy.

The man who would take it upon his self to rid Italy of its dictator, Marco Columbera, was perfectly aware that Mussolini remained hugely popular but he was convinced, as were the others in his group, that most Italians were happy with Mussolini's occupation of Albania in April 1939, aping Hitler's *anschluss* and that the assassination of Mussolini would not be universally applauded. They knew that they dare only kill Mussolini if he was on the point of dragging Italy into war, believing that most Italians did not want to see a repeat of the First World War with the likely enemy being their neighbour, France. Relations between the two countries had already become strained with Italy threatening to seize Tunisia, Corsica, Djibouti and even Nice in the South of France!

Following the German invasion of Poland, and the subsequent declaration of war by Britain and France, Mussolini bided his time, waiting for the right moment to strike over the Alps and into Egypt and Sudan. Columbera and his team were also poised and waiting. Timing, for all concerned, was going to be crucial.

It was the sudden Blitzkrieg unleashed upon France and the Low Countries on 10 May 1940 that was the trigger. Columbera was convinced that Mussolini would immediately declare war on Britain and France. He had to act now.

CIVIL WAR

It was announced that Mussolini was to inspect troops leaving for Aosta, close to the French border, on 20 May. It would be Columbera's last, and probably only, opportunity to assassinate Mussolini before Italy was at war. He was provided with details of Mussolini's route through Rome and he decided that as two attempts at shooting the President had both failed, the best way of ensuring success was to throw a bomb into Mussolini's famous open-top red Lancia.

On the morning of the 20th, units of the Littorio Armoured Division were to be inspected by Mussolinin, before moving off to join General Umberto di Savoia's Gruppo Armate Ovest (Army Group West). The Littorio Division had just received seventy M11/39 medium tanks and Mussolini wanted to show off these new Italian machines.

Columbera waited by the Porta Pia, a gateway in the Aurelian Walls of Rome. At last the buzz of the crowd to his right suddenly increased and moments later the cavalcade appeared. Mussolini's car was the second of the convoy, the bright morning sun illuminating the polished red paintwork. Columbera ignited the fuze and lobbed it into the slow-moving open-top Lancia. It really could not have been easier. The bomb landed in the back seat, and bounced onto the floor. Mussolini and General Giovanni Messe scrabbled around their feet to grab the bomb. It exploded just as Mussolini got his hands round the device. The explosion blew apart the Lancia, its rear doors being propelled more than thirty feet through the air. It also blew apart Benito Mussolini.

For Colunbera there was no escape. But the police lining the streets were quick to respond and managed to arrest the assassin before he was beaten to death. There would be no quick end for the man who had killed the great and beloved Il Duce. He was going to have a long and very painful life.

The Communists had often dreamt of this day, and their propaganda machine, which they had developed in France, moved quickly into high gear. Leaflets and posters appeared almost miraculously overnight, adorning walls, lampposts and windows:

THE FASCIST DICTATOR IS DEAD!
LONG LIVE FREEDOM!
Workers Unite
End injustice. Demand Workers' Unions

Before the nationalist press could print long eulogies extolling the almost innumerable achievements of their dead leader, word had spread across Rome, Mantua, Milan and Turin, though notably not in Naples, that there would be marches on the evening of 21 May. Vast crowds certainly appeared thronging the streets of northern Italian towns and cities. But, in what was a move that surprised most observers, there were as many carrying communist red flags as were waving the green, white and red of the Italian Empire. Mussolini had a somewhat strained relationship with King Victor Emmanuel III, who, as head of state, was still seen as the embodiment of Italian values – that of family and loyalty – unlike the adulterer Mussolini. The majority of Italians wanted a more moderate form of government overseen by the King.

In line with the Italian Constitution, it was only the King who could appoint the Prime Minister, and Victor Emmanuel wanted to move quickly to prevent the anarchists from exploiting the instability resulting from the assassination. But many groups now saw their chance to seize power.

The first of these groups to move were the antifascist organisations, such as Giorgio Amendola's *Partito Popolare Italiano*, and Pietro Nenni's *Partito Socialista Italiano*, which marched on Rome. The first clashes of the Italian Civil War broke out with the Fascists determined to retain their position. The Italian Communist Party formed Patriotic Action Groups (*Gruppi di Azione*) to unleash urban terror through bomb attacks. In the words of their statement, in effect their manifesto: 'To the tyranny of Fascism, that claims to reduce slavery through violence and terror, we must respond with violence and terror.'

The Civil War lasted for twenty months. Though casualty figures were hard to collate, something in the region of 70,000 were killed before the left-wing groups achieved victory. Despite his popularity, the Communists could not allow the continuation of a monarchy and the Italian Socialist Republic was formed. Victor Emmanuel abdicated and went into exile.

THE SECOND WORLD WAR

Whilst Italy was embroiled in its internecine struggle, the Second World War pursued its course almost unnoticed by the Italians. By the time the Socialist Republic had become established Germany was all but on its knees. The United States had thrown its vast resources into the conflict in 1942, putting every effort into its 'Europe First' strategy. The Italian Republic declared its neutrality, to confirm what was already an accepted fact.

With just one enemy in Europe to fight – the Third Reich – the Allies were able to mount an invasion of France in 1943 in overwhelming numbers which, fifteen months later, saw British and US troops marching up the Unter den Linden. One can only wonder what might have happened if Mussolini had survived the assassination attempt and joined forces with those of Germany. Britain might well have found itself forced to defend Egypt against a combined German-Italian army and might have had to divert considerable naval resources into the Mediterranean. It might indeed have been the case that US and British armies had to invade Italy, thus delaying the Normandy invasion until 1944. One bomb, one death, may well have saved millions of lives. We shall never know.

THE REALITY

It really was the case that a bomb was thrown at Mussolini's car as it passed the Porta Pia in Rome. The would-be assassin was Gino Lucetti, who after leaving the Italian Army at the end of the First World War, became increasingly dissatisfied with the growth of the right-wing in Italy and he migrated to France. There he met other like-minded exiles and Lucetti became an active member of anti-fascist groups. When their propaganda efforts across the border failed to arouse much support in Italy, the decision was taken to kill Mussolini.

With logistical help from other anarchists, a plan was devised in which Lucetti would throw a bomb at Mussolini as Il Duce drove through Rome on 11 September 1926. Having been provided with details of the route Mussolini would take, Lucetti waited near the Porta Pia. When Mussolini's famous open top red Lancia reached the old gateway, Lucetti threw the bomb at the car. The bomb hit either the windscreen or a wheel, depending on the different versions of the incident, but just bounced off, exploding a few yards away on the pavement.

In the ensuing confusion Lucetti tried to hide, but he was soon apprehended by Mussolini's police bodyguards, and, of course, given a good kicking. On him they found another bomb, a handgun with six dumdum bullets poisoned with muriatic acid, and a dagger. He received a thirty-year prison sentence, with lesser terms for his principal co-conspirators.

Mussolini survived that attack and he declared war on Britain and France on 10 June 1940. The war did not go well for Italy, suffering reverses in North Africa before being invaded by US and British forces in September 1943. By then it was already too late for Mussolini, who was arrested on the King's orders on 25 July 1943. Four days later he celebrated his sixtieth birthday.

Though the newly-appointed Prime Minister, General Pietro Badoglio, told Hitler that Italy would continue to fight on Germany's side, Allied bombing of Italian cities, especially Rome, brought pressure upon him from many quarters across Italy. On 8 September Badoglio announced that Italy would accept the peace terms that had been offered by the Allied governments.

By this time German troops had occupied the whole of northern Italy and Hitler decided to re-install Mussolini as head of the government. Mussolini was being held at a disused hotel on the highest point of the Gran Sasso mountain range near L'Aquila, and he sent paratroopers to rescue the former dictator. Mussolini was whisked away to Munich, along with his wife and two children.

German troops occupied Rome and Victor Emmanuel and Badoglio abandoned the capital, setting up the government in Brindisi. Mussolini saw this as an opportunity to re-establish his position in Rome. But the capital was dangerously close to the front line, and Mussolini had to re-form his government at Salò on Lake Garda. In November 1943, he became head of the 'Italian Social Republic'.

As the Allies advanced up the boot of Italy, so the territory of Mussolini's Social Republic shrank. By the spring of 1945, with Germany on the brink of defeat, Mussolini was asked to surrender to the legitimate Italian Government which had returned to Rome.

Mussolini asked for certain guarantees, including that the soldiers of the Italian Social Republic would not face prosecution. No such guarantees were forthcoming, so Mussolini made a bid to escape to Switzerland.

On 27 April, with a number of members of his government, he headed for the Swiss border, joining a group of 200 German soldiers who were also setting out in their trucks for Switzerland. Mussolini sat in the back of the last truck wearing a German helmet as a disguise.

The convoy drove up the west side of Lake Como, but was stopped at Musso by a large band of partisans. The leader of the party said that the Germans could continue their journey, but that no Italians would be allowed to escape. The trucks were inspected and, no doubt to the great delight of the partisans, they discovered Mussolini. He was arrested and taken to Drongo, along with his mistress Claretta Petacci and was placed under armed guard in a farmhouse.

CONSPIRACY THEORY

Exactly what happened to Mussolini in his final moments has never been satisfactorily established. We know that the other Fascists traveling with Mussolini were immediately shot, and that in the official account of Mussolini's death the Council of the Resistance decided that he should also be summarily executed, following a radio message from Rome. The fear was that Allied forces might try to capture Mussolini. Strange as it may seem, numerous American and British politicians had, in the past, praised Mussolini for his suppression of the communist movement in Italy and, with Fascism all but dead the Western powers were now seeing communism as the next great threat to democracy. So, President General Cadorna signed the order for Mussolini to be killed, making the execution legitimate.

Colonel Valerio (real name Walter Audisio) went to the farmhouse on the afternoon of 28 April with a number of his partisans. He took Mussolini and Claretta, who refused to leave him, to the road outside the gates of Villa Belmonte a short distance from the house. Valerio read out the death sentence of the Resistance Council and Mussolini and Claretta were shot by Valerio and his men.

There is another version of this story which is that when Valerio arrived at the farmhouse he found that Mussolini and Claretta had already been shot by the partisans earlier in the day in the courtyard of the farm. This would have meant that he had been executed before his death had been officially sanctioned. With the Resistance Council keen to be seen as acting in a fair and legal manner, they could not reveal to the world that the former dictator had been murdered by people loyal to the Resistance.

This was witnessed by a young girl who was sworn to secrecy for fifty years. She lived to tell the tale when released from her promise fifty years later. The motive for the killing seemingly, was that a few weeks earlier eighteen members of the partisan group that captured Mussolini had been taken prisoner and shot by Fascists. This was their revenge.

Whilst this sounds quite a plausible tale, the rest of the story is more difficult to believe. So that Mussolini could be executed 'officially', two locals, one who looked like Mussolini and a girl who was similar in appearance to Claretta, were dressed up and taken outside the Villa Belmonte to take part in a mock execution with blank rounds.[3] It seems an unlikely charade.

The bodies of Mussolini and the others of his entourage executed by the partisans, fourteen in total, were taken to the Piazzale Loreto in Milan. The sorry sight was witnessed by a young Swiss journalist:

> Four of them, including Mussolini and Petacci, hung by their feet, head down, like butchered animals from a girder above an adjacent petrol station ... What had once been their shirts now dangled down, leaving the chests of the four white and exposed. The crowd was huge, monstrous and eager, seething and pressing in the immense piazza with a kind of constant, low, indistinct roar.[4]

The crowd surged forward to kick and spit on the corpses. It was an ignominious end to the man who had restored Italian pride.

It might have been thought that the Mussolini story would end there, but on 29 August 2004 a documentary was shown on RAI, Italian state television, in which it was claimed that Mussolini was executed by British secret agents under orders from Winston Churchill, not by the group of partisans.

The film's credibility hinges on the evidence of former Italian partisan Bruno Lonati, who says he was one of the two-man team given the task of getting rid of the Mussolini and Claretta. Lonati claims that he acted along with a British Special Operations Executive agent codenamed Captain John, a Briton of Sicilian descent, real name Robert Maccarone, who had been sent to Italy with the specific mission of eliminating Mussolini.

Mr Lonati says that they went to the house near Lake Como where the couple had been held since their arrest, escorted them down a lane that led to the lake, stood them against a fence and opened fire with Sten guns.[5]

The reason given for the British Prime Minister wishing to have Mussolini assassinated is one that had been circulating for some years. It is alleged that when he was captured Mussolini was carrying documents that he hoped to use in his defence at his trial as a war criminal. These included letters from both Churchill and Austen

41

Chamberlain declaring their admiration for the Fascist leader before the Second Italo-Ethiopian War in which Italy conquered Ethiopia (or Abyssinia) and absorbed it into the Italian Empire. It is claimed that Mussolini 'aligned Italian foreign policy with Britain's'.[6]

There were also, it is claimed, letters from Churchill in which he had tried to induce Italy to make a separate peace with the Allies. This was in defiance of his agreement with President Franklin Roosevelt at Casablanca that the war could end only with the unconditional surrender of all the Axis powers. No *proven* documentary evidence of this has so far emerged.

NOTES:
1. *Belfast Telegraph*, 2 April, 2016.
2. Quoted in Jasper Ridley, *Mussolini* (Constable, London, 1997), p.183.
3. *Sunday Times*, 14 July 1996.
4. Christopher Duggan, *Fascist Voices, An Intimate History of Mussolini's Italy* (Bodley Head, London, 2012), p.417.
5. Taken from the *Independent* of 28 August 2004.
6. Richard Lamb, *War in Italy, 1943-1945: A Brutal Story* (St Martin's Press, 1994), p.303.

Chapter 4

Bullets in Birdcage Walk
The Assassination of Winston Churchill, July 1940

By Adrian Gilbert

The murder of Winston Churchill on Tuesday, 23 July 1940, shook Britain to its very core. That the Prime Minister of the United Kingdom could be gunned down in the streets of the capital, with the prospect of invasion by Nazi Germany ever-present, seemed unbelievable. But the doleful news bulletins of the Prime Minister's death were to prove only too accurate.

Churchill had attended a routine audience with the King on the evening of the 23rd, before leaving Buckingham Palace for the five-minute drive back to 10 Downing Street. While on Birdcage Walk, an apparently broken-down removal van suddenly veered across the path of Churchill's car, forcing it to a halt. A powerful Wolseley 18/85 then rammed the car from behind. Three men leapt from the Wolseley, and with revolvers in hand shot at the now trapped car, while a shotgun fired by the driver of the removal van smashed its windscreen.

Inside the Prime Minister's car, the driver and John Martin, one of Churchill's private secretaries, had been incapacitated by the crash and the shotgun blast. Sitting in the back, Churchill's veteran bodyguard, Walter Thompson, reached for his own revolver. Simultaneously he tried to shield the Prime Minister and prevent him from opening the car door. Churchill was having none of it. He shook off Thompson and clambered out into the street to confront his attackers.

From the subsequent post-mortem examination, we know the first bullet hit Churchill in the arm, followed by two shots to the chest, one of which fatally penetrated his heart. Amidst the noise of gunshots and the shouts that rang across Birdcage Walk and Green Park, it was claimed that he had called out, 'Not now!' before falling to the ground.

Thus ended the life and career of Winston Spencer Churchill, the political maverick who, against all odds, had achieved supreme office. He had spent just seventy-five days as Prime Minister.

Thompson, meanwhile, had been shot in the face, a .32in bullet breaking his jaw, but spitting out blood and broken teeth he pushed the car door open and fired back. Thompson had been Churchill's bodyguard for nearly twenty years; he was thoroughly trained in close-quarters combat, and his well-placed shots brought down two of the attackers. But in so doing he became a stationary target, taking a second bullet to the stomach.

The remaining assailant, who had fired the shots that killed Churchill, fled the scene. He ran from Birdcage Walk and through the passageway of Cockpit Steps. There he slipped into a waiting car that drove away along Dartmouth Street. The removal-van driver jumped from his cab, but was tackled and restrained by an alert member of the public.

The arrival of the police was followed a few minutes later by that of an ambulance to assist the wounded. Martin and the driver both survived, the latter permanently blinded through his injuries. Thompson – 'the Prime Minister's bulldog' – was rushed across the river to St Thomas's, but in an age before the advent of antibiotics, septicemia proved fatal; he died three days later.

WHO?

Once the fact of Churchill's death had been established, the immediate question was who was responsible? The first, obvious assumption was that it was the work of German secret agents. In previous weeks, British cartoonists had made great play of the idea of German parachutists landing in Britain, poorly disguised as nuns, in the light of rumours from the German conquest of the Netherlands. The drawings of stubble-chinned nuns with jackboots under their habits suddenly seemed less amusing.

During the long night of 23/24 July, the government was forced to come to terms with the loss of its leader. The armed forces were put on full alert, in the expectation of attack from air and sea, but to general relief there was only silence from the German side. The real answer to the question came readily enough.

The captured van driver, who gave his name as Brown, was a former Army sergeant who held a minor clerical position in the Cabinet Office. He co-operated with the police and identified the two dead assassins as officers from his old regiment. The other attacker was discovered to be a First World War veteran, Major H. J. Read. He was not to remain at large for long; the 'getaway' car broke down at Shepherd's Bush, less than three miles from the scene of the attack. As the driver – Read's former batman, R. Hunt – attempted to restart the car, a policeman passed by on foot patrol. At that point, an emotionally exhausted Read stepped forward and gave himself up to the rather surprised local bobby.

With the surviving suspects locked up at Cannon Row police station, the Metropolitan Police and the politicians attempted to make order from the chaos of the day. Meetings of both the War Cabinet and the wider full Cabinet were immediately called. They were informed, from a preliminary interrogation, that the assassins vehemently denied having any ties with Germany, insisting that they had acted alone.

While appeals for calm were issued to the nation through Fleet Street and the BBC, the War Cabinet convened with a single item on its agenda – to choose the next Prime Minister. With Churchill dead, the War Cabinet comprised just four members: Neville Chamberlain, the former Prime Minister and leader of the Conservative Party; Viscount Edward Halifax, the Foreign Secretary; Clement Attlee, Lord Privy Seal; and Arthur Greenwood, Minister without Portfolio, who with Attlee comprised the two senior Labour members in the otherwise Conservative-led coalition government.

Taking the chair, Chamberlain hardly needed to remind the others of a similar meeting held on 9 May that had also chosen a new Prime Minister – the painful encounter that followed his own resignation as premier after the debacle in Norway. On that day, the choice had been between Halifax and Churchill. Halifax had been the preferred candidate, supported by the majority of the Conservative Party and by King George. When canvassed for its opinion, the Labour Party had replied that it would back either man in place of Chamberlain. That Churchill got the job was a consequence of Halifax standing aside.

Halifax deferred to Churchill's greater knowledge of military matters and easy ability to appeal to the British public, although he maintained his own reservations, confiding to a friend, 'I don't think WSC will be a very good PM'.[1]

Despite stepping down, Halifax was not without political ambition. R. A. Butler, the undersecretary of state for foreign affairs, wrote: 'He told me he could do the job. He also felt that Churchill needed a restraining influence.'[2] Halifax believed that by continuing in his role as Foreign Secretary, he was best placed, in the words of his biographer Andrew Roberts, 'to dissuade Churchill from disastrous over-reactions'.[3]

But now, Churchill was no longer in charge. Chamberlain made it clear to Halifax that he alone commanded the necessary levels of support in both houses and from all parties, and, turning to Attlee and Greenwood, he emphasised the necessity of total unanimity in the choice of Prime Minister; any hint of discord would undermine the already shaken morale of the British people and provide vital ammunition to Britain's enemies. Both Labour politicians assented to the choice of Halifax.

Britain's strategic position was now far worse than it had been on 9 May – to lead the country was indeed a poisoned chalice – but Halifax had no hesitation in accepting, for reasons of simple duty and his quiet yet firm belief that he could run the country better than his erratic predecessor.

In the early hours of the 24th the King and the Cabinet confirmed Halifax's appointment, too late for the first editions that all carried the terse front-page statement from the Ministry of Information that a criminal gang had murdered the Prime Minister.

Whether Halifax managed to sleep at all during the remainder of the night is unknown, but at 11.00 hours, he called his first Cabinet meeting. All ministers were requested to remain at their posts – regardless of their private feelings towards the new Prime Minister – while the now vacant position of Minister of Defence (created by Churchill for himself in May 1940) was assigned to Anthony Eden, currently minister responsible for the Army. Matters of policy were not discussed; the only decision being to 'carry on as usual'. The conduct of the war would be left to Halifax and his immediate advisors.

Even before the new cabinet had convened, the first responses to Churchill's death were reverberating across Britain and around the world. Radio broadcasts from the BBC repeatedly called for calm, insisting that the assassination was an isolated, criminal event, and while most of the population was simply stunned by the news, marches and demonstrations took place in London and other major British cities. As largely spontaneous outpourings of anger against the killing of the nation's leader they had no political programme and simply withered away over time.

Of more immediate importance was the overseas' reaction. The states of the British Commonwealth and Empire expressed their continuity of support for Britain and its struggle against Nazi Germany (although not a view shared by nationalist movements within the Empire, who saw the demise of the arch-imperialist as an opportunity to renegotiate the colonial contract). In the United States, President Roosevelt immediately conveyed his personal condolences to the British people, condemning the murder of his old friend as 'an act of infamy'. The US Congress was joined by the governments of the remaining democracies in expressing their revulsion at the assassination, although no commitments were made, all waiting on the course of events.

Of Britain's enemies, the Pétain government in France was perhaps the most gleeful in reporting Churchill's death. The humiliation of defeat had been exacerbated on 3 July, by Churchill's decision (albeit made with great reluctance) to turn the guns of the Royal Navy on the French fleet at Mers-el-Kébir in Algeria to prevent the possibility of it falling under German control. But it was Germany's response that counted for most.

The Nazi leaders were as astonished as anyone else by the news. At first there was disbelief, and it was only a full twenty-four hours after the official BBC announcement that Goebbels' Propaganda Ministry declared that Churchill had fallen victim to 'the righteous anger of the British people, provoked beyond endurance by the antics of the drunken war-monger'. Ribbentrop, at the Foreign Ministry, kept his councel, conferring with the Führer over an appropriate official reply for a wider international audience.

WHY?

The interrogation of Churchill's assassins continued. Led by Special Branch, who were assisted by officers from the Security Service (MI5), the authorities found it difficult to believe the assertion made by Read and the two other survivors (Brown and Hunt) that they had acted on their own initiative. While it was accepted that there was no connection with Germany, it seemed impossible not to believe the assassination was part of a wider conspiracy designed to topple the government. But despite their best efforts, the police and MI5 failed to establish any direct connection with far-right groups, notwithstanding the knowledge that during the 1930s the accused had variously been members of the British Union of Fascists, The Link and the Nordic League. There was some suggestion that they had ties with shadowy Nazi sympathisers within the British establishment, but nothing was proven.

Throughout their interrogation and subsequent trial for murder and treachery, the assassins maintained the position that they had acted as patriots to get rid of Churchill, whose reckless and fundamentally wrong policies, had pushed the country to the point of military disaster.

They hoped their actions would arouse the nation to act, and that a new prime minister would realise that the true enemy of Britain was not Nazi Germany but Stalin's Russia.

They argued that Churchill had not been given a proper democratic mandate to lead the country, his appointment rubber-stamped by a cabal of Conservative and Labour politicians. Once in office he had usurped his powers by taking on the role of Minister of Defence, becoming a virtual dictator with almost unlimited powers.[4] The assassins also brought up Churchill's chequered military past, which, they claimed, made him a liability in time of war. They looked back to his role in the Antwerp fiasco in October 1914 and to the serious failings of the 1915 Gallipoli expedition. Of more concern to the authorities, however, was the suggestion that the recent setbacks in Norway and France could be laid at the door of the late Prime Minister.

We now know that there was truth in the assassins' accusations, subsequently made public by Churchill's opponents after the war and confirmed with the opening of the relevant state archives. But at the time, they were kept from the public, a policy encouraged by the authorities. Yet despite the government's D-notice muzzling of the national press and BBC, the assassins' 'manifesto' had been widely circulated immediately after the murder, and extracts were published in pre-seizure editions of the *Daily Worker*, the official paper of the British Communist Party – taking its line from Soviet Russia that the war was a conflict between imperialist powers at the expense of the working class.

Initially, the three defendants were reluctant to accept the authority of the court, but they finally pleaded guilty to the charges. Once the plea had been made, the trial was swift; the only outcome was a sentence of death by hanging. The three men had hoped for clemency, but nothing was forthcoming from a government determined to neutralise any potentially dangerous consequences from the assassination. The sentence was duly carried out at Wandsworth prison on the morning of Friday 2 August.

Halifax, meanwhile, was grappling with the supreme task of leading a country at war. He had originally been on the side of appeasement, but Germany's cynical repudiation of the Munich agreement and seizure of the remnants of Czechoslovakia in March 1939 led to a change of heart. From that point onwards, Halifax became an opponent of German aggression, supporting the territorial integrity of Poland against Nazi claims for Danzig and the 'Polish Corridor'. But, at the same time, he was a political realist, aware that changed circumstances called for new responses.

Halifax's attitude towards the war, following the devastating panzer breakthrough in France, had been revealed in a series of stormy cabinet meetings during Churchill's premiership. On 25 May, the still neutral Italian government had offered to mediate between the warring powers, and while this proposal was little more than a cynical ploy to seize territory from France, it did raise the idea of Britain making a settlement with Germany. Churchill was obdurately opposed to any peace terms – unless they came as an offer from Germany. Rightly or wrongly, he believed that any concession to Hitler was the first step on the slippery slope to Nazi enslavement.

At the initial War Cabinet meeting on 26 May, Halifax demurred from Churchill's insistence that Britain fight to the end regardless of consequences, believing that 'we had to face the fact that it was not so much now a question of imposing a complete defeat upon Germany, but of safeguarding the independence of our own Empire'.[5] The argument continued into the next day, with Churchill still refusing to accept any other policy but his own. Halifax recorded in his diary that 'Winston talked the most frightful rot'; he was at the point of resigning when Churchill begged him to remain in place and not 'do anything silly'.[6]

The other members of the War Cabinet were undecided, but on 28 May Churchill outflanked them all by delivering one of his more inspiring speeches to the full Cabinet, making any thoughts of seeking peace terms appear tantamount to defeatism. He finished with a typically melodramatic flourish: 'If this long island story of ours is to end at last, let it end only when each one of us lies choking in his own blood upon the ground.'[7] The Cabinet was won over, with Halifax and the other moderates pushed from centre stage.

But on 24 July Lord Halifax was left to formulate a realistic policy that had to take into account the capitulation of France and the loss of other friendly European nations, as well as the declaration of war by Italy on 10 June, which threatened British possessions in the Mediterranean and the vital Suez-Canal link to the Far East. Although Halifax cloistered himself with his advisors and the War Cabinet for two days, he had made up his mind from the outset that a middling course of action must be followed.

Even while Churchill was Prime Minister there had been limited discussions regarding the possibility of peace with Germany. On 17 June, Halifax's undersecretary R.A. Butler had met Björn Prytz, a

Swedish diplomat in London, to discuss the general international situation. In a subsequent telegram to Stockholm, Prytz wrote that Butler had informed him that 'no opportunity for reaching a compromise peace would be neglected if the possibility were offered on reasonable conditions and that no "diehards" would be allowed to stand in the way in this connection'. Prytz continued: 'During the conversation, Butler was called in to see Halifax, who sent me the message that "Common sense not bravado would dictate the British Government's policy".'[8] While Churchill remained in office the 'bravado' continued; with the arrival of Halifax and the restoration of 'common sense' peace feelers were extended to Germany via Sweden, with King Gustav V acting as mediator.

PRACTICALITIES AND REALITIES

In the short term, Halifax faced considerable diplomatic embarrassment. By unfortunate timing, on the evening of 22 July – less than twenty-four hours before the assassination itself – Halifax had broadcast a rebuttal to Hitler's famous 'appeal to reason' speech, made to the Reichstag on the 19th. Halifax had countered Hitler's 'offer' of peace with the rejoinder that 'we shall not stop fighting until freedom is secure'.[9] The broadcast and earlier negative comments in the British press seem not to have unduly influenced Hitler, although all of this was swept aside by the news of Churchill's death.

Hitler's attitude towards Britain was ambivalent. As a 'Germanic people' the British were not considered to be beyond the racial pale, and in his more relaxed moods he would often make favourable comments about Britain, especially regarding the administration of the Empire in India. On 15 July, the Propaganda Ministry had issued a briefing for the editorial departments of German newspapers that threw interesting light on official thinking: 'Germany's views about the possibility of a political peace, already mentioned [via Sweden], involved Britain withdrawing from Europe, i.e. the Continent and the Mediterranean and agreeing to a complete revision of the colonial sphere in Africa. In the Führer's view, sooner or later the racially valuable Germanic element in Britain would have to be brought in to join with Germany in the future secular struggles of the white race against the yellow race or the German race against Bolshevism.' The briefing concluded: 'the Führer wants an early end to the war'.[10]

But Britain was still Germany's enemy, and on 16 July Hitler had issued Directive 16, whose aim was 'to eliminate the English motherland as a base from which war against Germany can be continued'. If necessary, this would culminate in an invasion of Britain. Throughout June, the Luftwaffe had attacked British shipping in the English Channel and skirmished with the Royal Air Force. During July, the air attacks against southern England increased in scope and intensity, but to the Luftwaffe's dismay they found the RAF a determined and skillful opponent; German losses mounted steadily.

Yet even as Germany's armed forces began to make preparations for an amphibious assault against Britain, Hitler's mind was, in fact, turning eastward, to the destruction of the Soviet Union (the invasion order was issued on 29 July). Thus, when the German Foreign Ministry received news from Sweden that Britain might be prepared to come to 'an understanding' with Germany, Hitler was receptive to the idea. If a successful and lasting peace was achieved, then the implicit question within Directive 16 would have been answered: Britain would no longer be a base for a war against Germany. This would give Hitler a free hand to confront Stalin, without the dangers and distractions of a two-front war. And, as Hitler mused, once Bolshevism had been crushed he could deal with Britain at his leisure.

As the opening moves were made towards establishing a peace, both sides considered their options. In contrast to more usual settlements – where one side dictated terms to the other – both Britain and Germany held strong hands. Although the British Army had been unceremoniously bundled out of Europe with great loss of equipment, loss of life had been minimal. More to the point, the powerful Royal Navy remained in being and the RAF was proving a hard nut to crack.

While Germany dominated continental Europe, the thin strip of water separating it from Britain was as troublesome to the chiefs of the Wehrmacht as it had been to Napoleon and other would-be invaders from the past. Goering's bombastic promises of easy victory for the Luftwaffe were evaporating into the very skies he was failing to command, while Admiral Raeder was positively gloomy about the Kriegsmarine's ability to protect the amphibious landing force, especially in the light of unrealistic demands from the Army, unused to the complexities of maritime operations.

From Britain's perspective, Germany had overrun Western Europe and there was no way of changing that fact. By taking up the Swedish offer of mediation in a peace settlement, Britain was tacitly accepting the unpalatable truth that the centuries-old British strategy of maintaining the balance of power was lost. A German-dominated Europe was the new reality.

Secret negotiations were begun within the Swedish royal palace of Drottningholm, and when formalised on 20 August, an armistice brought overt hostilities to a close: German aircraft remained on their airfields in northern France, while Doentiz's U-boats were recalled to base. Under R. A. Butler's leadership, the British negotiators played a good hand, even though their position was weakened by the knowledge that nearly 40,000 British servicemen remained in Hitler's PoW camps, while Britain held a mere handful of Germans. It was this factor, more than anything else, that forced the British negotiating team to tread warily, and yet there was measured satisfaction in the Foreign Office when the Treaty of Stockholm was eventually signed on 26 September 1940, marking the official end to the War in the West.

The British had worked on the basis that they were negotiating from a position of strength. An initial German claim was put forward for parity in naval forces, as an amicable resolution (it was suggested) to previous aborted naval treaties. This was a clumsy manoeuvre that foundered on British intransigence that all its armed forces would remain at present strengths, unless, the British countered, Germany might adopt a similar reduced parity with its other arms of service. Britain also insisted that all foreign troops and governments-in-exile in the country would continue to enjoy British protection (although withdrawing their claims to governmental legitimacy) and that no individual who was resident in Britain in 1940 would be forced to leave the country for Germany or any German-occupied state.

That Germany would do as it wished in Europe was not even discussed, although the division of spheres of influence within the Mediterranean proved more difficult as Italy jostled for whatever possessions might fall its way. Corsica was 'handed back' to Italy, a move that proved a painful thorn in Mussolini's side when his rapacious and inept 'army of liberation' encountered the Corsican people. Italian demands against Britain for Malta and for the administration of the Suez Canal were rejected, the Italian position weakened after an 'invasion' of Egypt was chased back to Libya with heavy Italian losses. As a sop to Mussolini, a German request that Malta and Cyprus be declared as demilitarised zones was accepted by Britain.

German insistence on the restoration of their pre-1914 overseas colonies was also agreed by Britain, and by the other territorial beneficiaries, South Africa and Belgium (although the latter, occupied by Germany, had no say in discussions). For Germany, this was an important, symbolic step in the overturning of the last, vestiges of the Versailles Treaty. Thus, the old colonies of South-West Africa (Angola) and East Africa (Tanganyika) were returned to Germany, as were the German Cameroons and Togoland. After complex negotiations between Germany and the British, Australian and New Zealand governments, former German possessions in the Pacific islands also saw the swastika flying overhead.

In the economic sphere, Nazi calls for reparations from Britain for having been the 'aggressor' in 1939 were transmuted into agreements to supply strategic raw materials, notably oil, rubber and precious metals for German industry. German demands for favourable terms of trade – standard practice in continental Europe – were a continuing source of dispute that grumbled on well beyond the end of the European conflict.

The reaction of the British people to the Treaty of Stockholm was predictably varied. Only a few fanatics on the left and right had rejoiced at Churchill's death, but the establishment of the new Halifax-led government and the successful conclusion of peace negotiations produced relief that the fighting was over, with Britain still an independent, sovereign state. Yet, at the same time, there was a profound sense of anti-climax. Churchill's arrival had transformed the mood of the nation, as described by author Margery Allingham: 'In those weeks in May and June, I think 99 per cent of English folk found their souls, and whatever else it may have been it was a glorious and triumphant experience.'[11] The Britain that emerged from the war was a far duller if safer place.

TURNING SWORDS INTO PLOUGHSHARES

The new government's main task was to manage the transition from war to peace. During the first year of hostilities, the economy had been subordinated to the demands of war. The sudden onset of peace inevitably caused economic dislocation. Demand for war materials ceased overnight, and the overall reduction in international trade – with the United States slipping back into recession – adversely affected the British economy more than most. Admittedly, the markets of the Empire remained under British control, but trade with Europe was dependent on Germany as economic gatekeeper. Beating the swords back into ploughshares would prove a slow and frustrating business; it was only towards the end of the 1940s that renewed industrial activity and the expansion of international trade threw off the blanket of economic depression.

In the political sphere one of the first acts of the government had been to forcibly despatch the troublesome Duke of Windsor and his wife to the relatively safe backwater of the Bahamas. The former Edward VIII had been an inveterate Nazi supporter before the war and his renewed enthusiasm for Hitler was an embarrassment for both his brother, King George VI, and the government.

This was followed by the release of those interned who had been seen as potential dangers to the wartime state. Some 27,000 'enemy aliens' – ranging from Italians employed in the restaurant trade to émigré German Jews – emerged anxiously from their barbed-wire camps into an uncertain world. Britain's own 430,000-strong Jewish population looked on in rising alarm at the tide of anti-Semitism sweeping across Europe, which turned to horror when news of the fate of their fellow Jews in the extermination camps of Eastern Europe began to filter through to Britain.

Those extreme right-wingers released from British war-time internment numbered little more than 750, but they were rather more confident, many of them, including the British Union of Fascists (BUF) leader Oswald Mosley, foreseeing a bright political future.

During the interwar period, the fascist lunatic fringe – lurking somewhat to the right of the BUF – had been mocked by the British public, in so much as they knew of its existence at all. The Imperial Fascist League, The Nordic League, The Right Club, Mosley's old January Club, The Link and the Anglo-German Fellowship and many other more transient groups had been suppressed on the outbreak of war. They now began to flex their muscles.

The Anglo-German Fellowship came to the fore, described as 'a mixture of English fascists, appeasers, anti-Semites, hard-headed businessmen, fanatical anti-Bolsheviks, eccentric aristocrats and neurotic Mayfair Society women.'[12] Encouraged by Nancy Mitford's father, Lord Redesdale, the Fellowships's success owed much to the backing of Goebbels from the German side and to the assiduous work of former *Times* reporter H.A.R. Philby, who had returned to the Fellowship after a brief wartime spell with the Secret Intelligence Service (MI6).

The early 1940s was a time of marches and demonstrations, where Union Jacks and the flags of the dictatorships – Germany, France, Italy, Spain, Finland and Portugal – were intertwined in a new form of

European Union. Away from the streets – with their mob oratory and battles with the left – the self-censorship that had formerly inhibited the owners of so many of England's great country houses was cast aside in favour of public protestations of support for the New Order. Julia Stoner's childhood memoir of her aristocratic family reveals a depth of feeling for the fascist cause that was far from atypical. She recalled being given a charm bracelet, complete with dangling gold swastikas, as her mother strutted drunkenly through the house at Assenden Lodge crying out, 'Heil Hitler!' – even while the war was still ongoing.[13]

The new British 'fascistorcracy' drew strength from the many Nazi supporters of the period, who had included the Dukes of Westminster, Wellington and Buccleuch, the Marquis of Tavistock ,the Earl of Athlone, Lord Lothian, Lady Cunard, Lord Derby, the Marquis of Londonderry and Lords Allen and Stamp.[14]

Hitler's invasion of the Soviet Union acted as a beacon for the British Right during the years of German success. Within weeks of the opening of the German assault on 2 June 1941, British volunteers flocked to Germany. Goebbels enthusiastically seized upon this to develop his grand concept of a pan-European crusade against Bolshevism. When the war eventually turned against Germany, the Nordic volunteer formations were sacrificed in holding the line against the Red Army. To more jaundiced eyes in Britain, the destruction of the 'Wiking' Panzer Army (complete with the British Panzer-Grenadier Division and the League of St George) outside Moscow in February 1944 was a salutary lesson in the dangers of volunteering in the armed forces.

The promise held out to the political right during the first year of peace was not to last, however. Halifax's coalition government refused to be pushed from its centre ground. It enjoyed the broad support of the British people and proved more resilient than envisaged. While elements of the far right certainly had money and influence, they failed to gain electoral support and were thus denied the chance of power. Mosley was the only figure from the fascist 1930s to gain a parliamentary seat, and his by-election victory was overturned at the next general election. There was talk of fascist coups, but they came to nothing, especially as the Security Service – a few crackpots excepted – stood behind the government.[15] By the mid-1940s the extreme Right had withdrawn to its more natural habitat in politics' nether regions.

For those on the Left – ranging from the Labour Party to the communists and beyond – the immediate reaction to the peace might be described as that of a sullen silence. Such was the general feeling of demoralisation, that rising unemployment and some severe government measures in the economic sphere failed to provoke the trade unions and other left-wing associations into action. But this apathy was transformed by the German assault on the Soviet Union. Following instructions from Moscow, the Communist Party shrilly demanded action against Nazi Germany (much to the fury of Dr Franz Six, the recently appointed German ambassador). But the War in the East also revitalised the entire Left, as it did much of Britain, whose distaste for Nazi Germany had not simply ceased with the end of hostilities. The government meanwhile looked on, refusing to be drawn into the conflict in any direct manner.

During the autumn of 1941 the first calls for a general election were made, becoming increasingly stronger during the remainder of the year. As there was no war to justify the existence of a wartime coalition government, Halifax was persuaded to call a general election in the spring of 1942 (the first since 1935). Although it was generally agreed that Halifax had performed well in extricating Britain from the war, it was also widely believed he was not the right man to lead the country forward in the new peace-time era. The ensuing Labour victory saw the new Attlee government move towards a rebalancing of social inequality, with the country's limited resources devoted to improving public health, the extension of the pension system and overhauling state education. In matters of foreign policy, Attlee followed Halifax's 'wait-and-see' approach as the War in the East became ever more destructive, with both sides reluctantly forced to accept a compromise peace.

'WHAT-IF?'

Looking back to the summer of 1940 it is tempting to wonder what might have happened if Churchill had survived the assassination attempt. Novelists, film-makers and historians have all been drawn to consider alternative futures based on Churchill continuing to stand firm against Nazi Germany. Some of these works have a touch of wishful thinking about them,[16] although others can be taken as more serious counter-factual histories.[17]

Several have described a successful German invasion (Churchill falling this time to a German soldier's bullet) and the terrible fate that would have befallen the nation under Nazi rule. Others have suggested that the invasion failed (the RAF and Royal Navy destroying the landing force on the beaches) or that Hitler suddenly got cold feet and abandoned the whole amphibious invasion plan – although still being prepared to attack the Soviet Union and accept a two-front war. Variants on this latter theme include Britain allying itself with Soviet Russia, and Churchill forging a pact with President Roosevelt to launch a massive Anglo-American amphibious invasion of German-occupied Europe.

Central to these accounts is the idea of Winston Churchill as a great war leader, inspiring his people to the heights of valour and self-sacrifice, while calmly directing his armed forces with all the military skill of his famous ancestor, the Duke of Marlborough. From his short time in office, we have ample proof of his great skills as an orator and the way in which he gave heart to the ordinary people of the United Kingdom. But this would not have been enough on its own to win the war against the might of Hitler's Germany.

During the World War of 1914-18, total fatalities for the United Kingdom and Empire stood at just under one million. If Britain had fought on in 1940, possibly joining the Soviet Union and other combatants in what might have developed into a second world war, British casualties would almost certainly have been far higher than those of 1914-18. As things turned out, the list of British fatalities among the three armed forces was mercifully low, amounting to just under 16,000, the majority (11,000) sustained by the Army in France in 1940. The British economy – as we have seen – had been severely disrupted by the war, and had the conflict continued the country would have effectively been declared bankrupt, all assets – both at home and abroad – sold off to pay the impossible financial demands of modern warfare.

THE REALITY

During Churchill's premiership, the lack of regard held for him by many within the Conservative Party and the major state institutions was kept from the population at large. The well-known MP, diarist and Chamberlain supporter 'Chips' Channon – like his colleague R.A. Butler – was mortified by Churchill's surprise accession to power on 10 May: 'Perhaps the darkest day in English history. We were all sad, angry and felt cheated and outwitted.'[18] Lord Hankey – a close advisor to Chamberlain – memorably noted that the 'unreliable' Churchill was a 'rogue elephant'.[19] On 23 May, Lieutenant-General Henry Pownall, General Gort's Chief of Staff in France, was sufficiently exasperated by Churchill's interference in military affairs to exclaim, 'The man's mad.'[20]

These negative remarks were backed by other, firmer evidence of Churchill's wayward character. Halifax had been wrong to defer to

Churchill's apparently greater military knowledge; as it turned out, he was a consummate armchair strategist, repeatedly confusing a dramatic 'arrows-on-the-map' approach to war with real and effective military action.

The fiasco in Norway owed much to Churchill's strategic failings. He was lucky to escape censure – something he privately admitted: 'It was a marvel. I really do not know how I survived and maintained my position in public esteem while all the blame was thrown on poor Mr Chamberlain.'[21]

More damning still was his decision to continue sending British troops to France after the Dunkirk evacuation, as part of a vain attempt to prop up the wavering French government. While his generosity of spirit in helping France might be applauded, it was made at great cost to Britain with no successful outcome. The 51st (Highland) Division was one of the formations despatched to France, only to be promptly captured en masse by the German Army on 12 July. When an evacuation was eventually sanctioned – the decision to quit France owing much to the personal intervention of Lieutenant General Sir Alan Brooke – the converted liner *Lancastria* was sunk by German bombers on 17 June with the loss of over 3,500 lives – the greatest disaster in British maritime history.

When France capitulated on 22 June, Britain had lost her last significant military ally and now faced the prospect of defeat. Churchill's defiant stand against a barbaric enemy earned him the admiration of millions around the world, but this was hardly an appropriate policy for the nation to adopt in such difficult times.

Most rational people would agree that Halifax's peace was far preferable to Churchill's war.

NOTES:
1. Halifax, in Max Hastings, *Finest Years* (Harper Press, London, 2009), p.3.
2. Butler, in Andrew Roberts, *The Holy Fox: A Biography of Lord Halifax* (Weidenfeld & Nicholson, London, 1991), p.199.
3. Roberts, ibid.
4. See, by way of amplification, R.A. Butler's angry quote on Churchill taking power: 'The good clean tradition of English politics … has been sold to the greatest political adventurer of modern political history…. [T]his sudden coup of Winston and his rabble was a serious disaster and an unnecessary one.'
5. Halifax, in John Charmley, *Churchill: The End of Glory* (Hodder & Stoughton, London, 1993), p.403
6. Halifax, ibid, p.404.
7. Churchill, ibid, p.406
8. Prytz, in Thomas Munch-Petersen, 'Common sense not bravado', The Butler-Prytz interview of 17 June' in *Scandia* (2008).

9. Halifax, *The Times*, 23 July 1940.
10. Dr Hans-Joachim Kausch, German Propaganda briefing, in Jeremy Noakes and Geoffrey Pridham (eds), *Nazism 1919-1945*, Vol. 3 (University of Exeter Press, 2001), p.172.
11. Margery Allingham, *The Oaken Heart* (Michael Joseph, 1941), p.163, in Andrew Roberts, 'Hitler's England' in Niall Ferguson (Ed), *Virtual History: Alternatives and Counterfactuals* (Picador, 1997) p.320.
12. Philip Knightley, *Philby: The Life and Views of the KGB Masterspy* (Andre Deutsch, 1988), p.51.
13. Julia Camoys Stoner, *Sherman's Wife: A Wartime Childhood Among the English Catholic Aristocracy* (Bennett & Bloom, London, 2006). See also, Richard Griffiths, *Fellow Travellers of the Right: British Enthusiasts for Nazi Germany* (Constable, London, 1980).
14. Hastings, p.27; Roberts, 'Hitler's England', p.292.
15. See Christopher Andrew, *The Defence of the Realm* (Allen Lane, London, 2009), Chapter 3 (Section B) and Introduction (Section C).
16. Novels include *Loss of Eden* (Faber, London, 1940) by Douglas Brown and Christopher Serpell and *SS-GB* (Cape, London, 1978) by Len Deighton, while among 'fictional' histories are Kenneth Macksey's *Invasion* (Arms & Armour Press, 1980) and Adrian Gilbert's *Britain Invaded* (Century, 1990).
17. Counter-factual histories include *Invasion 1940* (Rupert Hart-Davis, London, 1957) by Peter Fleming; *If Britain Had Fallen* (Hutchinson, London, 1972) by Norman Longmate; and *Virtual History*, op. cit.
18. Channon, in Hastings, p.8.
19. Hankey, in Charmley, p.408.
20. Pownall, in Hastings, p.22.
21. Churchill, in David Reynolds, *In Command of History* (Penguin, 2004), p.126.

Chapter 5

The Assasination of Jan Smuts

Operation Weissdorn, January 1942

By Nigel West

The codename for the Abwehr plot to assassinate South Africa's Prime Minister Jan Smuts was *Weissdorn* ('Hawthorn') and was prepared by the organisation's sabotage branch, Abteilung II. Headed by the Austrian aristocrat Erwin von Lahousen, Abt.II was based at Quentzsee, near Brandenburg, and consisted of a highly trained elite force which had proved itself on countless covert operations conducted during the Blitzkrieg campaigns of 1940.

The decision to initiate *Weissdorn* was taken at the highest level in Berlin and was inspired by the success achieved by the Afrika Korps in Libya where the capture of Cairo looked imminent. Although the Suez Canal was still in use, a combination of the Kriegsmarine's U-boats, the Luftwaffe's bombers and the Italian navy had effectively closed the Mediterranean to Allied shipping and when Malta finally succumbed to the Axis siege, as seemed inevitable, Britain's sea-routes to the Empire would be largely dependent on the Cape of Good Hope. However, if Capetown and Simonstown were denied to the Royal Navy, the blockade of British ports could only be broken by the transatlantic convoys evading the submarine wolfpacks. What the Kaisermarine had come so close to accomplishing in 1917 was now a very real prospect, and was a major strategic incentive for the undertaking.

Weissdorn was an ambitious scheme, but was eminently practical. South West Africa had been a German colony until the invasion of 1915 when it had been effectively annexed by the Union. There was still a large German community, and much of the Afrikaner population in the region smouldered with anti-British resentment after two Boer Wars. This had been fuelled by shortwave propaganda broadcasts from Berlin by *Deutschlandsender Zeesen*, and a well-established network of agents run by Leopold Werz, the German consul in neutral Lourenco Marques. Portuguese Mozambique provided the Axis partners with a safe-haven from which they could infiltrate agents across South Africa's vast, unguarded land borders, and spies could operate with impunity throughout most of the Union because of the Afrikaner support and the lack of any security infrastructure. Furthermore, South Africa's instinctive neutrality in the current conflict had only been abandoned with the resignation of the former Prime Minister, General Hertzog in September 1939, and both the country and the United Party cabinet were divided on the question.

A former Boer guerrilla commander who had opposed South Africa's involvement in the Great War, Hertzog had been elected Prime Minister in 1924, and again in 1938, and had only lost his Parliamentary motion on neutrality by a margin of just thirteen votes. It had been Smuts who had rejected neutrality, thereby pushing the country reluctantly into another world war. The German plan was to restore the constitutional position to the moment before the Governor-General had refused to dissolve parliament and call an election, putting the neutrality issue squarely before the elections. That controversial decision had plunged the country into an unpopular war with Germany on behalf of the British Crown, and the removal of Smuts would create an opportunity for Hertzog's return, or a plebiscite. Abwehr II was to facilitate this objective, while Abwehr I had already prepared the groundwork.

The Abwehr had already established a clandestine organization in South Africa led by Lambertus Elferink, a Dutch journalist married to a South African wife, Gerita Johanna, and acted as a link between the pro-Nazi *Ossewa Brandwag* (OB, the 'Guards of the Oxwagons') movement founded in February 1939 to celebrate the Great Trek to the interior, that was committed to re-establishing the Orange Free State and the Transvaal Republic. The OB's paramilitary wing consisted of the brown-shirted *Stormjaers* ('Assault Troops') who engaged in the widespread sabotage, often bombing railway lines, telegraph communications and electricity pylons with dynamite stolen from the mines. There was also opposition to military service for the British Empire, leading to a major riot in Johannesburg in February 1941 in which 140 soldiers were injured, and this dissent was interpreted in Germany as evidence that South Africa was on the brink of a fascist revolt that would rid the country of Field Marshal Jan Smuts' coalition government and the repression introduced by the Interior Minister, Harry Lawrence.

The OB's leader, Hans Van Rensburg, was a shrewd lawyer who took great care not to overstep the fine line between political opposition to Smuts, under whom he had served in the Ministry of Justice in 1933, and outright subversion, which might provoke wholesale internment under the terms of the sweeping War Measures Act. Always conscious of *agent provocateurs*, he employed a subordinate, Bernard Gerling, to maintain contact with the fanatics, thereby insulating himself from any direct contamination. Having met Adolf Hitler and Hermann Göring, whom he admired in equal measure, Van Rensburg knew his own destiny, and had been assured during a personal meeting with Elferink that an important emissary would arrive from the Reich Chancery in June 1941 carrying details of *Weissdorn*. To ensure recognition, Elferink had entrusted van Rensburg with a *parole* or codeword that would guarantee the envoy's authenticity.

THE BLOOD OATH

The administration in Pretoria had been unprepared for the disorder and in the absence of an internal security apparatus the police, which was anyway heavily penetrated by anti-war OB sympathizers, proved powerless to cope with the highly disciplined Stormjaers who took a Blood Oath of loyalty to the cause based on the Nazi version. The belated response was to conduct a purge of state employees, requiring any OB supporters to resign their membership or leave the civil service, an ultimatum which prompted large numbers to abandon their police posts.

Smuts was reluctant to take decisive action against the OB as he feared civil war. He recalled the execution by firing-squad of the Boer rebel Jopie Fourie in December 1914, which he had ordered as Minister of Defence, that had been the catalyst for lasting anger within the Afrikaner community, and his suppression of the March 1922 miners' strike by deploying troops, tanks, artillery and aircraft, had also led to great loss of life. As Prime Minister of a fragile coalition, Smuts was anxious not to split the nation further. He was also fearful that any heavy-handed, premature intervention might unite Nico Diederichs' Broederbond and the National Party to form a grouping on the right to rekindle the *voortrekker* spirit.

The *Weissdorn* plan centred on a former Empire Games heavyweight boxing champion, Robey Leibbrandt who attended the 1936 Olympic

Games and met Adolf Hitler. In 1938, after working as a boxing instructor at a police college in South Africa, he returned to Germany to train gymnasts, qualified as a glider pilot and joined the Wehrmacht. Of German and Irish parentage, Leibbrandt had been born in Potchefstroom in the Transvaal, and his father had fought the British in the Second Boer War. He took up boxing while still at school, at the age of thirteen, and quickly established a reputation for strength and courage. He only missed the 1952 Olympic Games through injury, and on one occasion only narrowly lost a fight on points, despite only using his left fist, having broken his right thumb.

A committed Nazi, and convinced that he had been cheated out of another contest by biased British judges in Brighton, Leibbrandt volunteered to return to South Africa for *Weissdorn* on a mission to assassinate Smuts who, according to intelligence reports, had virtually no protection, either at Libertas, his official residence in Pretoria, or at his farm. His assignment was to establish contact with the OB, offer paramilitary training to the Stormjaers, and shoot Smuts with a sniper's rifle. As the recipient of a signed copy of *Mein Kampf*, Leibbrandt was a devoted adherent to the Führer, utterly devoted to ridding South Africa of British influence.

The issue of smuggling Lebbrandt back to South Africa represented a significant logistical challenge as there was no overland route available that avoided Allied controls. Travel to neutral Istanbul was an easy option, but entry into Palestine or Egypt without the required documentation made the task impossible. The alternative, by ship from the Far East, was also fraught with danger as neutral vessels were routinely stopped and searched for contraband.

Embarking in Lisbon without the proper papers would also be impossible, so the ingenious solution, dreamed up by Heinrich Ahlrich, of the Abwehr's naval branch, was to recruit a remarkable yachtsman, Christiaan Nissen, a member of the Cape Horners' Guild, who had great experience of smuggling agents across hostile waters. Indeed, he had spent much of the Great War in a British internment camp on the Isle of Man after he had been caught on the *Melpomene* off Queenstown while attempting to land agents. More recently, he had dropped three spies successfully from the converted trawler *Soizic* onto the beach in Baltimore Bay, County Cork, in August 1940. The three agents, two South Africans and a Belgian, had been quickly apprehended by the Irish police, but Nissen's contribution had been faultless.

To take Leibbrandt, alias Walter Kempf, and his radio operator, Emil Dorner to Africa, Nissen was assigned a confiscated forty-ton French yacht, the *Kyloe,* and in March 1941 he chose an experienced helmsman, Heinrich Garbers, as his skipper. The rest of the crew consisted of his brother Arndt Nissen, Paul Temme and an Abwehr officer, Hans Scharf, who had been employed as a liaison officer with Breton nationalists. The twenty-metre *Kyloe,* which had been built in England, sailed from Paimpot in Brittany on 1 April on an epic 8,000-mile voyage lasting sixty-seven days to land Leibbrandt in June at Mitchell's Bay, 150 miles north of Capetown.

During the voyage Leibbrandt siffered from a very debilitating seasickness and came to distrust his French wireless operator, to the point that he refused to go ashore at the designated site, Lambert's Bay, and insisted on choosing another location on the Namaqualand coast where he paddled ashore alone, carrying $14,000, and buried his transmitter. He then made his way to Capetown and stayed at the home of a friend until he could reach the OB. Lambert's Bay had been chosen because it was close to the family home of Elferink's wife, but Leibbrandt was unwilling to trust anyone.

Initially, because Van Rensburg was hard to reach directly, Leibbrandt was forced to deal with General Chris de Jager who was sceptical of the younger man's motives, He appointed an aide, Hendrik Erasmus, to accompany his visitor back to Mitchell's Bay to recover his transmitter, and only then did he accept that the envoy was all he claimed to be. An invitation to meet Van Rensburg followed, and this took place in conditions of great secrecy and security in the open veld halfway between Pretoria and Silverton where there would be no opportunity for eavesdropping or hostile surveillance. The conversation between the two men took place in Van Rensburg's car, out of earshot of any of the OB bodyguards, and opened with an exchange of Elferink's recognition parole. Having accepted his Leibbrandt's bona-fides, it was agreed that he should join a team of Stormjaers to train them for *Weissdorn.*

Over the next three months Leibbrandt assembled a trusted group of sixty gunmen he called the National Socialist Rebels, and traced an old friend and chemistry graduate, Dr Louis le Roux, to teach them the art of bomb-making. This was part of the second phase of *Weissdorn* which involved an escalation of the bombing campaign, with the dual aim of undermining the government's authority while demonstrating to potential supporters that there was organized, widespread opposition to Smuts. Roux worked in a laboratory in Potchefstroom which became the focus of incendiary devices which were planted across the Transvaal, concentrating particularly on railway bridges, and spread to Pretoria where Jewish-owned shops and five cinemas were attacked.

The objective was not to kill anyone, and thereby alienate potential supporters, but to orchestrate a series of incidents that would defy the government's authority and prove its impotence. This was the formula recommended by Abwehr II, arguably the world's most skilled purveyors of politically-motivated terrorist schemes. Under the direction of the Abwehr's headquarters in Berlin's Tirpitzufer, Leibbrandt arranged for the destruction of the railway line in a tunnel between Lourenco Marques and Pretoria on 14 December, just as a troop train was scheduled but, as the explosives were being laid beside the rails, the bomb detonated prematurely, killing Erasmus's brother Doors, and another accomplice, D.K. Theron. A third Stormjaer escaped the scene by car.

Another tactic favoured by Leibbrandt was the distribution of a five-page, professionally typed and Roneoed OB pamphlet which set out the movement's manifesto and presented cogent, impressively-presented arguments for a pro-neutrality, anti-war stance.

Leibbandt introduced a particularly effective test or initiation ceremony for new recruits, who were handed a revolver and ordered to execute a fellow-member said to be a traitor. The gun would be loaded with blanks, but the candidate would be unaware of the deception. Those that refused to go through with the ordeal were rejected.

Leibbrandt also found time to visit his parents in Bloemfontein, whom he had not seen for some years, and grew emboldened and a little careless. Word spread of Leibbrandt's return to the Transvaal, where he had been quite a celebrity, and he was forced to go into hiding at Ontmoet Farm, in the mountains near Makhado. He then moved on to a farm belonging to his uncle, Dominee Robey Joyce, but he was handicapped by two disadvantages. The first of these was that he had encountered great difficulty in changing his dollar bills into the local currency. The second was that he had only made intermittent radio contact with Berlin.

Nevertheless, with only a half-hearted investigation being conducted by the police into reports of armed men training in the mountains, in defiance of a newly-imposed government ban on privately-held firearms, Leibbrandt had no trouble in driving to Pretoria and undertaking a reconnaissance of the prime minister's official residence in the suburb of Bryntinion, which was surrounded by some three hundred acres of gardens and by a large park. Only completed the previous year, the residence had been constructed at the highest point on the property, making it an excellent target from a slightly lower angle.

Thus, at dawn on 20 January 1942, a date chosen because it was the eighth birthday of the declaration of the Third Reich, Leibbrandt settled into a sniper's hide he had constructed in the grounds, and prepared for Smuts to take his daily stroll in his garden before breakfast. The OB had supplied Leibbrandt with a complete floorplan of the property, and assured him that the gardens were not patrolled.

THE NEW ORDER

As soon as Smuts stepped down from the Dutch Cape terrace of his official residence he was felled by a single shot to the neck which left him dead before he hit the ground. It was an expert shot from a skilled marksman who had been practising for weeks and was fully prepared for his task. Within an hour 400 uniformed OB police, railway police and prison staff had seized control of the government buildings in and around Marshall Square, and the coup was underway with swift efficiency.

In London Winston Churchill felt the loss very personally as he had invited Smuts to join his War Cabinet and many regarded Smuts, newly promoted to the rank of field marshal in May 1941, as his chosen successor should anything happen to him.

The new administration in Pretoria was welcomed by the Axis, but greeted with dismay and disbelief by the Allies. All army units were confined to barracks and the Royal Navy was given twenty-four hours to steam out of Simonstown. There was a heavy police presence on the streets and an OB militia occupied the South African Broadcasting Corporation's radio studio and transmitter in Johannesburg. The new government declared the country's neutrality, while simultaneously inviting the old German embassy in Pretoria and consulate-general in Capetown to be reopened. Aged seventy-four, the former premier, General Hertzog, was persuaded to come out of the bitterly reluctant retirement he had imposed on himself to lead a temporary administration until elections could be held.

The British were powerless to respond, and there were certainly no troops to spare from the campaign in North Africa where General Erwin Rommel had begun his counter-offensive at El-Agheila. Six weeks earlier Japan had attacked the United States, and U-boats were now operating along the Eastern Seaboard. It was at this moment that the British were more isolated than at any time since the Battle of Britain, with the Japanese 25th Army sweeping down into Malaya, having sunk HMS *Prince of Wales* and HMS *Repulse*. Even worse, the Allied grip on the Middle East was critically dependent on Empire troops, and they included the 1st South African Infantry Division, the 2nd Infantry Division, the 6th Armoured Division and the 3rd South African Brigade. The sudden withdrawal of these units from the Allied order-of-battle would have disastrous consequences in the Western Desert.

In London the loss of South Africa as an ally would have the most profound impact on the prosecution of the war, and there were recriminations within the intelligence community because of what were perceived to have been a series of lost opportunities to interdict Leibbrandt, or at least penetrate the OB. MI5 had tried to post a Defence Security Officer to Pretoria, and had sent Bill Luke and then Michael Ryde to offer professional guidance to the local authorities, but Smuts had been uninterested in establishing a separate, internal security apparatus, and had preferred to leave the task of intelligence collection and counter-espionage to the police, an organization that had fallen heavily under the OB's influence. Indeed, the police Special Branch entrusted with combating German espionage was headed by the assistant chief of police, Lieutenant Bill Coetzee, who was widely distrusted as an ardent nationalist and a probable OB supporter. Previously Coetzee had spent much of his career monitoring what were termed native agitators, a group that posed an entirely different challenge. While the head of military intelligence, Colonel Ernie Malherbe, had recognized the broad OB threat, he had been powerless to persuade others to take the problem seriously.

As an expedient, the Secret Intelligence Service (MI6) had sent a representative, Mark Oliver, to Pretoria in an effort to support his counterpart in Mozambique, Malcolm Muggeridge, who supervised several operations against his local opponents, Leopold Werz and Umberto Campini intended to disrupt their activities.

According to MI6, Werz and his subordinate Ernst Paasche, had fled the embassy in Pretoria and moved to Portuguese territory to avoid internment. They had established themselves in the Polana Hotel in Lourenco Marques and acquired diplomatic recognition from the compliant Portuguese. Based on their daily cable bills, which averaged more than £100 a day, they were extremely active, and analysis of some of their traffic confirmed the existence of a large network mainly devoted to shipping reports. This would become a major preoccupation for the Allies as U-boats picked off merchantmen off the coast, and MI6's limited resources were concentrated on harassing Werz's LEO spy-ring, headed by a Greek journalist, Basil Batos, thereby underestimating the significance of the Abwehr's illicit support for the OB in the Union. The failure to appreciate the OB's political potential would have the severest consequences for both South Africa and the Empire.

Nor, it emerged, was MI5 totally uninformed about Leibbrandt. A double agent in Brazil, Hans von Kotze, codenamed *Springbok*, had volunteered information about the Abwehr's structure in South Africa, and had warned his handlers that Leibbrandt had been trained as a saboteur and should be regarded as extremely dangerous. Unfortunately, this tip had not been acted upon in London because, at the time, von Kote had yet to prove himself a reliable source, and policy dictated that intelligence reports of this kind were only circulated once an agent had been confirmed as dependable.

In the absence of any cooperation from the pro-Nazi Portuguese PVDE, MI5 had adopted the expedient of cultivating the police in neighbouring Swaziland, and also made approaches in Pretoria where the police chief, Brigadier G.R.C. Baston and his subordinate, Colonel de Villers, proved receptive to offers of unofficial assistance.

On the return journey *Kyloe* encountered Allied ships on two occasions, but avoided a search by flying the US stars and stripes. She finally docked at Villa Cisneros in the Rio de Oro in Spanish Sahara and the crew were met and debriefed by Weissdorn's controller, Sonderfuhrer Karl Haller, a peacetime lawyer burdened with a club foot. When Haller had completed his report *Kyloe*'s crew was flown to Rome, congratulated on their success, and assigned to new duties.

THE REALITY

Operation *Weissdorn* really was sanctioned by Berlin and only failed when Leibbrandt was arrested on the grounds of General Smuts' house outside Pretoria with a German sniper's rifle in his possession. The police had already been informed about Leibbrandt and had offered a reward of R1000 was for his capture, dead or alive.

He was sent for trial on 16 November 1942 and was found guilty of treason. Leibbrandt was condemned to death, but on 11 March 1943 this was commuted to life imprisonment by General Smuts himself.

Hans Scharf was interrogated by the Allies in July 1944 and disclosed for the first time details of the *Kyloe*'s extraordinary odyssey. Dr Haller, the Abwehr II controller, was interrogated in May 1945.

Following victory by the Nationalist Party in the General Election of May 1948, Leibbrandt and other political prisoners were pardoned and released. Leibbrandt married, ran a flower farm at Honeydew, near Johannesburg, opened a butcher's shop, and fathered five sons, one of whom was named Izan, which is Nazi spelt backwards. Later he moved to Bloemforntein where he ran a motor business, succumbing to a heart attack in 1966 at the age of fifty-two. Two months later, Van Rensberg also died.

Chapter 6

Mahatma Murdered
The Assassination of Mohandas Karamchand Gandhi, August 1942

By James Luto

It may have been the jewel in the British crown, but it was a flawed gem, divided by race, ruptured by religion and torn by caste. The vast sub-continent, still governed locally by disparate princes, Rajas, Ranas and Nawabs, had been unified under the British flag. Now it was unified with a common aim – independence. A people that could not live together sought self-rule so that they could live apart.

For 100 years, there had been movements and mobilizations to throw off the British yoke in a united battle of all Indians against foreign domination. But in the early 1900s, with the birth of the Hindu Mahasabha, the Muslim league and the RSS, these movements – which on different occasions actually collaborated with the British – were in constant battle with the larger national movement. Many blamed the fracturing of the independence movement on one man – Mohandas Karamchand Gandhi.

The deeply-religious Hindu leader of the Indian National Congress party, given the honorific title 'Mahatma', or 'venerable', held a vision of a secular, caste-free India. This put him in conflict with religious leaders and many in Indian society who refused to allow the lowest casts, the Dalit, or Untouchables, to rise above their station.

Little wonder, then, that in 1934, an attempt was made to assassinate Gandhi. On 25 June, Gandhi was scheduled to deliver a speech at Corporation Auditorium, Pune. He was travelling to the Auditorium in a motorcade of just two cars, along with his wife Kasturba, when a bomb was thrown at the leading car. Gandhi and Kasturba were in the second car. Ten people were injured in the incident, but, it seems, no arrests were made.

Gandhi was opposed to all forms of violence, and when war broke out in 1939, Gandhi offered Britain 'nonviolent moral support', seeing Fascism as a far greater evil then imperialism. But the representatives in the Indian Congress were appalled at being drawn into a war without being consulted. They argued that they could not be part of a war that was supposedly defending democracy if they were denied a democratic choice in the matter. The entire Congress resigned.

Following protracted discussions, Gandhi's stance changed. He demanded Indian independence, knowing that Britain had its hands full, and would not want to become bogged down in suppressing civil uprisings in India. Then everything changed – the Japanese attacked Pearl Harbor and invaded British-controlled Malaysia, their soldiers marching into Burma to threaten the very frontiers of India itself. Britain expected the Indian armed forces to support the British in defending India. Now, when Britain needed India as never before, was the time to exert the utmost pressure on the British to grant self-rule. In the eyes of very many Indians, Gandhi's practice of non-violence would never force the British to leave. Stronger measures were needed and if Gandhi was not willing to take the necessary action, others would.

'QUIT INDIA'

Aware of the growing sense of frustration, Gandhi moved to increase pressure on the British, and it was on 9 August 1943 that Gandhi launched the 'Quit India' movement, exhorting the nation to adopt 'ordered anarchy' and urging the Indians to 'Do or Die'. For the first time, he told his people that they should resist violence against them, albeit passively.

The day before he had delivered what was possibly his most famous speech at the Gowalia Tank Maidan Park in Bombay:

> Ours is not a drive for power, but purely a non-violent fight for India's independence ... The Congress is unconcerned as to who will rule, when freedom is attained. The power, when it comes, will belong to the people of India, and it will be for them to decide to whom they entrusted it ... I believe that in the history of the world, there has not been a more genuinely democratic struggle for freedom than ours ... In the democracy which I have envisaged, a democracy established by non-violence, there will be equal freedom for all. Everybody will be

his own master. It is to join a struggle for such democracy that I invite you today. Once you realize this you will forget the differences between the Hindus and Muslims, and think of yourselves as Indians only, engaged in the common struggle for independence.

I have noticed that there is hatred towards the British among the people. The people say they are disgusted with their behaviour … This hatred would even make them welcome the Japanese. It is most dangerous. It means that they will exchange one slavery for another. We must get rid of this feeling. Our quarrel is not with the British people, we fight their imperialism. The proposal for the withdrawal of British power did not come out of anger. It came to enable India to play its due part at the present critical juncture. It is not a happy position for a big country like India to be merely helping with money and material … Speaking for myself, I can say that I have never felt any hatred. As a matter of fact, I feel myself to be a greater friend of the British now than ever before. One reason is that they are today in distress. My very friendship, therefore, demands that I should try to save them from their mistakes. As I view the situation, they are on the brink of an abyss. It, therefore, becomes my duty to warn them of their danger even though it may, for the time being, anger them to the point of cutting off the friendly hand that is stretched out to help them.

Seeing the danger that the 'Quit India' movement would bring about in their rear whilst they faced the Japanese on their front, the British authorities decided to act swiftly, rounding up all almost all the Congress leadership within twenty-four hours.

Yet Gandhi was quite correct when he spoke of many people seeing the Japanese as liberators. Such was the hatred of the British, it was thought that nothing could be as oppressive as the rule of the Raj – and one man was going to do something about it.

THE FIRST INDIAN NATIONAL ARMY

Mohan Singh had been a Captain in the 1st Battalion, 14th Punjab Regiment of the Indian Army when his unit had been posted to Malaya on 4 March 1941. When the Japanese invaded Malaya, Singh's battalion was heavily defeated but he managed to escape into the jungle. After several days on the run he was captured by the Japanese. Whilst in captivity he was approached by Giani Pritam Singh who had earlier joined the Japanese. He and Major Fujihara, a Japanese Intelligence officer, asked Mohan Singh to form an Indian Army composed of captured Indian soldiers. After some hesitation Mohan Singh agreed, and he was placed in command of a number of Indians that had been captured by the Japanese. This was the start of the formation which eventually became the First Indian National Army.

Gandhi's speech on 8 August condemning the Japanese, and his earlier support for Britain, showed that Gandhi was not the man to lead his country away from the British and into the hands of the Japanese. Gandhi would have to die.

It may seem odd that many would wish to align themselves with Japan, but the two countries had developed close cultural ties over many centuries, mainly fostered by religion. Buddhism had spread from India, via China and Korea and since the eighth century monks and scholars often embarked on voyages between the two nations. This fostered strong cultural links, and many common themes in their respective folklore. Similarly, Hinduism, like Shintoism, is an animist religion in contrast to the Christian monotheism.

For many in India, the prospect of an alignment with Japan was far more appealing than the existing rule by Europeans with whom there were few shared values. Indeed, an independence movement, the Indian Independence League, was already firmly established in Japan under the leadership of Rash Behari Bose, a revolutionary figure who had escaped to Japan after he had attempted to kill the Viceroy of India, Lord Hardinge. There were also other Indian independence associations across South-East Asia, such as the Central Indian Association and the Singapore Indian Independence league, which, following the occupation of Malaya were brought together under Bose's leadership.

When Singapore was overrun by the Japanese on 15 February 1942, amongst the 85,000 British troops who surrendered, 45,000 were Indians. Mohan Singh asked for volunteers from the captured Indian soldiers to join what was then the *Azad Hind Fauj* (Free India Army) to fight for Indian independence from the British rule. Such was the strength of feeling amongst the soldiers that by 1 September 1942 Mohan Singh, now a General, had 40,000 men under his command.

Gandhi's speech was met with great anger in both Tokyo and Singapore. Gandhi, who had been a civil rights lawyer in British-governed South Africa, was obviously a British patsy. Rather than leading his people in a great fight for independence, he had told Indians not to use violence. His real motive was clearly to stop his people from rising against the imperialists. If Gandhi was permitted to continue as the moral leader of

India, the country would never be free. Gandhi had to be stopped. Mohandas Gandhi had to die.

THE INFAMOUS THREE

No-one knows for certain who gave the order, if indeed an order as such was ever issued. It may have been little different from Henry II asking who would rid him of Thomas Beckett? Rash Bose may have expressed his wish that Gandhi must be killed, and killed immediately, whilst the Japanese army was consolidating its hold on Burma and could soon be ready to march across the border into northeastern India. If so, his words were heard and his meaning interpreted literally.

Knowing he had to strike quickly, Captain Birbal Chandra gathered his men together. It would be a simple task to slip across into India and track down Gandhi, but they must move without delay. By 13 August, Chandra, along with fellow officers, Deepak Subramani and Giridhar Narayan, was working his way from Kohima to Diphu in Assam. On Monday 16 August, the three soldiers, all former members of the Rajput Regiment from Fategarh, had reached New Delhi. The men had many friends and family from Uttar Pradesh in the Indian capital, all of whom wished to see the end of the British.

Following his 'Quit India' speech, on Saturday 8 August, Gandhi's movements, and the action he was taking, were being carefully watched. It was known that he was due to attend evening prayers at Birla House. The place was unknown to the three conspirators and a reconnaissance was required.

They set off in two rickshaws at 08.30 hours the next morning to travel to the twelve-bedroom mansion on what was then Albuquerque Road, and today known as the Tees January Marg. They stepped from their rickshaws at the house, being prevented from entering by the gatekeeper. When asked who they wanted to see, Chandra said 'the secretary'. The gatekeeper went to find the secretary but the men did not wait, seeing that they could not bluff their way in through the front of the house. The prayer meeting was to be held in a pavilion in the back garden. They, therefore, walked round the estate and found a small gate which led past the servants' quarters to the prayer ground. There were few people in the prayer ground, but it was not uncommon for people to be visiting the gardens and no-one paid the three plainly-dressed young men any attention. Gandhi was in the house and may even have seen the three men who would end his life strolling around the grounds.

The assassins saw that the small pavilion was built of grey sandstone. It could only comfortably accommodate some twenty people, who would sit facing a raised wooden platform where Gandhi would lead the prayer meeting. It did not seem likely that an attack could be delivered from the front of the pavilion through a crowd of people who would be his most ardent followers and willing to sacrifice their lives for the revered Mahatma. But at the back of the pavilion was some brick trellis-work which was designed to allow air to pass into one of the small apartments of one of the Birla House servants. It was Giridhar Narayan who first saw the possible opportunity. If they could get into the servants' quarters, they would be able to shoot Gandhi in the back through the trellis.

They saw that there was a line of twelve servants' apartments at the end of the garden. Narayan measured the openings in the trellis with a piece of string and concluded that they were wide enough to enable them to throw a hand grenade through one of them into the pavilion. From that point the plan was quickly laid. They would sneak into the apartment and two of them shoot Gandhi in the back whilst the third would lob a grenade at him. They had also obtained a slab of guncotton, an item not difficult to obtain in wartime India, with the intention of exploding it to create mass confusion in and around the pavilion which would enable the assassins to get away unnoticed, dropping their guns in the apartment. All being well, one of the servants would get the blame.

THE ONE-LEGGED MAN

The three assassins now had to wait until the evening. Being well-trained infantrymen, they knew that the next thing they had to do was check their weapons. They went to the Hindu Mahasabha building, walking into the adjacent woods to practice with their pistols. This almost proved their undoing, as suddenly forest guards appeared through the trees. Chandra and Narayan quickly sat on their guns, and tried to appear as if they were resting casually on the ground. The guards were immediately suspicious of the three men, who, when asked what they were doing, replied that they were just tourists visiting Delhi. With nothing more to go on, the guards continued with their patrol. The story of the forest guards and how they allowed the three assassins to slip through their fingers has passed into legend, with many a conspiracy theory being concocted that the guards knew perfectly well what the assassins were planning.

In the late afternoon, the trio made their way to Birla House. Chandra had painted a red caste mark on his forehead to give him the appearance of a devout Brahmin. When he reached Birla House, he set about finding the servant whose apartment backed onto the pavilion. This, it transpired was a Chota Ram, who washed the automobiles in the Birla garage. The servant believed Chandra when he said that he had a friend who was a photographer that wanted to be allowed to take photos of Gandhi from behind, so as not to disturb the Mahatma at prayer.

Surprisingly, the servant saw nothing unusual in this and he agreed to allow the men into his apartment. All seemed set, but then as Chandra was about to step into the room he saw three men sitting inside and a one-legged man standing outside. He could not ask the men to leave the room as he was supposed to be merely a photographer and there could be no reason he would want them out of the way. The room was so small that the assassins might well become trapped inside by the four servants, but worse, in Chandra's mind was what was outside. A one-legged man traditionally meant bad luck.

Chandra stepped back, mumbled something to Chota Ram, and pulled his co-conspirators aside. There was a whispered consultation, and a hurried change of plan. The scheme they next contrived was to explode the gun cotton next to the pavilion. Everyone would rush out through the entrance where the three men would be waiting. As Gandhi left they would shoot him down and drop hand grenades.

The prayer meeting began on time, at 17.00 hours. Ten minutes later the slab of guncotton ignited with a violent explosion. Weapons ready, the three men braced themselves for the expected stampede. Nothing happened. Astonishingly, the devout Hindus continued their prayers as if nothing had happened. After a few moments servants and gardeners in the grounds rushed to see what had happened, but the three would-be assassins had already fled out of the grounds into the waiting rickshaws, disappearing into the jumble of Delhi's traffic long before the British Army truck arrived at Birla House.

17.15 HOURS, 18 AUGUST

The failure of the Birla House attempt did not dampen the enthusiasm of the conspirators, who now knew for certain that their bad luck was due to the presence of the one-legged man. As the men analyzed the events of the evening, they agreed that the plan had been too complicated and that a simple attack in the open would be far easier to carry out and more certain of success. Now that they were familiar with

Birla House and the routine of the evening prayer meeting, they could plan with greater knowledge.

The later edition of the *Delhi Times* of 18 August carried the story of the explosion in the grounds of Birla House seventy feet from where Gandhi had been leading evening prayers. The three men were relieved to read that no-one knew who had caused the explosion. This meant they could mount their next attack without fear of recognition, and few would ever consider that another assassination attempt would be made so soon after the previous effort.

At 16.30 hours, the three men arrived at Birla House and mingled with the 100 or so people in the prayer ground. The explosion of the previous day had brought even more to the meeting, no doubt to show their support for the Mahatma. It was a warm evening with a pleasant light breeze rustling the trees.

The men waiting silently, standing well apart to lessen the chances of their view being blocked. At 17.13 hours Gandhi emerged from the House with his grandnieces. Usually one of his attendants, Gurbachan Singh, would go ahead of Gandhi to clear a way through the crowd that always gathered wherever the revered leader went. But Gurbachan Singh had been delayed and was still trying to catch up with Gandhi as the Mahatma reached the steps of the pavilion. Chandra knew at that moment that his chance had come. Such an opportunity, of Gandhi being in the open without his attendant, might never come again. He felt a strange calmness, knowing that it was Shiva the God of both creation and, most importantly for Chandra, of destruction, who was guiding his hand.

He saw Gandhi smile which seemed to Chandra to be Shiva's signal. He darted out of the crowd, raised his pistol and fired three shots in rapid succession. He had seven bullets in his gun and would have kept on firing to make sure he killed the Mahatma if Sergeant Devraj Singh of the Royal Indian Air Force had not acted so quickly and thrown himself on Chandra. Others quickly fell on the assassin, aiming blows on his head and face.

With scores of people flocking round Gandhi there was no possibility of the two other conspirators getting anywhere near the wounded man, and seeing what was happening to Chandra, Subramani and Narayan left the grounds as discreetly as they could. They would, though, be arrested the next day when Chandra, proudly, through his cut and swollen lips, told the police why he had killed the most famous man in India.

END OF EMPIRE

The news of the death of Mahatma Gandhi created headline news around the world, but in the midst of the war, did not arouse much surprise. Death was always on the front page of every newspaper. In fact, the British authorities in Delhi had already considered arresting Gandhi for his provocative 'Quit India' speech and now that he was finally out of the way, well so much the better. Maybe now the Indians would fall squarely behind the British to stave off the Japanese forces that menaced the country. They could not have been more wrong.

On 20 August Rash Bose issued a statement to the world's press. It is considered to mark the end of the British Empire. Though it would be decades before Britain relinquished control of all its overseas colonies, that process began on 20 August 1942:

> The people of India have rejected the feeble leadership of Mohandas Gandhi. The man who told the people not to fight against the tyrannical rule of the British imperialists has met his end. Now it is British rule that is at an end. I say to every Indian – Hindu, Moslem, Buddhist, Sikh, Christian – now we fight!
>
> From this very day, I want every farmhand to lay down his scythe; every civil servant to put down his pen, and every soldier to take up his gun!
>
> I say to King George and to the warmonger Churchill, that you now have a new enemy, and he is 350 million strong. You cannot fight such an enemy. And be assured, non-violence is no more. At every street corner, in every house, you will find that enemy. And whilst you watch your back, the Indian National Army will be marching with its Japanese allies to liberate India.
>
> I will give you oppressors no time to consider your fate. From today all India will be against you. Either leave now, or die where you sit or sleep. Your empire is finished.

The response to Bose's statement across India was mixed. At first many Indians continued their lives as normal. Some depended upon the British for their livelihoods and simply could not afford to antagonize their bosses. Equally, many in the Indian Army loved their regiments, and their glorious history, and respected their British officers. But as the days passed, news of clashes between British troops and Indian solders increased. The movement very quickly gained momentum. The strength of feeling amongst the Indians of all classes surprised everyone. By the third week of September the situation had become critical, and it was on 23 September that the Japanese Fifteenth Army and the Indian National Army launched an attack on the British outposts in Mizoram.

Churchill immediately called a Cabinet meeting. It was a momentous event. With no preamble, the Prime Minister launched into a very solemn address. He was suffering one of his 'Black Dog' moods and had not left Chequers for days. It had taken a huge effort for him to dress and go out and face his ministers. 'I am heart-broken. This war has brought misery to the world, and to me. Everything that once seemed good and dependable has been blown away by the gun and the bomb. Now we see India, that rich, colourful and tolerant, yes tolerant, country, torn asunder. What depresses me more than anything is that we must withdraw from India, leaving this vast and beautiful country to the ravages of an evil regime.

'We have ruled that fine country with a handful of men because the Indians saw order and humanity in our administration and our laws. But those few men cannot now hold back the people who have been deluded into believing the Japanese will bring them freedom and independence. Soon they will realise they have been deceived – but they must learn this for themselves. We shall evacuate our troops, merchants and administrators without delay. Umm, I doubt any of you disagree?'

A few murmured their assent, such as Sir Stafford Cripps and Lord Moyne; most remained silent. There was really nothing to be said. India would one day have its independence anyway. This was not how anyone would have wished, but independence was inevitable. It was important to get the British troops and civilians out of India quickly. That had to be a priority. Then the consequences of the occupation of India by the Japanese would have to be considered. As these thoughts permeated the minds of the ministers, Clement Atlee, the Deputy Prime Minister spoke. 'Once the Chiefs of Staff have made the arrangements for the evacuation, we must meet again to discuss our next moves.'

'Yes, of course,' Churchill said quietly. 'I will also ask Brooke [General Sir Alan Brooke, Chief of the Imperial General Staff] to get the JPS [Joint Planning Staff] to prepare something. Once we have a plan from Brooke I will call a Cabinet.'

With that Churchill abruptly stood up, and Anthony Eden's 'I will prepare a statement for the press', was all but drowned by the noise of Churchill's chair toppling over. With a deep growl, Churchill walked out of the Cabinet Room and back to the dark recesses of Chequers and the even darker recesses of his troubled mind.

REMEMBER, REMEMBER

Eden's statement was delivered to the British press on 25 September. British forces would begin to withdraw within the next two weeks. It was expected that the British presence in India would be terminated by the end of November. There was no mention of either the Indian National Army, the Japanese or even the war in Eden's statement. The UK was granting the Indian people the independence they so earnestly sought, the implication being that they were digging their own graves. Britain, of course, 'wished the disparate peoples of India well, in their endeavour, knowing that they will always find the friendly hand of Great Britain stretched out in welcome.' The withdrawal from India, would allow Britain to concentrate its efforts at defeating the greater enemy 'on its doorstep'.

The announcement was received surprisingly well across the UK. The war in the East was far away and had little direct impact upon the lives of most people. The general view was that India had become an increasing burden upon the UK, with the Indians constantly agitating for self-rule. Eden's theme was readily adopted by most commentators and leader writers. The Indians would soon regret what they had wished for and before long they would realise their mistake.

The first problem was that of extricating the British forces. General Archibald Wavell, General Officer in Command, India, had just four British infantry divisions under his command (2nd, 5th, 18th and 70th) and he relied heavily on the Indian Army. Led in the main by British officers, many Indian regiments continued, for the time being, to obey orders. But the Indian National Army, the 1st Division of which had already advanced into the hills of North-East India with the aim of debouching into the Ganges Plain, was receiving deserters from British Indian Army in increasing numbers.

Wavell had to act quickly and already Vice Admiral Sir James Somerville's Eastern Fleet was making for Bombay. Every ship along the western coastal strip from Kochi to Karachi was being commandeered and taken round to Bombay, whilst on the eastern seaboard shipping was concentrating at Calcutta. The roads from central India were jammed with vehicles heading for the coast.

In what has been called the 'Indian Dunkirk', Wavell and Somerville achieved the almost miraculous feat of evacuating almost all the British expatriate population, as well as the four Army divisions ahead of the expected date. The last ship to sail, left the Bay of Bengal at 23.50 hours on one of Great Britain's most notable days – 5th November.

The loss of India in purely territorial terms was of no great consequence. The Japanese would have more than their hands full and would present no threat to South Africa, or anywhere else, for a long time to come. Japan could be left to the Americans, whilst Britain focused its efforts on North Africa and Europe. But there were other factors to consider. The first of these was that a large number of Indian Army regiments were serving with the British Army in North Africa and these could not be allowed to return to India. To avoid any thoughts of mutiny, all those Indian soldiers were promised British citizenship if they continued to fight alongside the British Army. Though there was some trouble amongst Indians in Cairo, those serving with Montgomery pushing westwards after the Battle of El Alamein, remained loyal to a man – the prospect of a new life in England was too tempting an offer. The populations of the northern industrial towns of today reflect this large-scale settlement of Indian soldiers who were proud to fight for their new country.

As is well-known the greatest challenge was still to come. For the loss of India meant the loss of Ceylon, which could not hope to remain in the Allied camp. This, in turn, meant that passage through the India Ocean was no longer possible, leaving Australia and New Zealand isolated. What surprised the British planners was how quickly the Japanese moved against the Antipodes. Rather than endeavouring to bring India immediately under its control, Lieutenant General Masakazu Kawabe allowed Rash Bose to form a new administration, the Indian National Government. The transition from one colonial power to another was remarkably smooth at first, and the Japanese, with the British gone and no-one to fight in the sub-continent, were able to divert a large proportion of their forces from garrison duties in Burma and Malaya to New Guinea and the Dutch East Indies. The bombing of Darwin began in earnest on 2 December.

The capital of the Northern Territory endured a 'mini-blitz', with large areas of the city, and especially the port and its facilities, being levelled to the ground. With the British unable to send any forces to help, it was to the US that Prime Minister John Curtin appealed.

Roosevelt was quick to respond, and squadrons of Curtiss P.40s and Vought F4U Corsairs were immediately despatched to Australia. It was in March 1943 that the Pacific Alliance was formed between Australia, New Zealand and the US, with the other Pacific countries joining both towards and after the end of the war. Australia and New Zealand withdrew from the British Commonwealth and remained part of what is now the Pacific Free Trade Area.

India proved to be a step too far for the Japanese who had already suffered serious reverses at the battles of the Coral Sea and Midway. From the very first sitting of the Indian National Parliament divisions between Moslems and Hindus were apparent. Within weeks, Moslem leaders were demanding their own 'self-rule'. Riots broke out in the Punjab, which General Kawabe made no effort to quell. With the United States' forces driving ever closer to Japan, India was left to its own devices.

Ultimately, the death of Mahatma Gandhi served no-one's end. The occupation of India stretched Japan's resources to breaking point and, left to its own devices, India broke into three, with Moslem East and West Pakistan being separated by Hindu India. Shorn of two of its most important members, the British Commonwealth ceased to exist in 1949 – post-war Britain, still suffering rationing, had more pressing matters.

THE REALITY

Mohandas Gandhi was indeed assassinated in much the same way as described above, but not until 1948, as he was arrested along with most of the Congress Party leadership the day after his 'Quit India' speech. He spent most of the rest of the war in prison.

Before he was finally killed Gandhi had been the target of three earlier assassination attempts. The first was made in 1934 at Pune, as referred to earlier. A second attempt was undertaken in May 1944, when Nathuram Vinayak Godse, tried to attack Gandhi with a dagger at Panchgani, a hill station near Poona, but was overwhelmed by Gandhi's followers. A third attempt, also involving a dagger, was made on 8 September 1944 at Sevagram, but this was stopped before the would-be assailant was able to approach Gandhi.

On 30 June 1946, an attempt was made to derail the train that Gandhi was travelling on between Bombay and Pune. A similar effort occurred on 31 July 1947 when a bomb was thrown onto the tracks at Phillaur Station when Gandhi's train was passing on its way from Delhi to Rawalpindi.

The next effort was again one by the persistent Godse at Birla House on 20 January 1948. By this time India had achieved self-rule, but it had led to the splitting of the country into two with Moslem Pakistan being declared a separate nation from Hindu India. The separation of the two resulted in terrible scenes of human misery, with millions – possibly as many as fourteen million – being compelled to leave their homes and hundreds of thousands being killed or injured in retributive genocide (figures for those killed range between 200,000 and 2,000,000). It was the largest mass migration in human history. Some believed that the separation of the country and the resultant deaths and destruction was caused by Gandhi's lenient views towards the Moslems. Further anger was generated when a large financial settlement was made by the Indian Government in favour of the new state of Pakistan.

Along with six others Godse did try to place himself in a servant's apartment at the rear of the prayer pavilion but was deterred by there being other men in the apartment – and, yes, because they saw a one-legged man outside. Godse and his co-conspirators tried to escape but one of them, Madanlal Pahwa, was captured by the Delhi police.[1] Pahwa admitted everything and the police went round to the two hotels where the conspirators had been staying, but the men had gone.

It was ten days later, on 30 January, that Godse shot Gandhi three times in the chest at another prayer meeting at Birla House. He, and the others, were arrested and put on trial. Godse admitted his guilt, stating that:

'I do say that my shots were fired at the person whose policy and action had brought rack and ruin and destruction to millions of Hindus … I bear no ill will towards anyone individually, but I do say that I had no respect for the present government owing to their policy, which was unfairly favourable towards the Muslims. But at the same time I could clearly see that the policy was entirely due to the presence of Gandhi.'

Godse was sentenced to death and, despite pleas of leniency from Gandhi's family, he was hanged at Ambala Jail on 15 November 1949.

Rash Bose was decorated by the Japanese but was killed in Japan towards the end of the Second World War. The Indian National Army, fought well against the British in the Arakan campaign and took part in the battles of Imphal and Kohima as well as at Irrawaddy and Meiktilla during the Fourteenth Army's successful re-conquest of Burma. Though it ceased to exist in September 1945, it became the rallying point of the independence movement, prompting a number of mutinies in the Indian armed forces against British rule.

NOTE:
1. Robert Payne, *The Life and Death of Gandhi* (The Bodley Head, London, 1969), p.627. It is also said that Choturam became suspicious and asked Madanlal Pahwa why he needed photographs from behind, and inquired about the absence of a camera!, p.126.

Chapter 7

'Hitler Dead!'

Operation Foxley, SOE and the Assassination of the Führer, March 1943

By John Grehan

He was young, blue-eyed and blond, and his *SS-Sonderkolonne* uniform fitted his large, angular frame well. Joachim Adalbert looked every inch the perfect Aryan male and walking purposely around Berchtesgaden he attracted little attention. He was there early, as he had to be – timing was everything. He could not arrive too soon as he would be obliged to hang around, which would look highly suspicious. But most importantly of all, he could not be a moment late. Adalbert swung his arms and strode out briskly, deviating past the former hotel Haus Türken, both to use up a few extra minutes and to check on the guards of the *SS-Wachkompanie Obersalzberg* posted there.

Adalbert moved towards the Gutshof where the two-man SS picket watched Hitler for around 1,000 yards along his regular morning walk to the Teehaus on the Moonslaner Kopf. He restrained himself from glancing at his watch and maintained his steady pace.

ALONE WITH HIS THOUGHTS
At a little after 10.20 hours the doors of the Berghof swung open and Adolf Hitler stepped out into the bright, clear Alpine atmosphere of the Obersalzberg. In late March, the snow still lingered in sheltered areas, but the Führer's path to the tea-house was always kept clear. Hitler valued his morning walk immensely, and he always insisted in walking alone. This was the only time that he could relax as an ordinary man, strolling through the lovely Bavarian countryside untroubled by the war that raged across Europe, to enjoy the simple pleasure of a glass of

Above: The Kremlin in Moscow, where Stalin presided over the Soviet Union and could have met his death. (Shutterstock)

Below: David Margesson at his desk at the War Office during the Second World War.

Above: Rome's Porta Pia, the gateway in the Aurelian Walls which was the site of an assassination attempt on Mussolini. (Mauro Carli/Shutterstock)

Below: Birdcage Walk in London – where the ambush on the newly-installed Prime Minister Winston Churchill is described as having occurred. (Lewis Clarke; www.geograph.org.uk)

Above: Known since 1994 as Mahlamba Ndlopfu, Libertas was, during the Second World War, the official residence for Jan Smuts in Bryntirion, Pretoria. (Hendrik van den Berg)

Below: The terrace in the grounds of Birla House, Delhi, which was the scene of numerous assassination plots against Mohandas Karamchand Gandhi. (Courtesy of Daniel Villafruela)

Above: The editor and author, John Grehan, standing on the so-called 'Teahouse Path' at Berchtesgaden, looking towards where the teahouse itself once stood in the trees across what is now a golf course. (Historic Military Press)

Below: An aerial photograph of RAF Hendon circa 1941-1942 – was this the site of an assassination attempt on the Free French leader General de Gaulle?

Above: Photographed in 1941, this Focke-Wulf Fw 200C-4 Condor, *Immelmann III* (*werke* number 3099), was Hitler's aircraft. Note the characteristic insignia of the *Fliegerstaffel des Führers*, Hitler's personal squadron which was commanded by Hans Baur, on its nose. Baur, who had complete control in selecting the personnel and equipment for the squadron, was the only pilot (with the exception of one flight in twelve years) with whom Hitler ever flew. (Deutsches Bundesarchiv)

Above: Wack Wack Golf Course, near Manilla in the Philippines, where President José Garcia was shot. (Courtesy of Jun Acullador)

Above: A hut near the entrance to Tito's personal headquarters, which was located in a cave complex about half a mile north of the centre of Drvar.

Below: The entrance to Tito's cave as it appears today.

Top Left: Claus von Stauffenberg, on the left, looks on as Adolf Hitler is greeted on his arrival at the Wolfsschanze, or Wolf's Lair, on 15 July 1944, five days before Operation *Valkyrie* was carried out. The individual shaking hands with Hitler is General Karl Bodenschatz, who was seriously wounded in the bomb's blast. (Bundesarchiv, Bild 146-1984-079-02/CC-BY-SA 3.0)

Centre left: The trousers that Hitler was wearing when he was caught in the blast of von Stauffenberg's bomb.

Below: Göring (third from left) and Bormann (far left) survey the conference room at the Wolfsschanze following the detonation of the suitcase bomb left by Claus von Stauffenberg, 20 July 1944. (Historic Military Press)

Above: A recent picture of a reinforced bunker at the Wolfsschanze, Hitler's command headquarters on the Eastern Front during the Second World War. (Szymon Mucha/Shutterstock)

Below: A view of part of the Imperial Palace in Tokyo. The primary residence of the Emperor of Japan, the Palace is a large park-like area located in the Chiyoda ward of Tokyo and contains buildings including the main palace, various private residences and administration buildings. (Robert Cicchetti/Shutterstock)

milk at the Teehaus. Though the SS guards watched him throughout most of his walk, they did so from afar, with a patrol following him discreetly at a distance, and if he spotted any of them he would turn on them angrily, shouting 'If you are frightened, go and guard yourself.' But this insistence upon privacy would prove his undoing. He would die in the one place he felt safe.

Hitler had purchased the Berghof villa from sales of *Mein Kampf* and after his rise to power in Germany had greatly enlarged it. By 1943 the estate included barracks and an SS guardroom, a theatre, a small farm, administration offices, and workers' accommodation, as well as the Haus Türken, the guesthouse Hoher Göll, and residences for Bormann, Göring and Speer. The estate was heavily guarded by the SS, with the *Reichssicherheitsdienst* (RSD) and *Führerbegleitkommando* acting as close bodyguards, the *Wachkompanie Obsalzberg* responsible for guarding the estate, and the *SS-Sonderkolonne* providing motor transport for Hitler and his entourage. With Hitler in residence at the Berghof, there was little for someone to do in a position with the *SS-Sonderkolonne*, such as that impersonated by Joachim Adalbert, which enabled him to move around the estate without undue suspicion.

There were ten static pickets around the estate plus one-man patrols, but only one of the former, that stationed at the Gutshof, had the specific task of watching Hitler during his morning walk. He was observed, though, by SS pickets at the Theaterhalle and Göring's residence as he crossed a concrete path from Oberau road to the Führerstrasse. These guards, however, were more than 500 yards from the path. After his breakfast of milk and toast at the Teehaus, Hitler was driven back down to the Berghof, so the only time that the Führer was alone and vulnerable was during that fifteen to twenty-minute stroll through the woods.

THE SNIPER

The Special Operations Executive (SOE) had considered many different ways of killing Adolf Hitler. These had looked at bombing his special train, the *Führersonderzug*, of poisoning him, and attacking his motorcade. It was, though, only at the Berghof that Hitler was alone and virtually unguarded. If a sniper could get within range, the chances of killing Hitler were very good. Fortunately, the trees through which Hitler walked were part of a forest which continued beyond the perimeter of the estate to the River Larosbach. The forest was dense and, as the trees were mainly non-deciduous they still held their leaves, and would provide excellent cover both in the approach to the perimeter and when the sniper waited for the arrival of the target. At the selected point in the woods, the sniper would only be about 100 to 200 yards from the path taken by the Führer. The wood beyond the perimeter was not patrolled or guarded.

The wire-mesh perimeter fence was 220 centimetres high, supported by steel tubes at three to five metre intervals. The tubes were bent inwards and laced with three or four strands of barbed-wire. This perimeter was patrolled by a *Reichssicherheitsdienst* dog team at 10.00 hours to make sure the area was safe before Hitler started on his walk. The sniper would not be able to take up his position until after the dog patrol had passed, which mean he only had a few minutes to get into position before Hitler left the Berghof. Timing was everything.

This was appreciated only too well by *Pope*, the field-name for a twenty-seven-year-old, devotedly-catholic Austrian who had lived in Vienna before the *Anschluss*, and who saw Hitler as the Anti-Christ. *Pope* volunteered for the SOE's Section X in 1942, and he saw his mission as a holy crusade. The main problem that his SOE assessors had with him was that he was willing, too willing it seemed, to die in his quest to rid the world of the hated German Chancellor. This disregard of personal safety could be disastrous in the field. Care, discretion and vigilance were the essential ingredients for a successful operation, not reckless bravery. Over the course of many months these attributes were slowly instilled in the young man. He was now ready to slip unseen through the woods to calmly and clinically kill the Führer.

INTO THE WOODS

The majority of the soldiers that could be found at Berchtesgaden were men of the *Gebirgsjäger*, the Alpine troops, many of whom were admitted to the military hospital, the Platterhof, and were a common sight around the village. Dressed accordingly, *Pope* was therefore able to slip through the buildings and into the wood unnoticed.

Soon *Pope* was in the trees and out of sight. He stared at his watch which gave a time of 09.53 hours. He would have to wait. The Austrian, who had been a school teacher in Vienna, burrowed as deeply into the undergrowth as he could. He did not dare look up or move until 10.05. Even if Hitler left the Berghof at exactly 10.00 hours, *Pope* would still have time to get into position before the Führer reached the desired point.

The seconds ticked by with *Pope* barely able to contain his growing anxiety – not of fear, but of failure. At last the hand flicked onto the '5'. *Pope* knelt up and looked over the top of the bushes. He was too far back to see the wire, but he could hear no sound of movement. He stood up slowly and began to tread quietly and carefully through the trees. His eyes watched for any loose branch underfoot, the crack of which might alert the patrol if the German guard had not passed out of earshot. With each step he stopped and glanced up towards the wire before taking his next, cautious move.

He reached the fence and, looking along its perimeter, he could not see the RSD dog patrol. Did this mean the patrol had gone or that it was about to appear just as he was about to climb up the fence? He who hesitates is lost, so *Pope* grabbed the mesh, and began to climb. It was known that the fence had been climbed at least once before. What was described as a 'mad' woman climbed into the estate before being apprehended. Despite this, or perhaps because she had been quickly and easily caught, no amendments or modifications had been made to the fence. *Pope* was quickly over the fence. From here he had only a few yards of forest to move through before taking up his pre-determined position.

At last he reached the approximate spot and carefully loaded his rifle. Trying hard to control his breathing, *Pope* settled into position with his telescope-fitted Mauser. Almost immediately a small, thin figure appeared on the path, dressed in a brown double-breasted jacket and loose black trousers. *Pope* had to act quickly, but carefully. His training fought against his natural impulse to start shooting at the man he had dreamt for so long of seeing over the sights of a gun. But as much as the forest concealed the presence of the SOE operative, so the trees hid the Führer.

'PLAN B'

The months of meticulous planning had resulted in the SOE compiling a huge dossier, some 131 pages long, with photographs and diagrams, detailing the exact layout of the Berghof estate and the position of all the guard pickets and the estate's routines. This had enabled the planners to identify two areas where Hitler might be vulnerable. The first was on his walk, the second was as he returned, by car, from the Teehaus. If *Pope* failed to kill Hitler, then an alternative plan would be undertaken. This was for a two-man team to fire a Projector, Infantry, Anti Tank (PIAT) at the Führer's car from the woods near the tea-house as he returned to the Berghof.

Already a Sudenten German, alias *George*, was in place in the woods where he would be joined by Adalbert if something went wrong with

Pope's effort. Adalbert was to be the eyes and ears. If Hitler completed his morning walk undisturbed, then it was evident that something had prevented the Austrian agent from completing his mission. That being the case, Adalbert would enter the woods to join *George*. The latter, who had made his way to the Obersalzberg along a path through two 1.8 metre-high tunnels and along the south bank of the Larosbach to reach the woods on the Mooslanger Kopf, was also equipped with hand-grenades and smoke bombs which, it was hoped, would help cover the escape of the two agents through the woods after the attack.

This, though, was more than could be expected. In view of the large number of troops in the area, and the extraordinary efforts that would be made to capture the assassins, there was, in reality, almost no chance of the two men escaping. Both had been provided with the SOE's 'L' capsules – cyanide pills. The two men were of German extraction, and therefore no direct link could be attributed to Britain, especially if they were both dead and unable to reveal any of their secrets under torture.

THE FATAL SHOT

Again, Hitler's slim frame emerged from behind the trees. He was now almost directly opposite *Pope*. The density of the trees had only been considered by the planners at SOE Headquarters in Baker Street as an advantage, not as the hindrance it now clearly was. *Pope* permitted himself a quick glance to his right, and saw that very shortly Hitler would disappear from view again. It was now, right this very moment, or not at all. Remembering his training, *Pope* inhaled as his index finger curled round the trigger. With the exploding bullets *Pope* had been issued, one shot would be enough. With the slow-moving figure large in his sights, the assassin exhaled and squeezed the trigger.

Almost instantly, it seemed, the most hated man in Europe, was flung sideways through the air. *Pope* could scarcely believe the impact the bullet had. Hitler was evidently the weak and increasingly ill man that rumour said he was. As Hitler bumped onto the ground, the report from the Mauser rang around the woods. It had been agreed in London that the use of a silencer would affect accuracy, and to risk missing Hitler made the entire enterprise pointless. *Pope*'s best, though slim, chance of escape rested on the confusion – the pandemonium – that would immediately follow the execution.

Already the shouting had begun, as the guards realised that something terrible had happened. These men were responsible for Hitler's safety and if the Führer had been shot whilst on their watch, the consequences for them would be dire. Though *Pope* wore *Gebirgsjäger* uniform, *George* was dressed as a Czech worker and it was unlikely that anyone would link the two. They both left their weapons behind and joined the throng of people now running around the outside of the estate, hoping to blend into the crowd. Adalbert had been stood by the guard at the Gutshof and so was plainly not the man who had shot Hitler and was therefore under no immediate suspicion. Soon, he would pretend to join in the hunt for the unknown assassin.

LITTLE FOXLEY

There was, of course, no point in simply killing Hitler for the sake of it, although ridding the world of such a monster was no bad thing. But if the Nazi Party remained in power, the war would continue as before, and possibly to the Allies' disadvantage, as Hitler's decisions had become increasingly bizarre and his insistence on refusing to allow his generals to conduct strategic withdrawals in the East had cost the *Wehrmacht* dear. With saner heads and wiser council, Germany might well recover from the reverses it had recently experienced.

The regime in Berlin had to receive such a shock that it would be driven into a realisation that its leading figures could be killed off whenever the Allies decided. So, to coincide with the assassination of Hitler, further strikes would be made against leading Nazi members. The targets, though, would not be the likes of *Reichsmarschall des Grossdeutschen Reiches* Herman Göring, or *Reichsführer-SS* Heinrich Himmler. These were the men most likely to take over power once Hitler was dead, and it was seen that these two had the most to lose if Germany was defeated. Their desire to keep their wealth, power and influence would induce them, it was believed, to approach the Allies with an offer of peace. The alternative, might be also be to die at the hands of an assassin, a point that would be made abundantly clear to them by the other assassinations planned by SOE under the codename *Foxley II* or *Little Foxley*.

The man at the top of the list of *Little Foxley* was Reich Minister of Propaganda Joseph Goebbels. Surprisingly, he was seen as an easy target. He rarely left Berlin except at weekends and much information had been gathered on his official and private addresses, his usual travel arrangements, the men he was normally in company with and, most importantly, the occasions when he was not closely guarded.

With his 'diminutive stature and clubbed foot' Goebbels was instantly recognisable, more often than not wearing civilian clothes. He usually arrived at one or other of his Berlin offices between 09.00 and

10.00 hours in the winter months. Anyone wishing to see the Reich Minister, other than well-known members of the Party, had to make a written submission. This application was vetted by his personal adjutants. When in, and whilst travelling to, any of his official addresses he was closely guarded, with his personal bodyguard, *SS-Untersturmführer* Wilhelm Kruse always close by.

It was in his off-duty moments that Goebbels was most vulnerable. He entertained a considerable number of 'bathing belles' from the Universum Film AG at his various residences around the city when his wife Magda was out of town. Access to any of these, when Goebbels could, quite literally, be caught with his trousers down, though, would be virtually impossible.

He was known to frequent a few bars, cafés and clubs, and it was at one of these that the SOE would strike. These included private clubs, where access would be difficult, and the Jockey Bar which had been taken over by the Propaganda Ministry. There was one place, however, which was open to the public. This was the Kunstlereck am Zoo (today simply the Hotel Zoo) on the Kurfürstendamm. Shooting Goebbels there would be comparatively easy, but there would be little or no chance of escape for the assassin.

Eventually, it was decided that it would be one of Goebbels infrequent visits to his residence outside Berlin, the Sommervilla Waldof, which was on a road that joined the Prenzlaur Chausee to the Berlin-Stettin Autobahn. This single-storey white house with a grey-blue roof, was set in large grounds surrounded by a two-metre-high fence topped with barbed-wire. Though a strike on his car whilst travelling to or from the villa to Berlin was considered, the dates and times of such a journey could not be discovered by SOE. So it was whilst he was at the villa, that the British agent struck.

As the wire around the villa was not electrified, it was a simple matter to cut through and sneak into the grounds, the entire place being guarded only by six men – uniformed SS and Gestapo in civilian clothing. Gaining access to the villa itself was a different matter altogether. As it transpired the villa backed onto the western shore of the Bogensee lake and Goebbels' study in the main wing had a large glass wall facing the lake.

It was more by luck than judgement that on the Saturday that Hitler was in residence at the Berghof, 20 March 1943, that Goebbels was also at the Sommervilla Waldof. Luck, though, is an essential ingredient in any such operation.

THE SHATTERING OF THE GLASS

Again, it was to be a lone gunman who would fire the fatal shot. Precise details of the assassination are not available as the agent, whose details remain classified, was never seen again. What is known is that the unnamed agent was scheduled to take a plain, ordinary rowing boat, the smallest and least significant he could find, and row past the villa at the time Goebbels usually began work, which at the villa, was a little earlier than when at his office.

The Minister of Propaganda was killed by a single bullet at 09.36 hours. Witnesses stated that they did not hear a shot, only the shattering of the glass in the study. No-one, by all accounts, saw a boat or had any idea who shot Goebbels. The lone gunman sailed off into the distance and into history. His SOE file (subsequently tagged HS 9/1823/4) was officially closed for 100 years, until 2043.

Because of the death of Hitler, the killing of Goebbels went almost unnoticed in Berlin amidst the chaos and confusion. As Hitler had frequently been the subject of assassination attempts over the years by German Communists and ordinary men and women driven by religion or conscience, no immediate thought was given to the possibility of British involvement. What most feared was that it was the Army, the *Heer*, which had decided to topple Hitler. The prospect of a military coup was very real, and no-one in any position of authority knew the consequences of such an eventuality which, it was presumed, would mean a clear-out of many who owed their posts to support of Hitler. To a considerable number, Hitler really was their Führer.

Until it was known who was responsible, fear, as much as confusion, reigned throughout every ministry and every office in Berlin. Himmler immediately stepped forward, Göring being in Pomerania, to try and contain the rumours that Hitler was dead, but this proved utterly impossible. What was needed now was a calming speech from the Propaganda Minister. It was really only then that the news of Goebbels assassination penetrated through to the Reich Chancellery.

Himmler seemed stunned with this latest news. Clearly something big was afoot. As he was not involved in a coup, someone else who commanded considerable resources surely was. Himmler called all the SS troops he could gather in Berlin to defend the *Führerbunker*, expecting to be attacked at any moment. Indeed, no official message was sent to inform Göring of the two assassinations until the 22nd, in case the *Reichsmarschall* was involved.

When, on the 23rd, Göring turned up at *Führerbunker*, he was received in the Chancellor's office surrounded by armed SS.

By this time, Himmler had called most of the senior *Heer* officers to the *Führerbunker* individually, and all seemed as surprised as he was that Hitler was dead. Being slightly more suspicious of the air force, it was only when he had assured himself of the genuine loyalty of the army officers, that he asked the various heads of the *Luftwaffe* to go to the bunker to be questioned.

When it became apparent that there was no revolution in the offing, though some officers struggled to suppress their delight at the death of Hitler, thoughts turned to outside interference. Though the assassination could have been carried out by any of a number of groups from almost any country, backing would, almost certainly, have to come from Britain. The Occupied territories lacked the resources to mount such a complex operation, and the US had not developed the kind of sophisticated covert skills that the UK had mastered over the course of 200 years. The double assassination had to be the work of the British, and the world needed to be told.

'HITLER DEAD'
The words 'Hitler Dead' formed the headlines of every newspaper around the globe. Each one also carried the statement by Himmler, calling himself Deputy Führer, mocking the words of Winston Churchill:

> Never in the course of human history was so much owed by so many to one man. Adolph Hitler transformed an embarrassed and betrayed German people into the mightiest nation in the world. But England, zealous of its waning power, sought to destroy Germany before its industry and commerce was pushed aside by the ever-increasing might of the Reich.
>
> While the Führer wanted only to right the wrongs of the treachery of Versailles, Britain sought to stop Germany from its natural path as the leader of Europe. The Führer wanted peace – Britain wanted war.
>
> That war proved disastrous to England. Her army was driven from the Continent in disarray, and now she hides behind her navy, sending her cowardly aircraft to bomb the houses of the innocent women and children of the Reich. But she knows that Germany will never be defeated and so tried petty revenge for her losses.
>
> I have to tell you now, my *volk*, that whilst the Führer was walking alone through the lovely woods of the Berghof, he was

gunned down by a British assassin. We do not know how many British agents were involved, but those we have captured revealed the plot to kill both the Führer and Reich Minister Goebbels.

Never has a nation, one once so strong, stooped so low. Killing two unarmed men in their own homes. Never has a nation made such a mistake. For these acts will only stiffen our resolve. Listen when I say, Mr Warmonger Churchill, that you have stirred up emotions that can never be extinguished. GERMANY WILL FIGHT UNTIL THIS WAR IS WON!

Himmler, possibly more than any other, knew how hollow these words really were. Germany was losing the war. The combined military and industrial resources of Britain and its Empire, the vast Soviet Union, and the young energetic United States, far exceeded those of Greater Germany and the Occupied countries. Hitler knew that the Allies would never negotiate with him and there is no doubt that he would never surrender, and would keep on fighting until Germany was destroyed.

The death of Hitler changed everything. Now there was a chance of peace and Himmler and his confidantes knew that the German people wanted peace above all things. The great 1,000-bomber raids by the RAF's Bomber Command had destroyed Cologne, Hessen and Bremen in horrific firestorms. These presaged worse to come. Peace or death and destruction. Both would result in humiliating surrender, that was inevitable. But peace would save Germany, and as she had risen once, so she would again. Peace it must be.

THE STOCKHOLM SYNDROME

As direct communication with Great Britain was impossible – as Hermann Hess had so amply proved in 1941 – contact would have to be made through a neutral country. Switzerland was an obvious choice, but too obvious. Suspicions would be roused if unusual activity was seen around Bern and Himmler did not want to be seen by his people as going cap-in-hand to offer up Germany to its enemies. So Sweden was chosen. Germany had good relations with Sweden through the iron ore which it shipped across the Baltic to the Ruhr, and it was a long way from the agents and the intrigue of land-locked Switzerland.

Felix Kersten, Himmler's personal physical therapist and *SS-Brigadeführer* Walter Schellenberg, chief of *Sicherheitsdienst* foreign intelligence were despatched to Stockholm. The inclusion of Kersten in this mission may seem strange, but Himmler had become dependent on Kersten because of the masseur's unique ability to alleviate his chronic, sometimes unbearable, stomach pains, and he exerted unusual influence upon the *Reichsführer*.

The two emissaries made their presence known and were able to meet with Abram Hewitt, an OSS officer in Stockholm under cover of the United States Commercial Company, and a longtime friend of President Roosevelt. Hewitt penned a message to the President, which went in secret through the diplomatic pouch, straight to the White House. Himmler offered to make peace with the Western Allies and then together the US, Britain and Germany could fight the true menace to civilisation, the Bolsheviks of the Soviet Union.

Of course, Roosevelt was not going to turn on Stalin, who, at this stage of the war would prove a far too formidable foe. But if he could obtain a peace settlement advantageous to the US without risking the enormous loss of life that would result if Allied ground troops had to invade Germany, he would take it.

Roosevelt knew that Churchill would never deal with the Germans at any level, so the negotiations which continued in Stockholm were kept very secret throughout. The news of a deal, if indeed one could be brokered, would be presented to Winston only when the ink was dry on the parchment.

THE HEWETT MEMORANDUM

It was not until July 1943 that an agreement was reached. A meeting of 'The Big Three' was held in Cairo on 18 July. Stalin and Churchill immediately denounced the arrangement as 'dealing with the devil'. In practice, though, there was absolutely nothing that the British Prime Minister could do about it, being by this stage of the war entirely in Roosevelt's pocket. As for the Soviet leader, he was allowed to keep all the territory he had gained up to the German border as delineated in 1918. There was also the promise of continued aid, both in terms of goods and finance, to help not only restore Russian losses and damage, but also to send American experts and businessmen, to modernize the country's industry.

The arrangement with Himmler was little different from that at Versailles, with the important difference that Germany would not have to pay reparations. The hope was that the Germans had finally learnt their lesson, and they would never again allow a man such as Hitler to come to power. If Germany could prosper peacefully, there would be no reason to fight. It was thought that one day there could arise a unified Europe, headed by Germany and France, in which democracy reigned supreme, where all countries could trade freely with each other, and where the peoples of all nations would be able to live and work in whichever country they chose. That, of course, was just a dream.

THE REALITY
So much of this story is true that many might be surprised how close to reality the events described above really are. Firstly, the SOE did indeed draw up plans to assassinate Hitler at the Berghof. Operation *Foxley*, was devised by an agent known as LB/X, whose identity has now been revealed as Major H.B. Court. The information gathered by SOE on Hitler, his habits and his movements, was extraordinary. How SOE was able to learn so much about an area that was so heavily guarded by scores of utterly devoted, fanatical Nazis, defies explanation. The positioning and number of all the SS pickets was known to SOE and most of the buildings inside the Berghof estate had been identified. The planners knew where their agents could stay in Berchtesgaden, and which types of person lived, worked and convalesced there, and where they could hide immediately before the operation.

The plan to shoot Hitler on his morning walk is almost exactly as devised by SOE, as was the fall-back option of using a PIAT or a bazooka to blow Hitler's car to pieces.

Another option was also considered – that of attacking Hitler's motorcade as it travelled from the Berghof to Saltzberg. The *Kolonne* usually consisted of three or more Mercedes-Nurberg six-seater limousines protected by armour and bullet-proof windows. The motorcade was usually preceded by an RSD motorcyclist armed with a sub-machinegun. Hitler's car was always the first or second in the *Kolonne* and was distinguishable from the others in that it carried a large swastika symbol on its right-hand side mudguard. Hitler, helpfully, always rode in the front passenger seat, unless he was travelling with a fellow dignity and then he rode in the back with his guest. Consideration was also given to dropping a parachute battalion into the Berchtesgaden area. A battalion of 800 men would be able to completely overwhelm the 300 or so combat troops stationed in and immediately around the Berghof estate.

The SOE also planned to assassinate a number of lesser individuals, which did include Goebbels, as well as *Generalleutnant* Bruno Ritter von Hauenschild, *Generalmajor* Otto Ernst Remer and *SS-Obersturmbannführer* Otto Skorzeny. Himmler, Kaltenbrunner, Bormann and Göring were all considered as other *Little Foxleys*, but no detailed planning was ever carried out.

Why then was Operation *Foxley* not carried out? The subject of assassinating Hitler had first been considered as early as 1941, though such ideas were shelved until 1943, when the subject was re-evaluated, and the *Foxley* plans drawn up in the summer of 1944. Opinions were divided amongst the SOE staff about the desirability of killing Hitler, and doubts about the morality of assassinating a head of state caused them considerable agony.

Even in the midst of the most devastating war in history, there was something unseemly about an assassination of that nature. Equally, there was a chance that with an enemy government assassinating Hitler he would be turned in the eyes of many from being a monster into a martyr, thus encouraging the patriotic Germans to fight on with even greater tenacity. Also, all the senior Nazis who might take over from Hitler were well aware that they were likely to face prosecution for war crimes if they lost the war; there was, therefore, little likelihood of a German surrender.

In his Foreword to the published *Foxley* files, the renowned historian Ian Kershaw pointed out that in a survey of public opinion in West Germany in 1952, a third of those interviewed condemned the famous *Valkyrie* attempt on Hitler's life on 20 July 1944. This attempt was conducted by fellow Germans, so it is easy to imagine how strong the response to an assassination of the Führer by Britain might be. That same survey, incidentally, also revealed that a quarter of those questioned still 'thought well' of Hitler.

It must also be borne in mind that at the end of the First World War, it was the German claim that they had been 'stabbed in the back' by their politicians who had surrendered, even though their armed forces had not been defeated on the battlefield. A similar outcome in the Second World War might produce the same conviction, with untold potential consequences. Germany's belief in its military strength had to be utterly demolished. Allied leaders fully understood this which is why they announced that the only terms they would accept was unconditional surrender.

On the other hand, it was argued that the entire Nazi structure had been built around Hitler and that his death would see the whole of that flimsy edifice crumble almost overnight. If this would have happened and the war shortened, even if only by a few months, hundreds of thousands of lives would have been saved, for it was in the latter stages of the war that the casualty count reached appalling numbers.

The strongest argument against the assassination of Hitler is revealed in the *Foxley* papers in a minute written on 9 October 1945 by Lieutenant Colonel Ronald Thornley:

> As a strategist, Hitler has been of the greatest possible assistance to the British war effort … his value to us has been the equivalent to an almost unlimited number of first-class SOE agents strategically placed inside Germany. Although the military situation has been temporarily stabilised on the western front and the German army appears to have regained cohesion, Hitler is still in a position to override completely the soundest of military appreciations and thereby help the Allied cause enormously …
>
> To remove Hitler from the wheel at a time when he and his fanatics have pledged themselves to defend every street and every house on German soil, would almost inevitably canonise him and give birth to the myth that Germany would have been saved if he had lived. If, as is almost inevitable in my view, the assassination was traced to Allied sources, the repercussions would probably be grave. It would be disastrous if the world came to think that the Allies had to resort to these low methods as they were otherwise unable to defeat the German military machine. From every point of view, the ideal end to Hitler would be one of steadily declining power and increasing ridicule.

There, then, is the reason why Britain decided not to assassinate Adolf Hitler.

The files on *Foxley* can be examined at the National Archives at Kew, London. They are referenced HS6/624 and 625. The *Little Foxley* papers are to be found in HS6/626 and 623. These, though are held on microfiche, which makes them far from easy to use. As a consequence, Mark Seaman has compiled a colour reproduction for the National Archives, entitled *Operation Foxley, the British Plan to Kill Hitler*. Further information on these assassination plots and others concocted by SOE can be found in Denis Ridgen's excellent book *Kill the Führer, Section X and Operation Foxley*, published by The History Press, in 2009.

Perhaps even more surprising than the elaborate plans to kill Hitler is the evidence that Himmler did indeed secretly approach the US, through Felix Kersten, without the Führer's consent. By early 1945, Himmler's relationship with Hitler had deteriorated and, with the defeat of Germany a certainty, Himmler used Kersten, who by that time had moved to Stockholm, to act as an intermediary in negotiations with Count Bernadotte, the head of the Swedish Red Cross. Letters were exchanged between the two men and Walter Schellenberg arranged direct meetings.

Himmler, whose record of atrocities is almost unrivalled as the man in charge of the concentration camps and responsible to a large degree for the Holocaust, was, no doubt, increasingly worried about how he would be treated if Germany was beaten into an unconditional surrender. He would not be permitted by the Allies to go into quiet retirement. He would have to answer for his sins. The only way he could avoid this was if he was the peacemaker and the head of an unbeaten country. When Hitler learnt of Himmler's treachery, he ordered his arrest. Himmler went into hiding, being arrested by British troops. Like Hitler, Himmler died of his own hand.

Chapter 8

A Mysterious Death
General De Gaulle, April 1943

By Martin Mace

It was three o'clock in the morning when the phone rang. General Charles de Gaulle, leader of the Free French forces and the symbol of French resistance to Germany, was quick to answer the telephone which lay on the table by his bed in the large room he occupied at 99 Frognal, Hampstead.

'Oui?'

'General de Gaulle?' asked a man with a pronounced American accent.

'Yes'. De Gaulle was puzzled. What was an American doing calling him at, God knows, whatever time it was? The stupid man probably forgot the time difference between the two continents.

'This is Reuters news agency. We have just received word that British troops have attacked Diego Suarez, and we would like to know what you have to say on the subject.'

This was not possible! He had repeatedly been assured by that fat bore Churchill that Britain had no plans to invade Madagascar. His heart began to thump in his chest. No, this was typical of those perfidious islanders. They had lied and cheated time and time again. Britain was determined to rob France of its empire, whilst France was occupied and divided. This was the end of all cooperation. Britain was the true enemy of France, and had, once again stabbed her in the back when she was at her weakest. But they will pay.

'General de Gaulle?', the Reuters man asked again. 'Were you aware of the intention to occupy Diego Suarez? Are Fighting French forces involved? Are you going there to take over the administration of the island?'

De Gaulle slammed the telephone down. He was not going to admit to being excluded by Churchill. He needed to consider his response. He leant over and switched on the bedside light. 03.03 hours. It would be, what, 01.00 in Madagascar?

He picked up his phone, and dialled quickly. The Free French would no longer deal with the Anglo-Saxons. They needed to plan.[1]

THE FALL OF FRANCE

Less than two years earlier, on 9 June 1940, General de Gaulle had flown to London on a mission from Prime Minister Paul Reynaud to help organise British operations in support of the French armies which, after the withdrawal of the British Expeditionary Force from Dunkirk, was vital if the Germans were to be stopped.

It was a Sunday when de Gaulle stepped onto English soil with his aide-de-camp Lieutenant Geoffroy de Courcel, but he was whisked straight round to Winston Churchill at 10 Downing Street. For the first time, the two fiercely patriotic men met face to face. Theirs would be a turbulent relationship, but at first it seemed to both men, that only they could save France.

De Gaulle returned to France assured of continued British support, only to find that the military and political situation was deteriorating by the hour. Defeatism was in the air. Churchill travelled to France to try and bolster the fading fortunes of Britain's ally. But seeing that the French forces were on the point of collapse, he offered the disintegrating French Government the only hope he could – that of an eventual victory: 'With our Air Force and our Navy we shall, with our Empire, be able to inflict the most serious blockade on Europe and hold on for years. What will happen in this case to the French fleet?' he asked the gathering of French ministers and military men. 'Britain has free use of the seas; her Empire and the French Empire are intact … We could develop rapidly a war of continents. It is possible that the Nazis will dominate Europe, but it will be a Europe in revolt, and it can be freed by the fall of a regime sustained above all by the victory of its machines.'[2]

With the 'stench' of defeat in the air, and the French soldiers throwing down their arms, de Gaulle saw Churchill as the only man who, true to his oft-repeated philosophy, was never going to give in. When he learned that Reynaud had been overthrown and Marshal Pétain had taken over, de Gaulle knew that France would soon be offering itself up to the Germans. On 17 June, de Gaulle, with a few sympathetic fellow officers and 100,000 francs handed to him by Reynaud, flew to England. He would not return.

THE FIGHTING FRENCH

With his 100,000 francs, de Gaulle took rooms at the Rubens Hotel in London, before announcing his arrival to Churchill. The British Prime Minister immediately agreed to allowing the general declare himself the leader of who de Gaulle termed the Free French, upon the news that Pétain had, as expected, capitulated to the Germans. De Gaulle made his announcement on the BBC: 'France is not alone. She has a vast Empire behind her. She can combine with the British Empire which holds the seas and is continuing the struggle.' He invited all French officers and soldiers on British soil to join him and very quickly the Free French movement, later to be re-named the Fighting French, was born.

But almost as soon as de Gaulle stood proudly side by side with Churchill, the British leader betrayed his new comrade in arms.

De Gaulle's vision for the fight to come included the French navy, the fourth largest in the world, which had not been involved in the Battle of France and remained undefeated. But, with the new French Government eager to agree terms with the Germans to avoid further conflict, Churchill was worried that the French fleet would be handed over to Hitler. Though the French Admiral Darlan gave Churchill a sworn commitment that he would scuttle his ships rather than surrender them to the Germans, Churchill demanded that the French warships must sail to the UK and place themselves under British control. This, though, would weaken France still further and, promoted to Minister of Marine, Darlan sought to retain his country's navy.

Suspicious of French intentions, and doubtful of their capacity to defy Hitler, Church took the bold, or in many eyes, reckless, decision to capture or sink the French navy. On 3 July, in what was termed Operation *Catapult*, all the French vessels already in French ports were taken by force, and the French warships in Alexandria were seized by Royal Navy personnel. At the port of Mers-el-Kébir in Algeria, where a strong French squadron was based, Admiral Marcel-Bruno Gensoul refused to agree to British demands, and the commander of a powerful British force, Vice-Admiral James Somerville, was ordered by Churchill to sink the French warships. The resulting bombardment saw more than 1,200 French sailors killed and a further 350 wounded.

De Gaulle had not been consulted and when he learned of this unprovoked attack, he was furious. The man who had declared that France would be great again, had already taken the first steps at reducing France to imperial impotence – for how could de Gaulle rally the French Empire if it had lost its fleet? Britain and France had fought for world dominance for almost 200 years, and Britain, it seemed, would lose no opportunity to attack France even when a greater enemy stood triumphant on the shores of the Pas-de-Calais.

But for now, de Gaulle needed Churchill. He would bide his time, and bite his tongue. Churchill had, with his unprovoked attack, demonstrated that he was determined to fight the Germans, and to take whatever action he considered necessary to win. This dispelled the belief of the Pétanists that Britain would find an accommodation with Germany, leaving France forever under Nazi control.

So, choosing to see Operation *Catapult* in a positive light, de Gaulle declared that Britain and France, 'will win together or they will both succumb.' The action against the French fleet, however, turned many Frenchmen away from Britain. It was seen as a stab in the back by the nation that was supposed to be its strongest ally. As a result, de Gaulle, who was seen at this stage by most people in France as being a deserter and Churchill's lackey, was not able to recruit as many of his country folk to his cause as he otherwise might have. The Pétain administration, which set up at Vichy in southern France, declared de Gaulle to be a traitor; was tried in his absence for treason, and condemned to death.

BRITAIN VERSUS VICHY

Whilst France became theoretically neutral, relations between Britain and France were severed, and the majority of the French colonies, which were beyond any possible German interference and which de Gaulle had expected to rally to his call, sided with the Vichy regime. The attack upon the French fleet at Mers-el-Kébir cost both de Gaulle and Britain dear.

This was made apparent when a combined Anglo-Free French military and naval force attempted to occupy Dakar in the French West African state of Senegal. De Gaulle hoped to free himself from British control by establishing himself in one of the colonies, but the Governor-General refused to allow the Free French into the port, and the attempt by force to seize Dakar was repulsed with not inconsiderable losses. The French had now turned on each other.

Relations between France and Britain deteriorated further when, in the summer of 1941, another combined Anglo-Fighting French force invaded Syria and Lebanon. The Vichy troops in the Levant numbered in excess of 30,000, backed by large numbers of tanks and artillery. In the ensuing fighting, there were more than 10,000 casualties before the Vichy troops surrendered. De Gaulle was permitted to take over in the Levant, but very few of the colonials chose to join the Fighting French.

None of this was what de Gaulle wanted. He had hoped to rally support, not to have to fight his own countrymen. Increasingly, the French people saw Britain, not Germany, as the real enemy, and de Gaulle's credibility in their eyes suffered by association. But he was almost totally dependent upon Britain for transportation as well as weapons and financial support. In effect, he was powerless without Britain, even though he was still cautiously suspicious of Churchill's ultimate objectives. Ideally, he would like to break away from Britain, but, as the course of the war remained uncertain, he decided to remain based in London. Soon, though, a telephone call in the early hours, would change everything.

DIEGO SUAREZ

On Sunday 7 December 1941, Japanese aircraft attacked the US Pacific Fleet at Pearl Harbor. The sudden entry of Japan into the war placed another French colony directly in the line of operations – the island of Madagascar, which is situated in the western Indian Ocean. Madagascar sits astride the shipping lanes that travel round the Cape of Good Hope to the East and was, in the days before mass air transportation, of immense strategic importance.

Already, even at this early stage of the war, hundreds of supply ships and more than 250,000 service personnel had travelled these routes. Oil from the Iraq and Iran, provisions to the Soviet Union via the Persian Gulf, troops and equipment for the defence of Egypt, aid to Australia and New Zealand – all crossed the Indian Ocean. The main French naval base on Madagascar, in Diego Suarez Bay, was the best-equipped outside metropolitan France.

As the Japanese pushed ever further westwards over the course of the following weeks, taking Hong Kong, Singapore, and invading Burma, their naval forces extended their operations deep into the Indian Ocean. If the Japanese could occupy Diego Suarez, they would be able to sever Britain's communications with India and Cairo.

It was obvious to both Churchill and de Gaulle that Madagascar would very shortly become a target for the Japanese. De Gaulle pressed Churchill to help him take the island on behalf of the Fighting French. But Churchill had seen the way that the colonialists had resisted the Fighting French at Dakar and Syria. If de Gaulle's troops tried to take over Diego Suarez, the colonialists were certain to resist, and Britain could not afford to become embroiled in a prolonged battle in the fourth largest island in the world. There was, Churchill believed, a far better chance of the troops in Madagascar submitting if a British-only force was sent, and the despised de Gaulle kept well out of it.

De Gaulle became increasingly concerned about Madagascar but every time he mentioned the subject, he was told that although Britain was keeping an eye on the situation, there were no plans to make a pre-emptive move against the island. Meanwhile, Churchill had ordered plans to be drawn up in the strictest secrecy for an assault upon Diego Suarez, under the name of Operation *Ironclad*. 'It is of the greatest importance that de Gaulle's people should be misled about Ironclad.' The official line was that 'while, of course, we are watching the situation carefully, we are doing nothing for the present.'

IRONCLAD

A force, which included a battleship, aircraft carriers, cruisers and flotillas of destroyers and mine-sweepers, with some 13,000 soldiers in transports and assault ships, sailed for Madagascar towards the end of March 1942. By 5 May the British force was off the northwest coast of Madagascar. As the troops landed, aircraft dropped leaflets, asking the colonists to accept a peaceful takeover. The French replied with their guns.

After two days of hard fighting, Diego Suarez was taken, but the Vichy Governor-General, Armand Annet, refused to surrender the island and he remained at large in his capital in the centre of Madagascar, Antananarivo. When de Gaulle was woken with the news of the British invasion in the early hours of 6 May, he knew he had been intentionally misled by Churchill, and he was convinced that Britain had every intention of keeping the island for itself, just as it had taken other French territory from the days of Wolfe at Quebec to Grey in the West Indies. De Gaulle was convinced that if he stayed chained to Britain, neither he, nor France, would ever be permitted to rise again to take its former place in the world.

So it was that de Gaulle rang Maurice Dejean immediately he had absorbed the news of the British betrayal. Dejean, who would later become the Commissioner for foreign affairs of the self-styled French *Comité français de Libération nationale* which replaced the *Comité national français* (French National Committee), received de Gaulle's words calmly. He agreed with a quiet '*Oui*', de Gaulle's repeated insistence that the Fighting French movement would soon become irrelevant if it remained under Churchill's thumb: 'We are a convenient cover for Churchill. By claiming he is acting on behalf of the Fighting French, he can take any of our possessions, and who would not believe him, for here we are? By sitting here, it seems to all the world that we are endorsing his actions.'

For a few moments there was silence. Dejean knew that the egotistical general sought only affirmation of his own views, not the ideas of others. 'We must plan this with care, Maurice. Churchill will not let us go willingly, and without British ships or aircraft there is little we can do.'

Dejean knew that he could now speak. 'When you give your next broadcast, you could denounce the perfidy of the British to the world. Then there would be nothing Churchill could do, for everyone would know what the British are doing.'

'No!' replied de Gaulle angrily. 'This will only show how weak we are. We will be the butt of all of Laval's pathetic jokes and he will use it to show Hitler that he is more important than I.' Dejean had heard this all before. De Gaulle believed himself to be 'the man who is France', and he saw the Machiavellian Pierre Laval, recently-installed as Prime Minister, as a threat to his ambitions. De Gaulle had already adopted a presidential air, and none doubted he dreamed as much of victory over Germany as he did of entertaining heads of state at the Élysée Palace. 'President de Gaulle' had a certain ring about it.

'For now we should imply that we were fully informed about the invasion of Madagascar and that we will in due course take over the administration of the island. We will see what Churchill makes of that. But I am not going to give Churchill or Eden the satisfaction of lodging a protest. I will simply ignore them. Let us plan, Maurice, and let Churchill stew.'

PARTITION

True to his word, de Gaulle refused to meet either Churchill or his Foreign Minister, Anthony Eden, but a letter was handed to Sir Alexander Cadogan, the Permanent Under-Secretary at the Foreign Office, by Maurice Dejean, on 6 May. 'The action now going on may have direct and imminent repercussions,' ran the wording of the letter, denouncing what it called 'Anglo-Saxon imperialism', and wondering if this was just the start of Britain's move against other French colonies: 'Applied, tomorrow, to Guiana, in French West Africa or in French North Africa, the method used for Madagascar would, in fact, result in a dislocation of the French Empire, in which the people of France might be led to see the beginning of a partition.' The note continued in a threatening tone, warning that the action against Madagascar might have 'direct and imminent repercussions.'[3]

After considering his options, de Gaulle wrote to the leaders of French colonies that were under Fighting French administration. These were General Catroux in Beirut, Governor-General Éboué in Brazzaville (French Equatorial Africa), and High Commissioner d'Argenlieu in Noumea (New Caledonia). Referring to the British takeover of Madagascar, de Gaulle wrote: 'my suspicions were realized', telling the colonials that he 'would not consent to remain associated with the Anglo-Saxon powers.' He then instructed them to 'make it clear, as from this moment, to the Anglo-Saxon representatives in your vicinity, that such is your resolution.'

De Gaulle then outlined his plan: 'To reassemble, as best we might, in the territories that we have liberated. To hold these territories. Not to entertain any relations with the Anglo-Saxons, whatever that might cost us. To warn the French people and world opinion, by all the means in our power, particularly by radio, of the reasons for our attitude.'[4]

True to his word, de Gaulle told the world what he thought, with a report in *The Times*, of 28 May, under the headline 'Gen. De Gaulle's View', he declared that, 'It was impossible for them [the Free French] to restrict themselves to providing the cannon-fodder and the firing parties for the war against the Axis'.

He told the British Foreign Office that he was going to 'visit Equatorial Africa but Eden was wary of the general's motives. On 27 May he wrote to Churchill: 'I induced him (de Gaulle) to postpone his proposed trip to Africa. I fear, however, that a further attempt on my part would merely increase his suspicions of us which are seldom far below the surface ... I hope you will agree that for the sake of our future relations with him it would be best to let him go.'[5]

Churchill did not agree, telling Eden that, 'There is nothing hostile to England this man may not do once he got off the chain.'[6]

De Gaulle, however, quickly realised that by moving his base to one of the African colonies the Fighting French would soon run out of money and equipment and quickly become forgotten and marginalised.

He would have to remain at the centre of affairs, and if he wanted to have nothing to do with Britain or the US, the only possible place where the Fighting French could get the support it needed both in terms of finance and military hardware – was the Soviet Union. Stalin had already announced his support of the Free French and there is no doubt that they would be welcomed in Russia with open arms. However cordial relationships might be between the Western Powers and the Soviets, both sides knew that their social and governmental philosophies were incompatible and that the current cooperation was a temporary expedient. If Stalin had a grateful post-war France on its side, it would have an ally in the very heart of the West. The Soviet leader would see having de Gaulle based in Leningrad as a major victory.

De Gaulle also knew that if he was to move from Britain he would have to do so secretly. It had become quite apparent that if Churchill became aware of his intention to relocate elsewhere he would be stopped.

SUM OF ALL FEARS

De Gaulle continued with his plan for a move north. With no large air force, the only way in which the Free French could move, en bloc to the Soviet Union was by ship. Though lacking any major warships, *les Forces Navales Françaises Libres* possessed a number of patrol boats, escort vessels, and the large submarine *Surcouf*, certainly enough capacity to move all the men. De Gaulle presented an outline of his plans to a select group of the Committee:

'You have seen what I have often told you. For Britain this is a welcome war. After every war her empire expands – it is no coincidence. The only nation that can hold her ambitions in check is, as it has always been, France. Always the English lords, the haters of *liberté, égalité, fraternité*, have sought to dominate the world. Always they meet the forces of *la Belle France*.

'Never have England had such an opportunity to succeed in her desires. Now she can take whichever of our country's possessions she wishes in the name of military expediency, and by remaining here in London we give their actions legitimacy. The Americans ignore the Free French people and deal with the cowardly dogs in Vichy.

'What then can we do? The answer is simple. We will transfer to Leningrad.'

For a second there was complete silence. Then Émile Henry Muselier, Georges Thierry d'Argenlieu, and Philippe Kieffer burst into shocked response.

De Gaulle waved his hands to quieten the three naval officers, but Vice Amiral Muselier was not a man to be silenced by such as de Gaulle: 'There is no question that we are seen as Churchill's poodles, and I wish as much as you to be free. But surely we must set up in our own territory. Let us go to the Levant?'

'And there we would have the Royal Navy on one side and the British army on the other. What could we do? But the British and Americans would not dare touch us in Russia. And Stalin could provide us with aircraft and heavy weapons – all supplied from the US! What a joke that would be. Roosevelt, who refuses to talk to us and who sends materials to Leval, would be giving us all we need.'

De Gaulle laughed and continued laughing longer after the smiles had died on the faces of the others. *Capitaine de vaisseau* Georges d'Argenlieu asked the question that was already forming in the minds of the others. 'But how do we know that Stalin will welcome us?'

'Do you not think that Lenin despises the Anglo-Saxons and their perversion of democracy? Do you not think that Stalin sees the British and Americans as a threat to his rule? When this war is over, the next battle will be Communism against Capitalism. Will Stalin welcome us? He would have the broadest smile that had ever spread under that pathetic moustache.'

All this time, *Lieutenant de Vaisseau* Kieffer had kept his thoughts to himself. Kiefer actually admired the British, and had formed the *Fusiliers Marins Commandos* which he trained along the lines of the SAS. De Gaulle turned to Kieffer, staring, suddenly mirthlessly, at the forty-one-year old. 'Georges?' Was all that the Free French leader said. De Gaulle always demanded loyalty but always suspected treachery in all of those around him.

'It is a risk. But in war there is always risk.'

De Gaulle did not push Kieffer further, but then continued: 'You will see I have called you three because you control our naval forces. I dare not tell anyone else until I know you have got all our vessels close together in British ports and fully prepared for the voyage to Leningrad. When I make my statement I want to sail that evening. By the time Churchill and Eden have met to discuss their response we will be far at sea, and when they try to contact me to discuss the situation we will be beyond their clutches.'

'Ask no more questions now. Think carefully together and present me with your arrangements, and your questions, when you have considered what you must do.'

De Gaulle left the room abruptly. He did not want to hear the three sailors' objections. He knew only too well how correct Churchill was when he observed, 'you may take the most gallant sailor, the most intrepid airman or the most audacious soldier, put them at a table together—what do you get? The sum of their fears.' But if they had no-one to complain to, they would simply get on with the task. The very future of France was at stake.

MAKING ENEMIES

The prospect of transferring to Russia lay uncomfortably upon Émile Muselier. He believed as firmly as de Gaulle that the France should not have capitulated as it had and that a government-in-exile should have been formed in Britain, just as countries such as Holland and Belgium had done. France had not done this, and the position of the Free French movement was precarious at best. The United States continued to deal with the Vichy regime, refusing to recognise the Free French as the legitimate government of France and, as Britain was wholly dependent on the Americans, if Churchill was told to drop his support for de Gaulle, the Free French would have its legitimacy torn away.

De Gaulle's behaviour placed the entire Free French movement in jeopardy. Already Churchill's highly-perceptive wife Clementine had warned de Gaulle 'General, you must not hate your friends more than you hate your enemies.' De Gaulle, showing what he really thought of Great Britain, merely replied, 'No Nation has friends, only interests.'[7]

De Gaulle believed, like Napoleon, that 'I am France and France is me', and that only he could save the country. Yet if he continued on his present course he would alienate all those that sought to help France. Somehow he would have to be stopped.

Muselier waited for three weeks before making his move. He personally called Eden to ask for a discreet meeting as soon as possible. Muselier knew that the perpetually suspicious de Gaulle would be watching the actions of his three naval leaders. De Gaulle demanded complete loyalty yet distrusted everyone. Muselier could not be seen meeting the British Foreign Minister, so it was in the shadows of the trees in St James' Park that the two men, out supposedly on an evening stroll, met alone, coat collars upturned, nondescript trilby hats pulled far down.

No-one knows exactly what was said in the sombre exchange, but Eden, despite the late hour, went straight to 10 Downing Street. Predictably, Winston was still pontificating to the small gathering in the cigar-smoke-filled Cabinet Room. Amongst that number was General Alan Brooke, Chief of the Imperial General Staff, who had little time for de Gaulle. When Eden described his meeting with Muselier, Brooke declared: 'What a horrid mistake we made when we decided to make use of him!'[8]

He continued, complaining of his 'overbearing manner, his "megalomania" and his lack of co-operative spirit.' He spent his time 'concentrating on how he would govern France, as its Dictator, as soon as it was liberated!'[9]

There was little, though, that could be done about the problem of de Gaulle, in whom Eden placed great hope. Obviously, an eye would have to be kept on the Fighting French leader, and Muselier encouraged to continue to maintain his secret meetings with the Foreign Secretary.

OUT IN THE OPEN

Churchill and the War Cabinet had more to worry about that internecine struggles within the Fighting French movement or the blustering threats of the pompous de Gaulle. But then Muselier suggested that he and Eden might like to take a stroll one evening.

This time Muselier told Eden that on 19 June, de Gaulle was due to give an address at the Royal Albert Hall a meeting organised by 'Francais de Grande Bretagne' marking the second anniversary of his appeal to Frenchmen to fight on in spite of the armistice.[10] Muselier provided an outline of the speech to Eden that de Gaulle was to give. It would, as might be expected, open with highly nationalistic words, but then de Gaulle would conduct a prolonged denunciation of the Anglo-Saxon allies.

Though the move to Russia was not going to be specifically stated, the dissatisfaction with the manner in which the Fighting French were being side-lined was to be made abundantly clear. This would be the beginning of a programme of continual criticism of the treatment of France by her so-called ally and of Britain's true motives. When the news would eventually break of the departure of the Committee, all those who heard or read de Gaulle's statements over the months would, by then, understand why. Churchill would be the man blamed for driving the Fighting French out of Britain.

De Gaulle continued this theme, addressing a number of Fighting French officers:

'I have now become a political man and as a politician I am frequently obliged to say the exact opposite of what I actually think and feel … I pretend to be a good friend of Britain in order to create a good impression ...You all remember how, when you joined me, you were told by my Secret Service that England, like Germany, is our hereditary enemy. This you must always keep in mind. Russia will undoubtedly win the war in the field ... When I am in power in France after the war, I shall ask Russia for time to re-organise without her intervention. Russia will agree to this as she needs a strong France to balance the power in Europe. I shall then have accomplished what Hitler failed to do – become master of Europe.'[11]

Eden did not want to see a split between Britain and the Fighting French, and urged Churchill to hand over Madagascar to de Gaulle. The Fighting French, though, were hated in the French colony and such a move would have been resisted by the colonialists, and Churchill wanted to avoid any further bloodshed. Many in the War Cabinet were extremely worried with the direction events were taking and with Eden's efforts to try and appease the implacable Fighting French leader. On 2 June General Brooke wrote that 'Eden's support of de Gaulle will go near losing the war for us if we do not watch it.'[12] A third meeting with Muselier, however, made the Foreign Secretary realise that de Gaulle had to be dealt with.

A few weeks had gone by with no word from the Fighting French headquarters at Carlton House or from Muselier and, with a war to fight, the difficulties with de Gaulle had been pushed into the background. The shock came when Muselier and Eden met under the trees once again in St James' Park. Eden was shocked to hear that far from the subject of abandoning the UK, de Gaulle's plans were almost reaching fruition. He had been in contact with the Soviet Ambassador Alexander Bogmolov with a view to transferring Fighting French headquarters to Moscow. Stalin had happily agreed to the proposal.

THAT FATAL DAY

At last the preparations were complete. Rather than make any further inflammatory statements de Gaulle had adopted a seemingly conciliatory approach to relationships with his British hosts. He realised that his original plan to make a bold announcement on the eve of his departure to Russia might put Churchill on his guard. It was wiser, he calculated, to slip quietly away.

Under the guise of going to present medals to the officers and men of the fleet at Greenock, de Gaulle was, unusually, going to fly to Scotland rather than travel by train. A Wellington bomber, which had been converted to passenger transportation in 24 Squadron, Transport Command, was placed at his disposal, the party being scheduled to fly to the airfield nearest to Glasgow, which in those days was Abbotsinch.

After a security check on the aircraft at 09.30 hours, General de Gaulle's party arrived about a quarter of an hour later.

They were met by the Squadron commander of 24 Squadron, and ten minutes later all of them boarded the converted Wellington bomber after being properly fitted out with Mae Wests and parachute harness. The pilot started the twin engines and taxied onto the runway, where he ran up his engines, testing his flight controls in the prescribed manner. Everything was functioning normally, and at 10.05 hours he was granted permission to move onto the head of the runway and take off.

Loat held the aircraft on its brakes as he powered up, the geodetic airframe quivering and the thudding beat of the Rolls Royce Merlin engines rising to a deafening pitch. Releasing the brakes, the Wellington sped down the runway, climbing swiftly. After just four minutes the aeroplane had reached 4,600 feet when suddenly the elevator control column became loose in the pilot's hands. For a few seconds the Wellington continued upwards, then levelled off before starting to tip nose-down. The pilot said nothing as he fought to stabilize the Wellington as calmly as possible. He glanced across at his co-pilot, whose face had turned deathly white, and muttered, 'I've got not control from the stern. Have a look, quick.'

Before the co-pilot could move, the aircraft lurched over its' nose and tumbled towards the ground. Seconds later it hit the ground, exploding in a glaring flash of searing white and yellow flames. The black smoke that drifted back across the outskirts of Boreham Wood marked the funeral pyre of General Charles de Gaulle.

EPITAPH

It was a mere twenty-four hours later that General Giraud announced his leadership of the French people in their struggle for freedom. Giraud, who had not abandoned France at the moment of her greatest peril as it was seen by many in France that de Gaulle had, but he had fought on and been taken prisoner by the Germans. Giraud had become a national hero when he escaped captivity to return to Vichy. He was also well-respected by Roosevelt and the British.

Suddenly the situation in France and her colonies changed. All Frenchmen of every persuasion could support Giraud. Now the Germans had a nation seeking to resist the invaders at a time when

Hitler's armies were facing repeated reverses on the Eastern Front. More troops were transferred from Russia to try and halt the Resistance movement in France which was expanding beyond German control as the French people, unified at last after years of division and accusations and recriminations. As the Resistance moment grew in France so it inspired the other Occupied countries to take to arms. Europe, for so long acquiescent under the German jackboot, was now aflame with an unquenchable desire to throw off the Nazi yoke. The so-called Thousand Year Reich was coming to a premature end.

THE REALITY

It is a well-documented fact that following the British attack upon Diego Suarez, de Gaulle threatened to leave the UK and re-establish his Fighting French movement in the Soviet Union. On 6 June 1942, Ambassador Bogmolov was approached by de Gaulle with a view to relocating the Free French to the Soviet Union.[13] All the statements that are referenced in the footnotes are authentic and can be easily verified – and it really is true that Churchill asked the Cabinet to consider whether the Frenchman should be 'eliminated as a political force'. Perhaps what is even more surprising is that the attack on de Gaulle's plane does really appear to have happened, and was revealed to the British press some years after the war.

On 11 May 1967, a letter from William Lucien Bonaparte-Wyse was printed in the *Daily Telegraph*. Bonaparte-Wyse was an aide to Muselier. In this he stated that an aircraft in which de Gaulle and his staff were travelling from RAF Hendon to Glasgow to 'inspect' the Fighting French Navy when the aircraft aborted on take-off due to mechanical failure: 'A few moments later, the General's ADC, very white in the face, told me that an attempt at sabotage had been made.'[14]

In an interview with historian David Irving, the retired captain, Flight Lieutenant Peter Edgar Alfred Loat, D.F.C. (Service No. 42010), confirmed that he checked the weather at about 09.00 hours, and half-an-hour later the security officers came to check the aircraft, a converted Wellington Mark IA; these carried three crew and ten passengers, normally. There were five such Wellingtons in Loat's Flight at the time.

'His Wellington had no sooner lifted its tail off the ground than the elevator control column went loose in his hand, and the tail dropped back to the ground. Loat throttled back the engines at once, thankful that he had not begun his take-off run; he looked out of his side window, and operated his control column, but there was no movement from the elevators at all. Somewhere the controls had parted. He informed the control tower that the aircraft was unserviceable, and returned to the tarmac …

'The pilot and his maintenance Flight Sergeant climbed into the aircraft's tail, together with the Wing Commander, who was the airport security officer. Here they discovered that the controls had parted at the bolt line of the plate which connects the control rods to the elevator: from the nature of the fracture it was concluded that a powerful acid had been employed, and in this way the control system had passed muster during the routine maintenance inspection.'[15]

There was a secret investigation but no-one was ever brought to account for the attempted assassination.

Muselier did in fact see Giraud as a more realistic leader of the French forces in exile and he abandoned de Gaulle to join Giraud in Algiers in June 1943 (very shortly after the failed assassination on de Gaulle) and it is said that Muselier 'appeared to act as the head of an anti-Gaullist putsch'. The interweaving of suspicious events at this stage of the war is compounded by the fact that Giraud only became the French leader in North Africa following the assassination of Admiral Darlan, in which British involvement was suspected though never proved.

As for de Gaulle? He never flew in Britain again.

NOTES:
1. For details of the British amphibious assault on Madagascar and de Gaulle response, see John Grehan, *Churchill's Secret Invasion, Britain's First Large-Scale Combined Operations Offensive 1942* (Pen & Sword, Barnsley, 2013).
2. S.F. Clark, *The Man Who is France* (Harrap,1960) pp.105-6.
3. General de Gaulle, *War Memoirs, The Call to Honour, 1940-1942, Documents* (Collins, London, 1955), pp.344-8.
4. ibid, p.353-4.
5. TNA PREM 3 120/7, Eden to Churchill, 27/5/42.
6. ibid, Churchill to Eden, 30/5/42.
7. Peter Yapp (Ed)., *The Travellers' Dictionary of Quotation: Who Said What, About Where?* (Routledge Kegan & Paul, London, 1983), p.143.
8. Danchev, Alex and Todman, Daniel, *War Diaries 1939-1945, Field Marshal Lord Alanbrooke*, (Weidenfeld & Nicholson, London, 2001), p.212.
9. ibid, p.101.
10. *The Times*, 20 June 1942
11. Quoted in Simon Berthon, *Allies at War* (HarperCollins, London, 2001), p.245.
12. Danchev and Todman, p.263.
13. See François Kersaudy, *Churchill and de Gaulle* (Atheneum, New York, 1982), p.187.
14. Picknett, Lynn; Prince, Clive, Prior, Stephen, *Friendly Fire: The Secret War Between the Allies* (Mainstream, London, 2005), p.301.
15. http://spikethenews.blogspot.co.uk/2015/07/trouble-brewing-sikorski-de-gaulle.html.

Chapter 9

Crash of The Condor
The Death of Hitler, May 1943

By Andy Saunders

The war had been raging across Europe for three years and Germany was facing defeat. Everyone knew it, though none dare speak it. Hitler's intransigence, and his refusal to permit his generals in the East to make tactical withdrawals when the situation deemed such moves absolutely necessary, was leading to one disaster after another. The snow on Russian steppes was turning red with German blood. There was only one way that Germany could be saved – Hitler would have to be killed.

Many had sought to assassinate Hitler even before his rise to power in 1932. Political killings were commonplace in the social and economic upheavals that followed the end of the First World War which plunged Germany into a period of unprecedented instability. But Hitler seemed to have a charmed life, and every attempt, or planned attempt, at killing the despised leader of the Nazi Party had failed.

Shortly after being granted the Chancellorship Hitler instigated a ruthless programme to eliminate all opposition to his brutal regime. With informants and agents of the Secret State Police the *Geheime Staatspolizei*, or Gestapo, infiltrating every walk of life, resistance was hazardous, and often fatal. Yet, under Hitler's strong hand, order was quickly re-established and the naturally industrious German people to prosper. They began to see Germany, as they had before the First World War, as the leading nation in Europe. Most supported Hitler's remilitarization and were overjoyed when Hitler reoccupied the Ruhr. At last, after years of doubt and self-recrimination, the Germans could feel proud again, and as their self-belief increased so did Hitler's popularity. Resistance to the Führer became even more dangerous.

Hitler's expansionist foreign policy, however, started to cause anxiety amongst a number of leading figures in Germany, both in the business community and the army. Germany had reasserted itself and was on the path to becoming the foremost industrial power in Europe. No good would come from provoking another war. After the *Anschluss*, or annexation, of Austria, Greater Germany became by far the most populous country in Europe. Hitler, though, was not content to stop at that, and concern grew within Germany that Hitler was going to provoke the other European Powers into taking action to prevent any further expansion.

It was because of such fears that *Generaloberst* Ludwig August Theodor Beck, Chief of the German General Staff publically denounced Hitler's foreign policy. As a consequence, Beck was forced to resign.

Beck's fears seemed justified when Britain and France declared war on Germany in 1939, but the easy victory over Poland and then the remarkable success in May 1940 when France and the Low Countries were overrun and the British army forced to flee back to the UK, raised Hitler to almost god-like status in Germany. Hitler had achieved in weeks what the Kaiser had failed to do in years. Any attempt at removing Hitler at the very peak of his popularity would have been madness. Hitler, though, saw the Soviet Union as the arch-enemy of National Socialism. He had declared that he wanted *Lebensraum*, or living space, for his people in the East, and Stalin's Bolsheviks stood in the way.

WAR ON TWO FRONTS
In 1940, Hitler ordered the preparations for the invasion of Russia to commence, even though Britain's determination to continue to fight on despite the surrender of France, presented Hitler with the problem of having to fight a war on two fronts. To the likes of Beck this spelt disaster and whilst he must have known that his movements would be watched by the Gestapo, he was able to gather together a number of like-minded individuals who sought to stop Hitler before he embarked on such a potentially destructive course of action. It would take many months of secret and careful planning before any kind of move could be taken against Hitler and by then the attack upon Russia would already have begun.

It was at this time that Deputy Führer Rudolph Hess undertook one of the most enigmatic solo flights of the Second World War. On the evening of 10 May 1941, Hess set off from Augsburg-Haunstetten in a specially-adapted Messerschmitt Bf 110. His intended destination was Dungavel House, the summer residence of the Duke of Hamilton. He had been led to believe that certain members of the British aristocracy might not be averse to a peace deal with Germany. Hitler had repeatedly tried to make peace with Britain but his approaches had been ignored. The British, and especially Winston Churchill, would never negotiate with Hitler. But Hess hoped that if he could speak face-to-face with influential people in Britain he might be able to broker some form of peace arrangement. Any deal with Britain, even if it was disadvantageous to Germany, was better than no deal at all.

Hess, however, misjudged both the mood of the British people and the Duke of Hamilton, who had already joined the RAF. Hess' entreaties were rejected and he was to spend the rest of his life in captivity, much of it in solitary confinement.

THE PRUSSIAN

As the Germans pushed deeper into Russia, the treatment of the prisoners of war and the civil population appalled many of the German officers. Orders had been issued that 'partisans are to be ruthlessly eliminated in battle or during attempts to escape', and all attacks by the civilian population against *Wehrmacht* soldiers were to be 'suppressed by the army on the spot by using extreme measures, till [the] annihilation of the attackers.' The instructions issued by the *Oberkommando der Wehrmacht* included the statement that 'Every officer in the German occupation in the East in the future will be entitled to perform execution(s) without trial, without any formalities, on any person suspected of having a hostile attitude towards the Germans.'

Many who had reluctantly tolerated the extremes of the Nazi Party now found themselves being repelled by what they saw. Ordinary decent men also saw themselves being implicated in these excesses by association. It was the officers of the army, the *Heer*, who saw that it was up to them to put a stop to these horrors or they would be as guilty as those that had issued the orders, and the only way this could be achieved was by assassinating Hitler. It was at this point in the story that one promising young officer comes to the fore – *Oberstleutnant* Hermann Henning Karl Robert von Tresckow.

Born in Magdeburg, von Treschow was the son of a cavalry general and was steeped in the Prussian military tradition. Initially impressed with Hitler's militarism, by 1938 Treschow was another of those that saw the Nazi leader was dragging his country into a calamitous war.

There was, of course, no means by which he could influence events and once the fighting began, as a patriotic German, he put all his endeavours into securing a German victory.

As first General Staff officer (Ia) of Army Group Centre in Operation *Barbarossa*, Tresckow was well aware of the atrocities that were being perpetrated against the Poles and the Russians. Serving at Headquarters also meant that he had contact with the senior officers of the Army Group, and was able to quietly learn which of them held similar views to his own.

He also sent one of his adjutants, Fabian von Schlabrendorff to Berlin to see if Ludwig Beck, or anyone else of such standing, was still willing to act against Hitler. Von Schlabrendorff did indeed find such a group centred around *Generalmajor* Hans Paul Oster the deputy head of the counter-espionage bureau in the *Abwehr* and later *General der Infanterie* Friedrich Olbricht Chief of the General Army Office in the *Oberkommando des Heeres* (OKH). Knowing that he had powerful supporters, Tresckow felt confident that he could make a move against Hitler.

Tresckow could not take such action unless his commanding officer was in league with the conspirators. *Generalfeldmarschall* von Bock, though, was not prepared to be drawn into such an act, especially as Hitler remained immensely popular across Germany.

A reversal of German fortunes on the battlefield, as many believed was inevitable, gave Tresckow his opportunity. During the winter of 1941-2, the Soviets mounted a counter-offensive which saw the German army suffer its first defeats of the war. Buoyed by expectations of continued success, the sudden setback in the East came as a severe blow to the people of the Reich. This had two beneficial effects for the conspirators. The first was that Hitler's popularity waned for the first time in many years and the second was that von Block was replaced by *Generalfeldmarschall* Günther von Kluge who had been against Hitler's occupation of the Sudetenland in 1938 and had argued against the attack upon France and the Low Countries in 1940. Though von Kluge was unwilling to plot against Hitler in the midst of a titanic struggle against the Soviets, Tresckow knew that he was free to plan the demise of Hitler without fear of being denounced. It was around this point in time that the conspirators called their plot *Valkerie*, after the Norse legend of the host of women who were the ones that in warfare decided who should live and who should die on the battlefield. The conspirators had decided – it was Hitler who must die.[1]

THE PLAN

The fortunes of war once again swung back in favour of the German armies in the East in the summer of 1942, and likewise, Hitler's popularity rose accordingly. It did not last long. The winter of 1942-3 saw the Soviets return to the offensive, and German casualties mounted to unprecedented levels, and Hitler's orders to his general became increasingly unrealistic. The conspirators knew that the moment had come. Unless Hitler was assassinated Germany faced utter ruin. How, though, could the conspirators kill the most closely-guarded man in Europe?

Hitler had become increasingly reclusive and an audience with him either in Berlin or at the Eagle's Nest at Berchesgaden practically impossible. The only possible way that the conspirators could get close to Hitler was if he could be persuaded to leave the safety of his various headquarters and travel to Army Group Centre headquarters at Smolensk. Tresckow made repeated suggestions to Hitler's staff that the Führer should visit the front to assess the situation for himself. Eventually, Hitler agreed. He would indeed visit Army Group Centre.

The worsening military and logistical situation at the front had also forced von Kluge to change his mind. He wanted to see the end of Hitler, but was understandably worried about the repercussions, particularly if any attempt on Hitler's life failed and all those involved were arrested. A painful death was certain. He told Tresckow that he would join the conspiracy, but only after Hitler had been killed. Nevertheless, this was an important step forward for the conspirators for it meant that the leader of an entire Army Group would support them, making it impossible for the SS to stand in the way of the new government which would declare itself immediately it was known the Hitler was dead.

A 'shadow' administration had already been decided upon, with Beck as the new head of state. Backed, therefore, by an army in the field, a senior figure at the OKW in Berlin as well as in the *Abwehr*, any opposition to the new government would find itself facing a formidable organisation. This was essential if any solid advantages were to be gained by killing Hitler. Nothing would be achieved if the likes of Himmler or Goebbels stepped into Hitler's shoes. The assassination would have to be followed by a full-scale coup and the displacing of the Nazi Party. The stakes could not have been higher.

The conspirators knew that Hitler had been enticed into their trap, all they needed now was a plan to kill the Führer. Like von Kluge, they feared failure more than anything else. They had to conceive a foolproof method of killing Hitler. Many ideas were proposed. The most obvious to army officers was to shoot Hitler. A sniper would be able to choose his moment and even the place where he could easily target Hitler. The problem with this method was that Hitler's bodyguard, who would willingly sacrifice their lives for Führer, would form a barrier around the Führer making him a difficult prey. The most certain way would be for an individual to get close to the Führer, draw a hand-gun and shoot Hitler at an unmissable close range.

Few men were willing to attack the Führer in this way. Many regarded Hitler as a liability but they still saw him as their leader, their Führer. They had also sworn an oath of allegiance to him as army officers and such an act would mean breaking that oath. It also seemed an underhand and cowardly act, hardly befitting German officers. It was somewhat hypothetical, anyway, as Hitler would be surrounded at all times by a strong bodyguard and the chances of getting anywhere close to the Führer without permission was extremely remote. Another take on this, and a more honourable one in the eyes of Captain Georg Freiherr von Boeselager, was to overwhelm the SS bodyguard and kill Hitler in a 'fair' fight. In this attack all those that had committed themselves to the conspiracy would take a hand. It would be all for one and one for all. This was vetoed by von Kluge who did not want to see large numbers of Germans fighting each other. This evolved into all the conspirators attacking Hitler as he sat down to the pre-arranged lunch that was to be prepared for his visit. This plan was also dropped, allegedly von Kluge disapproved of killing a man at dinner.

It was Tresckow who conceived the now famous scheme that saw the end of the Hitler regime. It was indeed, an exceptionally clever plan. Tresckow had seen that Hitler usually travelled long distances by aeroplane. All he needed to do was plant a bomb on the Führer's aircraft. As Hitler would be flying over areas where Soviet partizans were known to be active, all Tresckow had to do was set the fuze for around thirty minutes after placing the bomb and the aircraft would be brought down in hostile territory. Not only would the perpetrator of the incident be unidentifiable, and most likely attributed to the Soviets, it would most likely be days before the wrecked aeroplane would be discovered. The conspirators could then quickly form a new government with all the trappings of legitimacy, untainted with the stain of usurpers and murderers.

With the help of Fabian von Schlabrendorff's cousin Rudolph-Christoph von Gersdorff who was in the *Abwehr*, Tresckow gathered together the necessary explosives and fuzes for the assassination attempt. This was no easy task, as the timer had to be silent (a loud hissing noise or a ticking noise within the confines of an aeroplane would be certain to cause alarm) and the explosives had to be both compact and therefore easily hidden or disguised whilst being powerful enough to cause damage that would bring the aircraft crashing to the ground. This is where von Gersdorff proved invaluable. The *Abwehr*'s Section II dealt with, amongst other things, sabotage, and here he was able to obtain all that Tresckow desired. Von Gersdorff gave as his reason for needing such items was that he wanted to equip a White Russian (i.e. anti-Communist) partizan unit being formed unit, formed under George Boeselager, known as the 'Boeselager Brigade'.[2]

Section II duly handed over the items von Gersdorff requested. This included a powerful plastic explosive from stock captured from the British. The RAF had been dropping large quantities of explosives to the SOE and resistance movements across Occupied Europe which had been seized by the Germans. A comparatively small amount of this substance would be quite adequate for the job. He was also given some British fuzes. These were more sophisticated than the German fuzes, and they worked by the release of acid from a capsule. When the fuze was set the acid ate through a wire which then released a spring which drove the firing pin on to the detonator. The speed at which the acid ate through the wire was determined by temperature – the colder the temperature, the longer the period of time before the acid worked its way through the wire. To make sure that he gauged the correct length of time for the operation of the fuze and the amount of explosive and how it could be carried and contained, Tresckow practiced in fields close to the front line where explosions would not attract any especial attention.

For these field trials von Gersdorff was able to obtain a variety of explosives, including a special small British bomb called a 'clam' which was attached to its target by magnets. Filled with plastic tetryl and TNT, it had the power to penetrate 2cm steel plate.[3] According to Fabian von Schlabrendorff, these 'clams' were 'extremely powerful, but not bulky. A package no bigger that a thick book was capable of tearing apart everything within the space of a fair-sized room.'[4]

Tresckow also made contact with Captain Ludwig Gehre, a member of the group in Berlin, and asked him to obtain drawings of Hitler's aircraft. Through a fellow conspirator who worked for Lufthansa, Otto John, Gehre learned that Hitler's aircraft was always closely guarded and anyone who approached it, even the usual mechanics who worked on it, were searched. John reckoned it would be impossible to plant a bomb on the Focke-Wulf Fw 200 Condor. He did, however, manage to obtain drawings of the aeroplane which were passed onto Treschow.[5]

As a precaution, in case placing a bomb on Hitler's aircraft was impracticable, Tresckow had other schemes prepared. The first of these was that of putting a bomb in Hitler's parked car during his visit. The second was to have Boeselager's Brigade ready to open fire on Hitler and his retinue if the opportunity arose, despite von Kluge's desire not to see Germans fighting and killing each other.[6] Tresckow had arranged for Boeselager's men to stand by the SS troopers as 'additional security'. He knew that he might never get another chance to eliminate Hitler and he was determined that, one way or another, the Führer would never leave the East alive.

SECURING CONTROL

Meanwhile, back in Berlin, Beck and his co-conspirators put in place the method by which they would seize control of the reins of government as soon as word was received that Hitler's aeroplane had crashed. The public statement that would be released would declare that the army had taken control of the government on the grounds of national security. One of the conspirators' principal concerns was with the Reserve Army. Whilst the conspirators knew they had Army Group Centre on their side, that body was hundreds of miles away and engaged with the enemy.

Von Kluge could not, realistically, simply disengage and march back to Berlin to provide military support for the coup. The *Heer* body within the Reich was the Reserve Army and if this force refused to accept the change of regime, the conspiracy would be certain to fail. Army Group Centre, however supportive of the conspiracy its officers might be, would never contemplate fighting fellow German soldiers. A minimum requirement, therefore, was that the Reserve Army would remain neutral, or passive during the change of administration. With this in mind approaches were made to *Generaloberst* Friedrich Fromm through Olbricht. Despite the growing disenchantment with the Führer throughout the army, Fromm refused to be drawn into the plot, but although he was now fully aware of the conspiracy, he did not betray his fellow officers to the Gestapo. The likelihood was that Fromm would wait on the turn of events before committing himself to supporting or opposing the coup.

That would, at least, give the conspirators time to put their plans into place in the key cities. Stationed in Berlin was the Brandenburg Division which was under the control of the *Abwehr*. Providentially, this division was undergoing reorganisation and awaiting a new commanding officer. Hans Oster and his commanding officer, Admiral Wilhelm Franz Canaris, who had been a secret opponent of Hitler for many years, managed to secure the appointment of *Generalmajor* Alexander von Pfuhlstein to the vacant post in the spring of 1943. A friend of Oster, von Pfuhlstein was willing to help secure the capital and prevent the SS division at Jüterbog to the south of Berlin from entering the city.

It was also essential that the SS in general were kept in the dark about the death of Hitler until after the new administration had taken over all the key government positions. This meant delaying knowledge about the crash both in reaching Hitler's advanced headquarters at the *Wolfsschanze*, the Wolf's Lair at Rastenburg and of that information being passed onto to Berlin. To cut telecommunications in and out of the Wolf's Lair, *General der Nachrichtentruppe* (General of Communication) Erich Fellgiebel, was to ensure that signal stations and telephone exchanges were occupied by men loyal to him who would ensure that Rastenburg was temporarily isolated from the outside world.

As far as possible, every contingency had been taken into consideration by the conspirators. There was a growing belief amongst the troops, especially those on the Eastern Front, that if the war continued to be prosecuted in the manner it was being fought, Germany was heading for certain defeat. On the Home Front the situation was equally depressing with the RAF and the USAAF bombing Germany day and night and systematically destroying one city after another. If Hitler was to die, seemingly at the hands of the Soviets, his death might be symptomatic of Germany's declining fortunes, but few, other than hardened Nazis, would be opposed to a change of government. At last, on 13 May 1943, it was announced that the Führer would visit Army Group Centre Headquarters for a briefing on the current situation on his way from his *Führerhauptquartiere* at Vinnitsa to Rastenburg.

OPERATION 'FLASH'

Three Focke-Wulf Condor aircraft of the *Regierungsstaffel* flew into Smolensk airport, where on the morning of 13 May, Tresckow waited in person to greet the Führer. Tresckow had prepared the bomb for the aircraft and at the controls of Hitler's aeroplane, coded D-2600, was his personal pilot *SS-Gruppenführer* Hans Baur.

'We knew Hitler's plane was equipped with special devices designed to increase its safety,' von Schlabrendorff explained. 'Not only was it divided into several special cabins, but Hitler's own cabin was heavily armour plated, and his seat outfitted with a parachute. In spite of all this, Trescow and I, judging from our experiments, were convinced that the amount of explosive in the bomb would be sufficient to tear the entire 'plane apart, or at least to make a fatal crash inevitable.'[7] With Hitler now in their presence, the codeword could be sent to Berlin to advise the other conspirators that the assassination was soon to take place. Von Schlabrendorff duly telephoned the words 'Operation Flash', receiving the reply that, 'the ignition can be switched on.' All that Trescow now had to do was find a way to get the bomb onto the carefully guarded aircraft.

The party drove to Army Group Centre Headquarters for the briefing in von Kluge's barracks and then went to the nearby officers' mess for lunch. Tresckow learnt that Lieutenant Colonel Heinz Brant was due to give a presentation to Hitler during the flight back to Rastenburg, so he made a point of sitting next to Brant during the meal. Here one witness described the scene: 'Hitler was sitting with his head hunched over his plate, shovelling in his vegetables, when Tresckow turned to Brandt, who was seated next to him, and asked if he minded taking two bottles of Cointreau back to headquarters on the flight.'[8] Brant happily agreed to take the liqueur back to the *Wolfsschanze*, Tesckow explaining that the bottles were part of a bet he had made with Colonel Helmut Stieff who was Chief of Organisation at the OKH. He told Brant that the package containing the Cointreau would be handed to him at the airport.

After the meal, Hitler took his leave. As so often with the highly suspicious and unpredictable Führer, he took a different route back to the airport and he invited von Kluge to travel in his car with him. This meant that any attempt at bombing Hitler's car or of an attack by Boeselager's Brigade was out of the question. Everything now, the whole course of the war and the future of Germany, and indeed that of Europe, depended upon the package Heinz Brandt would carry onto the aeroplane.

THE FATAL FLIGHT OF THE CONDOR

At Smolensk airport, Schalbrendorff pushed the detonator into the explosive which was parcelled up ready for Brandt, and just before handing the package over, he squeezed the acid detonator. The bomb was expected to ignite thirty minutes later which, Treschow and

Schalbrendorff calculated, would see the Condor flying over the area around Minsk.

D-2600 duly departed Smolensk with the other Condors in the flight plus the usual fighter escort. As it happened Brandt did not carry the package with him, but placed it in the cargo hold, which was considerably colder than the main cabin. It was, therefore, not over Minsk but just inside what had been Polish territory when the two 'clam' explosives detonated. The entire lower half and stern of the Focke-Wulf was blown off, the explosion taking the path of least resistance. Flying at its operational height of around 13,000 feet, there was nothing Hans Baur could do to save the aircraft.

Immediately, the leader of the Messerschmitt escort broke radio silence to report the destruction of the Führer's aeroplane. To his annoyance he could not make contact with Rastenburg, Fellgiebel's men having already moved to close down communications. Controllers at Smolensk airport were the first to learn of the disaster, immediately informing von Kluge's headquarters.

Though overjoyed and relieved, the conspirators could not be seen to be happy at the loss of the German Führer, and, indeed, disposing of Hitler was only half of the operation. There was therefore no celebration, merely confirmation of the news being passed to the movement in Berlin.

The news of Hitler's death was kept from the rest of the Army Groups whilst Beck and his men moved into action. Most Germans, including those on the front line, only learnt of the crash two or three days later when an announcement was made on Reichs-Rundfunk-Gesellschaft, the German State Radio. The telecommunications blackout during the first few hours worked perfectly, and Beck and his men swept into the Reich ministries, assuming command at the point of the bayonets of the Brandenburg Division.

Himmler, pragmatic as always, quickly saw that the rug had been pulled from under his feet, and he offered his services to the new administration. Equally, pragmatically, Beck, who declared himself temporary head of the Reich until the national emergency was quelled, accepted Himmler's offer, despite the protests of most of the conspirators. Himmler could cause more trouble than any other and if he, and his SS could be kept quiet during the early stages of the takeover, all the better. There was still a war to fight and an internal fight would be to no-one's advantage. Likewise, Goebbels and Göring were asked to continue as before stability, all were only too aware, was essential to avoid internal and moral collapse across Germany.

There was no declaration of an end to the Third Reich. The nation's great Führer had died, but the nation was still strong and would fight on with even greater purpose. The wreckage of D-2600 was quickly located and the presence of British explosives soon discovered. Hitler, it was evident, had been killed by Soviet or Polish partizans supplied by the British. There was no need for any further investigations. The conspirators had assassinated Adolph Hitler and got away with it.

D-DAY DEFERRED

The Allies had made it clear that the only terms that Germany could expect to be offered was unconditional surrender. But the new German Government was not the one that had precipitated war. Great, and immediate, efforts were made through Sweden, Switzerland and Portugal, to ask for high-level talks to begin to bring about the end of the fighting. Though Winston Churchill wanted to see the complete destruction of Germany, saner heads prevailed. Germany was not Hitler. Could the Allies, certain in the knowledge that they were going to win the war, simply keep on bombing the civilians of a country whose government wanted only peace?

The Allied leaders had declared that the Nazi leaders were war criminals, but if the Allies continued to kill thousands of people whose representatives had asked for an end to the killing, would that not be a crime? That Germany would have to accept harsh terms was indisputable, but Churchill and Roosevelt had little choice but to agree to hold high level talks with the new leaders of Germany, who were all known to have been opponents of Hitler. The deciding factor was that the Western allies were to launch the massive invasion of France, Operation *Overlord*. The outcome of this enterprise was far from certain and likely to see the loss of many thousands of lives. In case an agreement with the newly-appointed Chancellor Beck should not be reached, the troops were kept in readiness across the south of England but, for the time being at least, D-Day was deferred.

Joseph Stalin proved to be the hardest to convince. The Soviet leader cared little about saving lives and far more about expanding his power and influence. It was only when Roosevelt threatened to cut off all assistance to Moscow, that Stalin finally acceded. Nevertheless, throughout the negotiations at Berne in the summer of 1944, Soviet forces continued to push westwards driving in through eastern

Germany. The Soviets halted before they reached Berlin, but almost a week after an armistice had been signed.

UNEXPECTED CONSEQUENCES

Under the terms of the Berne Accord, German territory under Soviet occupation was to be included within a greatly expanded Union of Soviet Socialist Republics, along with the whole of eastern Europe, forming the largest power bloc in the world. As we all know, the weakened western half of Germany was soon overrun as Stalin extended his empire to the waters of the English Channel. With no British or American forces on the ground in Europe, there was nothing to stop the Red Army.

As had happened six years before, only the United Kingdom, backed by the industrial might of the US, stood as a bulwark against totalitarianism. It was hardly what Henning von Treschow had imagined when he plotted the assassination of the man who is now revered by the German people as their last and greatest leader.

THE REALITY

There were more than thirty known plots to kill Hitler between 1933 and 1945, and the attempt to blow up his aircraft on its return to Rastenburg after the meeting at von Kluge's headquarters was planned and conducted just as described above. The conspirators waited anxiously for news of the crash and were shocked and stunned when they received word that the Führer's aircraft had landed safely at Rastenburg. Their most immediate concern was that the package with the bomb inside would be discovered or that, even worse, it would explode and kill their brother officers at the Wolf's Lair. Either way, von Treschow's and Schalbrendorff's involvement would be obvious. The quick-thinking Tresckow telephoned Brandt at the *Wolfsschanze*. Luckily Brandt still had the package which remained intact. Tresckow told Brandt that there had been a mix-up and he had been given the wrong package. He asked Brandt to hold onto the item which Schalbrendorff would collect from him and exchange it for the correct one.

Schalbrendorff flew to Rastenburg on the daily courier flight the next day, hoping to be able to continue onto Berlin to report to the conspirators in the capital. He met the unsuspecting Brandt and, to his immense relief, made the exchange, which was two genuine bottles of Cointreau. Schalbrendorff boarded the waiting train to Berlin and once inside a closed compartment, he opened the package. What he found was that the acid had eaten its way through the wire holding the firing pin which had duly struck the detonator. Even the percussion cap on the detonator seemed to have worked but for some reason the explosive had not reacted. It is thought that this might have been because the temperature inside the Condor's cargo hold was too low for the explosive to function. It was not unusual for the heater in the aircraft's hold to fail. Hitler's life might have been saved through nothing more complex than a faulty heater.

Surprisingly, the failed bomb attempt in no way diminished von Treschow's resolve. Just eight days later, on 21 March, another opportunity presented itself and Treschow did not hesitate. Hitler was scheduled to view an exhibition of captured Soviet equipment and weapons at the Armoury in Berlin, and Army Group Centre was asked to send a representative who could answer any questions the Führer might have. This was an unexpected chance to get close to Hitler and so passionate in his belief was von Gersdorff, he offered to blow himself up as he stood next to the Führer.

On the day of the visit, Gersdorf arrived early at the Armoury. Gersdorff planned to lay a bomb with a short fuze at a spot where he could draw Hitler's attention to a particular item. The Armoury was filled with workmen all day and Gersdorff could not secret his bomb anywhere suitable. Determined to carry out his mission, Gersdorff decided to carry the bomb in his pocket as he walked round with the Führer. Gersdorff was to become the *Valkkyrie*'s suicide bomber.

Hitler arrived as expected, but he rushed through the display without stopping to inspect any of the exhibits. Gersdorff tried to draw Hitler's attention to some of the items but the Führer hurried on, as if sensing danger. Even though Gersdorff had used a ten-minute fuze, Hitler was through and out of the Armoury and into the street before the bomb could go off. There was no point in Gersdorff following Hitler into the street (which he was not authorised to do in any case, his duties being confined to the exhibition) as the effect of the blast would be vastly reduced, and a failed attempt by an officer of Army Group Centre would have thrown suspicion on all of Gersdorff's associates.[9] Poor Gersdorff then suddenly remembered that he was holding a bomb that was due to explode! He dashed into a toilet and removed the detonator with just moments to spare.

Though yet another plan had failed, the conspiracy remained undetected. Their chance would come again.

NOTES:
1. The adoption of this name was actually very clever, as there was an 'official' Valkyrie plan, approved by Hitler himself, to secure the key centres of government in the event of a civil uprising. Should the word Valkyrie ever be overheard then it would be assumed that it was in reference to the approved plan. This is discussed in more detail in a later of this book. See also Roger Moorhouse, *Killing Hitler, The Third Reich and the Plots against the Führer* (Jonathan Cape, London, 2006), p.194.
2. **This** unit was actually a force established to move into action to protect the conspirators should there be an immediate counter-coup.
3. Anton Gill, *An Honourable Defeat, A History of German Resistance to Hitler, 1933-1945* (Henry Holt, New York, 1994), p.207.
4. Fabian von Schlabrendorff, *The Secret War against Hitler* (Hodder & Stoughton, London, 1966), pp.232-3.7
5. James P. Duffy and Vincent L. Ricci, *Target Hitler, The Plots to Kill Adolph Hitler* (Praeger, London, 1992), p.127.
6. Joachim Fest, *Plotting Hitler's Death, The German Resistance to Hitler 1933-1945* (Phoenix, London, 1997), p.193.
7. Von Schlabrendorff, p.236.
8. Fest, p.195.
9. Helena Schrader, *Codename Valkyries, General Friedrich Olbricht and the Plot Against Hitler* (Haynes Publishing, Yeovil, 2009), pp.189-90.

Chapter 10

The Last Flight of The Bulldog
Winston Churchill and the Bay of Biscay Mystery,
June 1943

By Dan Mills

As Britain's Prime Minister, Winston Churchill threw himself into his premiership, and his love for travel and adventure led him to sail and fly his way around the world visiting troops and Allied commanders. In fact, during the five years of war he travelled no less than twenty-five times to foreign countries spending no fewer than 365 days (a whole year out of five) travelling. This led to calls in the Commons that too much official business was being missed by the premier. At one meeting Stalin once joked that Churchill must be the Holy Spirit, 'He flies around so much'.

It was soon noticed by the Abwehr (German Intelligence) that Churchill was exposing himself to great risk by leaving Britain so frequently, and a new element in the spy war began, with one side trying to target him, and the other to keep him alive.

Neutral airports of Spain and Portugal were soon to become a hotbed of spying networks, as was Britain's Rock of Gibraltar; all sides were watching who was landing where and staying with whom. In Portugal near Lisbon, was one of these neutral airports, Portelas. The Germans picked up on this and set out to target and kill Churchill.

Despite the obvious risks that Churchill was running, being his normal obstinate self, he gave short shrift to anyone who challenged his behaviour. Was it only a matter of time before his luck ran out? Many thought so.

The Luftwaffe almost dealt the Allied war effort that devastating blow on 13 June 1940, when two of its fighters were out hunting over the

Channel. The forecasted cloudy skies had cleared, and spotting fishing boats, they pounced in for the kill. Unknowingly, whilst Luftwaffe eyes were on their immediate prey, they missed an opportunity of huge consequence.

Sneaking past the scene was a RAF de Havilland Flamingo heading to Britain from France. It had no fighter escort due to fuel shortages during the crisis, and it carried Winston Churchill back from a conference at the French headquarters in the south-west of France. The observant RAF pilot had seen the enemy action below and immediately took evasive action by diving down to wave-top level, throwing the plane and its occupants about like 'salad in a colander manipulated by a particularly energetic cook'. Luckily, the Flamingo then met up with an escort and was safely landed at RAF Hendon.

In January 1942, Churchill again flaunted fate by taking a scheduled commercial flight into Britain from Bermuda, this time in a BOAC Boeing 314 flying boat. On his flight into Bermuda the day before his return to Britain he had taken the controls for a while and it may have been a similar occurrence that led to the BOAC flying boat veering off course almost onto German anti-aircraft guns in France. Once the error was noticed the pilot changed course, heading for the south coast of England. The Boeing then appeared on British radar as an enemy bomber causing six RAF Hurricanes to be scrambled. Fortunately, the fighters failed to find the flying boat and Winston, once again, landed safely.

Risks were taken time and again, with Churchill, as normal, apparently relishing the danger he was placing himself in. Nothing, it seemed, was going to deter the PM from flying to any war zone he wanted to visit.

BODY DOUBLE

After the outbreak of the war most of Britain's air companies were banned from operating, the one exception was the British Overseas Airways Corporation, originally flying from Hendon, London, then switching to Whitchurch, near Bristol. The government also restricted flights to service personnel and to those with specific approval.

BOAC flights into North Africa and Portugal were regular. Portugal was a neutral country and being conveniently located on the fringe of the European theatre of operations and not too distant from North Africa, its Portela airport in Lisbon was a hive of activity for both Allied and Axis diplomatic missions.

131

Both sides respected the neutrality of Portugal, with each leaving the other to go about his or her business unmolested. This courtesy also extended to the airspace above. For the Allied effort, this meant that the flight route from Portugal to Britain was invaluable and regular passengers flying home were diplomats, military personnel, intelligence agents and government employees, as well as associated family members. It also took escapees from enemy prison camps that had been passed to safety along the chain through France and Spain.

German and British civilian aircraft both used the facilities on offer and all outbound and inbound air traffic was scrutinized by the respective nation's spies. Airports such as these soon became a battleground in the information war.

Due to the very real threat of assassination, a body double operation was set up to help disguise the movements and whereabouts of Winston. Several doubles were used to great effect at all stages of travel both at home and abroad. The main body double was a Mr Alfred Tregear Chenhalls, a forty-three-year-old reverend's son who had an uncanny resemblance to the premier.

Chenhalls was hired by the Special Intelligence Service (SIS) to help in the effort to stay one step ahead of enemy agents and the British public. He regularly appeared as Churchill at events and at numerous locations to help fool everyone, even meeting dignitaries without anyone being any the wiser.

When he made an appearance as Churchill, the real one was often covertly travelling or resting. It helped his disguise immensely by also being a great cigar smoker. Chenhalls knew the risks he was taking by doubling up for the Prime Minister but was proud to be able to do his bit for his country when so many others were risking their lives too, and of course he was sworn to secrecy.

For eighteen years, between 1921 and 1935, Churchill had been allocated a bodyguard from Scotland Yard, Walter Thompson. In 1939 Thompson was called out of retirement by Winston to take up his former role. Thomson himself was also given a body double, the famous actor, Leslie Howard, to help thicken the smoke-screen deployed around his much sought-after client.

By a master stroke of coincidence, Chenhalls was also Leslie Howard's manager, therefore having known each other for a long time and working together, the show they put on was seamless. The problem was, Howard himself was also a target for the Axis forces, as he had mocked Goebbels during one of his film scenes. He was a marked man from that time on.

This was thought by some to be a foolhardy appointment as it was certainly believed by the Germans that Howard was also doubling up as a spy. He was also being used as a propaganda tool by the British. His screen work had been described as 'one of the most valuable assets of British propaganda'. Of course, the Germans could hardly have suspected he was acting as Thompson's double.

It was well known that Churchill had many enemies. Not just his current war adversaries, many organizations would have been happy to see him killed, and some were actively planning to do it themselves.

THE IRA

The Irish Republican Army was still seething about the break-up of its country only twenty-two years before, when the Anglo-Irish Treaty of 6 December 1921 had split Ireland in two. Winston Churchill was then the Secretary of State for the Colonies, and was a signatory of the treaty, and therefore a legitimate target for assassination by the 'original' IRA.

In 1940 the IRA leadership, aiming to provide information to the Abwehr, sent two members to Germany to canvass for support, also submitting invasion plans for Northern Ireland. The invasion plans, however, were discovered when an Irish courier was arrested on a train, carrying with him details of the parties involved. This led to the arrest of a German Intelligence agent who had parachuted into Ireland.

Undeterred, the IRA Army Executive met on 20 April 1941, and sanctioned requests for cash, arms and ammunition, and resolved to give information to those powers at war with England. In 1942 they then launched an armed campaign inside Northern Ireland to which the British Government quickly responded to by internment without trial of suspected and known IRA members, on both sides of the border.

THE STERN GANG

The Zionist forces in Palestine were also known to be actively targeting highly-placed British officials, including the incumbent Prime Minister. Seeking to bring an end to the British-mandated presence in Palestine, the Stern Gang targeted anything that was British, or connected to the British presence in Palestine. The more hard-line terrorists amongst its members wanted to take on the British Empire outside Palestine, wherever they found it.

The most prominent, successful murder carried out by the Stern Gang, took place in Cairo. Lord Moyne, the then resident minister for the Middle East, a close confidant and friend of Winston, was assassinated alongside his driver, British Army Lance Corporal, Arthur Fuller. The two assassins were caught, tried, convicted and then hanged.

It is also known that the Stern Gang recruited and trained agents to be sent to England to carry out assassinations. In 1941 they had written on two occasions to Adolf Hitler to ask for an alliance between themselves and the National Socialist Party. One of the signatories to the alliance offer was the then terrorist Yitshak Shamir, later to be the Prime Minister of Israel.

THE FLYING BULLDOG

The Secret Intelligence Service, ever mindful of an assassination attempt on Churchill, would often plant a bogus copy of the PM's travel itinerary knowing where it would be intercepted, in the hope that it would throw the Abwehr off the scent. This move, along with the body double arrangements, was thought enough to confuse any enemy agents.

However, despite their best efforts Winston still dismayed his protectors time and again with display after display of complete laxness regarding the security of his travel arrangements, most particularly over the telephone. During one such conversation with President Roosevelt Churchill said 'I mustn't tell you on the open line how we shall be travelling, but we shall be coming by puff puff'.

During late May 1943, Winston, Clement Atlee and some senior British and American officers flew to North Africa via Gibraltar to attend a meeting with United States General Dwight D. Eisenhower. The meeting was to discuss fighting in the European theatre of war, the Tunisian campaign as well as the decision to delay the invasion of France by twelve months.

On this trip, Winston was excited about using his own private, specially-adapted aircraft, an Avro York transport. With the serial number LV633, and named *Ascalon*, it even had its own conference room. The fact that he had adapted a plane to hold conferences was testament to the amount of time Churchill spent in the air. *Ascalon* arrived from Britain on its maiden flight, apart from the crew there was only one other on board, a male civilian.

Churchill again frustrated his personal staff by insisting on staying over for at least one night on the Rock and made no attempt to hide the fact that he had arrived. The staff had wanted to transfer and secure the

PM from one plane to another waiting at the end of the runway as quickly as possible, but were sent away. Winston was not for hiding.

Immediately the local La Linea-based Abwehr picked up on the news and all airports in the area were rigorously monitored for any sign of flights with 'Special' status. Waiting for yet another blasé travel plan, the German Intelligence set off to target the return flight from any of the nearby airports. Several hours later, reports had also started coming in from agents at Portela Airport, that Leslie Howard was there, on a propaganda tour; he was seen talking to Alfred Chenhalls, or was it Churchill?

Churchill was certainly either in Portugal or Gibraltar and, sooner or later, must fly back to Britain. The Germans were determined that he would never reach the UK.

A FATEFUL DAY

The Abwehr was running around in circles between Gibraltar and Portugal with one spy account seemingly contradicting another. The trouble was that they simply had to target both groups, either way, any success and they would bag one or the other – either the feared Churchill or the hated Howard.

Howard's return flight was scheduled for the evening of 31 May 1943, from Lisbon, Churchill's flight to Britain was due out of Gibraltar on 4 June.

By this time the Secret Intelligence Service had received information from the code breakers at Bletchley Park that the Abwehr were aware Churchill was outside the UK, though it mentioned the confusion over which location he was really at. Therefore, it was decided to get Churchill out of harm's way at the earliest opportunity, and he was moved to the Lisbon flight. Churchill travelled under the name Colonel Warden.

The security detail hoped the confusion over the personalities and the fact that his new personal plane had been recently reported as landing and waiting at Gibraltar, would be enough to divert attention from Lisbon. However back in Bletchley Park the code breakers had decrypted enemy traffic detailing the movements to Portugal of the Prime Minister. This caused a real dilemma. If the Lisbon flight was openly cancelled it might raise German suspicions that their coded signals could be read by the British. Nothing was considered more important than keeping the breaking of the Enigma code a secret. So, Winston himself ordered an aide to sabotage the plane under the cover of darkness.

At the scheduled boarding time the enemy spies watched as the passengers were led out of the passenger lounge to the waiting plane. Many eyes watched as Churchill, accompanied by his tall bodyguard, puffed on one of his large cigars as he made his way across the sun-drenched tarmac to the portable stairs, only to then watch them be led off again twenty minutes later.

Word was spread that the plane had mechanical problems, and in the warm interior of the airport terminal a chalk line was scored through the scheduled date and time of flight BOAC – 777 replacing it with 07.30 hours 1 June.

Roles were hastily swopped again, for some this would be fatal. Telephones were buzzing, spies were soon chattering, what is going on? Whilst Churchill was hidden from prying eyes Chenhalls lit a new cigar and headed out into a waiting car. He and Thompson were sent out as bait once again, the party were reported heading for Gibraltar to get a flight back to Britain. Enemy agents separated and observed the movements at both Portela and Gibraltar.

The morning of 1 June 1943, was cloudy with frequent showers. For the second time the passengers for flight BOAC 777 were led from the lounge to the waiting plane. The time was 07.20 hours, take off was scheduled for half past the hour.

Amongst the passengers walking to the plane was an unknown southern Irish Roman Catholic priest, another was one Wilfred B. Israel, a known Jewish activist and Zionist.

At 07.25 hours Churchill and Howard quickly boarded the plane and took their seats. The Irish priest then stood up and walked off the plane, missing the flight, why? Who was he? IRA? Was there a bomb on board?

As the plane was about to taxi off, Leslie Howard suddenly jumped up, exited the plane and ran to the terminal, he promptly collected a parcel from a desk then re-boarded the flight. By this stage so many theories were being bandied around, who was on the plane? Had Churchill gone to Gibraltar or not? Was that man Churchill's bodyguard Thompson? What was the package collected from the terminal? Was that the propaganda spy Leslie Howard really on board? What had happened to the Irish priest? Confusion reigned.

The Royal Dutch Airlines/BOAC Flight 777 heading for Whitchurch, England, taxied along the runway and finally took off at 07.35 hours on Tuesday 1 June 1943. As it did so, enemy agents scrambled to inform their superiors that they thought the Prime Minister of Great Britain was on board and that maybe the earlier reports of his departure towards Gibraltar were mistaken, or that their watching eyes had been duped by enemy agents.

Allied agents outside the loop were also now chattering like mad. They reported that Winston Churchill had got back on the flight to Bristol.

After taxi and take off, a regular stream of normal radio contact was kept with the plane until an alert came through at 10.54 hours – enemy aircraft had been sighted a short distance away, lots of them, and they were closing fast.

The unwritten rule of airspace neutrality on the Lisbon to Bristol route slowly lost favour with the Germans and by the end of 1942 the neutral airspace shared by both powers had shrunk. Attacks certainly happened on planes that had left the immediate neutral airspace above Lisbon, indeed, the DC-3 of Flight 777, named *Ibis*, had narrowly survived two such attacks in the past eight months. On both occasions, *Ibis* had been badly damaged by shell fire, one time only just managing to limp in to Lisbon.

The last message from Flight 777 over the radio was that they were being attacked, at longitude 09 degree 37minutes West and latitude 46 degree 54 minutes North.

At this stage into the flight the plane was about 500 miles from France and 200 from Spain. The pilot dropped the plane to wave-hop in the hope to avoid being spotted, but it was too late, they had already been seen.

Eight Junkers Ju 88 C6s of Gruppe V/KG40, based at nearby Bordeaux in Occupied France, were out on maritime escort patrol, and two of them were sent in to the attack. The brave Dutch pilots flew faster and did their utmost to avoid the cannon fire but were caught from both above and below, as tracer and shell tore into the plane. It was soon on fire, and with the pilots struggling to keep control of the plane, it fell in pieces from the sky into the Bay of Biscay.

Before it finally crashed into the sea three parachutists emerged from the plane, their silk canopies on fire. Did Winston take one of the crew members' parachutes and jump? If so, did he survive?

Word spread up the chain of command as soon as radio contact was lost with *Ibis*, and several flights of aircraft were scrambled hastily to search for the downed plane. No sooner had some of the Hurricanes reached the reported 'last contact' area than they spotted wreckage floating on the water 200 miles from the north-west coast of Spain. The worst had happened, the flying bulldog had chanced his arm once too often.

COVER UP

As the shocking reality of the situation sunk in, the SIS hasty arranged a meeting with the Cabinet at Number 10. If this terrible news was released to the public not only would morale fall drastically but the Germans would have scored a massive propaganda victory and a phenomenal boost to the flagging morale of the troops.

There was no other option then, Alfred T. Chenhalls had got away with bluffing the British public and the watchers so many times before, he would have to do it again – but this time it would be permanent!

Indeed, the SIS said that Chenhalls was at that moment 'getting away' with that very act in Gibraltar with Thompson by his side. Some argued that clearly, he had not got away with it because the PM had been targeted and killed successfully. In the end though those gathered felt they were left with no other option.

To maintain the deception, under the normal body double rules, the relevant security procedures afforded to the Prime Minister were assigned to any stand-in actors. So, there would be nothing unusual with Chenhalls and Thompson being whisked back to Downing Street as normal as soon as he landed – only this time he would be debriefed and then re-briefed on his critical future role.

Thompson was devastated at the news of the death of Winston, who had become a close friend. Personal feelings aside, he also knew his duty, and from then on, he would have to be even closer than normal to his 'client', taking an ever-increasing frontline role, being a confirmed, public figure in Winston's entourage. He would have to keep the proxy prime minister from the limelight. This was to prove difficult as Chenhalls had a flamboyant act to follow!

Whilst the German press reported, for a few days at least, the belief that the Luftwaffe had shot down Winston Churchill, in the British papers the following mornings pages were full of the story of the death actor Leslie Howard. An outraged press railed against the Germans shooting down an unarmed civilian aircraft. Another war crime to the mounting catalogue. The Germans were quick to deny any such accusations, claiming it was a case of mistaken identity.

Only after the British denial and then a public appearance of Chenhalls as Winston, did the Axis forces believe otherwise, then Goebbels gloated in his German propaganda paper that, 'Pimpernel Howard has made his last propaganda trip', referring to Howard's role in the anti-Nazi film *Pimpernel Smith*.

The British press also soon released the passenger list of those killed in the incident. Amongst those listed was one Alfred Chenhalls, accountant to Leslie Howard.

During the day, as the news was breaking, a Short Sunderland flying boat N/461 was tasked with carrying out a search for the downed plane. The crew had been specifically briefed to look for the inflatable dinghy belonging to the unfortunate *Ibis*, in the hope that any parachute survivors could be rescued. They were looking for Winston.

At this time, as if by a call to action, eight Ju 88s again swept down into the attack. However, after a furious air battle, the Royal Australian Air Force aircraft shot down three of the Ju 88s and escaped back to RAF Penzance.

The Bay of Biscay had gone from a neutral, safe flight area to being one of the most dangerous flying routes, and from then onwards all scheduled flights were switched to night time only. The reality now was that Britain's war effort was in big trouble, how would they prosecute the war with Winston dead and a civilian stand-in taking his place?

The truth is Alfred Chenhalls took on the role with enthusiasm. He tried to behave as patriotic and as eccentric as Churchill, he even started wearing his favourite velvet boiler suit, and began to practise his oration in front of the mirror. He became known to plan and act out past battles using match sticks to identify and manoeuvre units on the ground, whilst in the bath on the *Queen Mary* to the US he played out the D-Day landings whilst others splashed the water to make the action of the tidal waves!

For the rest of the war Chenhalls, with Thompson at his side, played the part of Winston Churchill very successfully. As Churchill, Chenhalls attended many top-level diplomatic meetings in Quebec, Moscow, Cairo, Teheran and Yalta without raising any suspicions.

He surrounded himself with many good advisors, and with experienced soldiers like Montgomery and Brooke at his side, Chenhalls helped steer Britain to victory. On 8 May 1945, Chenhalls stood on the balcony at Whitehall and announced to the nation that the war with Germany was over.

THE END

Shortly after victory in Europe, the Labour Party decided to withdraw from the national government which it had supported throughout the war, leading to the dissolution of Parliament by King George.

In the ensuing election, in July 1945, the Labour Party won by a landslide. It was widely reported that 'Winston' was surprised and stunned by his defeat. After all that he had achieved, he expected to stay in office after the war's end, he was wrong.

In fact, the ballot was fixed for Labour to win, it had been decided that Chenhalls had played the part of Churchill long enough. It was one thing to act out wartime leadership, with the benefit of his generals' advice and experience, but he could not be allowed to run a peacetime government.

THE REAL END

Winston Leonard Spencer Churchill passed away at home in Hyde Park, London, 1965, aged ninety, several days after a stroke. Alfred T. Chenhalls was killed alongside his good friend actor Leslie Howard when he was shot down over the Bay of Biscay on 1 June 1943. Or was he?

Chapter 11

Foul Play in The Philippines
The Assassination of José Laurel García, June 1943

By Alexander Nicol

Just ten hours after the attack upon the US Pacific Fleet at Pearl Harbor, Japanese bombers appeared over Clark Field on Luzon Island, around forty miles to the west of the capital of the Philippine islands, Manilla. Though the United States' Far East Air Force (FEAF), based in the Philippines, was aware of the aerial raid upon Hawaii, and its aircraft had been monitoring Japanese aerial movements, Major General Lewis H. Brereton's men were still taken by surprise when the Japanese attacked. Indeed, the Americans had planned to strike first by attacking the airfields on Formosa from where the Japanese were most likely to launch an assault upon the Philippines, but the Japanese acted too quickly.

Before he could launch a pre-emptive strike, Brereton had to get permission from Lieutenant General Douglas MacArthur, commander of the United States Army Forces in the Far East (USAFFE). Whilst waiting for permission, Brereton, not wanting to have his 'planes destroyed on the ground, ordered his squadrons into the air. Soon after this MacArthur confirmed the strike upon Formosa and had instructed Brereton to prepare his aircraft. This was received at 10.15 local time, with orders for the attack to be carried out just before sunset that afternoon, 8 December.

The American bombers and fighters were ordered to land and refuel in preparation for the afternoon attack. The men took the opportunity to have lunch. All but two of the US aircraft were on the ground when a radar station at Iba Field to the north of Manilla picked up two in-coming raids. US fighters were scrambled but confusion on take-off due to 'dust problems' and communication errors when airborne, resulted in the three Pursuit squadrons failing to intercept the approaching Japanese.

At 12.40 hours, twenty-seven twin-engine Mitsubishi G3M bombers struck Clark Field where one Pursuit squadron (the 20th) and two B-17 squadrons were on the ground. Behind the first wave was a second, consisting of twenty-six Mitsubishi G4M bombers, followed by Zero fighters which strafed the airfield for thirty minutes.

The second Japanese raid, of fifty-four G4M bombers, attacked Iba Field whilst the 3rd Pursuit Squadron's Curtis P-40 Warhawks were in the process of landing to refuel. A few P-40s managed to engage the enemy, but with little success against the overwhelming numbers of the Japanese.

The Japanese flew back to Formosa, having destroyed half of the FEAF. Most of the aircraft that had not been destroyed were lost over the course of the next few days. With the FEAF fighters unable to protect the few bombers that had survived, the B-17s were flown to Australia between 17 and 20 December. With little or no air cover, the US and Philippine ground forces were unable to fend off the Japanese invasion, which began on 8 December with landings on the north coast of Luzon. Though the invading forces were outnumbered by the defenders, the Admiral in charge of the US Navy elements in the region, Admiral Thomas Charles Hart, withdrew most of his submarine and surface vessels to Java because of losses to Japanese aircraft.

DEATH MARCH

Manila, the Philippine capital, was occupied by the Japanese on 2 January 1942, and US and Philippine forces were driven back to the Bataan Peninsula and to the island of Corregidor, where MacArthur hoped he could hold out until reinforced from the USA. However, Japan's complete mastery in the air and at sea across the Pacific meant that no help could be sent to the Philippines and the isolated American and Philippine troops on the Bataan Peninsula surrendered in April, with around 80,000 being taken prisoner.

This left just the Allied forces on Corregidor, but before the Japanese could launch an attack, they had to remove the prisoners from Bataan, many of whom were sick or wounded, plus a further 38,000 civilians who had been trapped in the region. Unable to find motor transport for such large numbers, the Japanese made them walk some sixty to seventy miles to the San Fernando railhead. In what was one of the most horrific episodes in human history, the prisoners were given little food or water throughout the march and were beaten, tortured and hundreds executed.

When they arrived at the railhead they were crowded onto trains and packed in so tightly that people could only stand and if they fainted or died, which some did, they remained trapped upright. When they reached the Capas train station, they had to walk the final nine miles to internment at Camp O'Donnell. Only 54,000 of the 80,000 reached Camp O'Donnell, and those who survived were in such poor condition they continued to die at the rate of hundreds a day. Possibly as many as 20,000 died in the camp. Most of the deaths were amongst the Filipinos.

The Allied troops on Corregidor surrendered in May. By the end of the fighting 23,000 American military personnel and around 100,000 Filipino solders had been either killed or captured. The loss of the Philippines is considered America's worst military defeat.

The Japanese set up a new puppet regime, headed by President José Paciano Laurel y García. Because of the brutality of the Japanese, with men being used as forced-labour and young women taken into brothels for the benefit of the occupiers, large numbers of Filipinos joined resistance groups and it is said that sixty per cent of the Philippines was under their control.

RESISTANCE

More than a quarter of a million Filipinos joined some 277 resistance groups throughout the islands. Even more engaged in anti-Japanese activities. When reports of the Filipino resistance reached Australia, Allied commanders began to supply the guerillas with equipment and even operatives to help coordinate the actions of the various groups. Predictably, the Japanese responded with brutal reprisals which only further added to the determination of the Filipinos to drive the invaders from their islands.

One of the most effective resistance groups was formed by Terry Adevoso. He was a cadet at the Philippines Military Academy when war broke out. He and the other cadets from the Reserve Officer Training Corps were told to go home, being too young to serve with the American forces. But Adevoso and the others were determined to do something, and so they gathered intelligence for the US forces and tried to organise and protect civilians. After the surrender at Bataan, the entire group took to the Antipolo mountains less than twenty miles from Manila, taking with them abandoned American weapons. They began attacking the Japanese, calling themselves the 'Hunters'.

The Hunters operated with another guerrilla group called Marking's Guerrillas, with whom they went about liquidating Japanese spies. As they acquired more weapons (the Hunters raided the Japanese-held Union College in Manila and seized 130 rifles) and more men, the resistance groups became bolder. Marking's Guerrillas even attacked a Japanese prison, releasing some captured resistance fighters as well as taking more weapons.

As the resistance movement grew it was evident that the only way Laurel's government could hold onto power was through the Japanese army. The Japanese high command, however, misread the situation. With the surrender of the US forces, they believed that the Philippines had been conquered and they had withdrawn the best of their divisions and the bulk of their aircraft to take part in their planned operations in Borneo and Indonesia. They had not appreciated how loyal to the US many Filipinos would prove to be, nor how they would respond to their treatment of the Filipino prisoners of war.

By the middle of 1943, the guerilla groups were strong enough to drive the Japanese forces from their lands, but they were spread around the Philippines and they found it difficult to coordinate their operations with the enemy holding key communication centres. The guerillas needed something that would trigger the various groups into simultaneous action.

If the uprising was general, there was nothing the Japanese could do to stop it. The invaders would simply be overwhelmed. That trigger would be the assassination of the despised Japanese puppet, President Laurel.

JOSÉ LAUREL

When Japan invaded the Philippines, the reigning President, Manuuel L. Quezon, escaped to Bataan, and when it became apparent that the US and Filipino forces could not resist the Japanese, he was flown to the USA where he set up a government-in-exile. Quezon did not want the entire Filipino government to abandon the country and he asked the rest of his cabinet to stay and try to mitigate the effects of the Japanese occupation.

Amongst the cabinet members was one man who previously had close ties with the Japanese, José Laurel, the Associate Justice of the Supreme Court. Laurel's son had studied at the Imperial Japanese Army Academy and Laurel had received an honorary doctorate from Tokyo University. He had also been a critic of the American control of the

Philippines. Understandably, Laurel, along with other Filipino officials, was asked by the Japanese to form a provisional government.

Laurel was happy to agree, (unlike his colleague, Chief Justice Abad Santos, who refused to cooperate with the invaders and was therefore executed) and, under pressure from the Japanese, the National Assembly elected Laurel to serve as President. To most Filipinos, Laurel headed an illegal regime, and any chance of winning the people round to his side was wrecked by the barbaric behaviour of the Japanese and a severe food shortage following the invasion coupled with spiraling prices. The dislocation of normal life, the reduction in imports and the activities of the resistance groups meant that food production and supplies continued to be disrupted. People began to go hungry, further stiffening opposition to the new government throughout the country. The Philippines was on the verge of rebellion. Now was the time to assassinate Laurel.

Whilst the vast majority of Filipinos were enduring great hardship, the members of the government that cooperated with the Japanese continued to enjoy life. President Laurel, it seemed, often relaxed with a game of golf. Away from the official buildings and his home, where guards were on duty, on the golf course he was exposed and vulnerable in an open space where there was nowhere to hide or escape.

It was on 5 June 1943 that Laurel was out on the Wack Wack Golf Course at Mandaluyong to the east of Manila. His playing partners included the President of the Far Eastern University, Nicanor Icasiano Reyes Sr. The party was playing the 7th hole when the assassin struck.

Concentrating on their game, the men had scarcely noticed the well-built young man walking diagonally across the light rough and onto the fairway. When just a few yards away from Laurel, the man turned, took three steps towards the President, raised his right hand and with a .45 calibre pistol fired four shots into Laurel's chest. The others were closer to the green and had to run back to the fallen Laurel. He was still alive but in a very bad way. No-one thought to run after the assassin who disappeared through trees to the left of the fairway.

They rushed him to the Philippine General Hospital where he was operated on by the Chief Military Surgeon of the Japanese Military Administration and other Filipino surgeons. Despite all their efforts Laurel died on the operating table.

The news of the assassination was the signal for the uprising. Led by the *Hukbong Bayan Laban sa mga Hapones* (or *Hukbalahap*) which translates as The Nation's Army Against the Japanese Soldiers, Japanese outposts were attacked and within days of the assassination the invaders had pulled back all their forces to Luzon Island, concentrating their strength to an area around Manila. With only light weapons, the Filipinos could not hope to defeat the occupying forces, but MacArthur, who was well-informed by Americans who had joined the resistance movement, saw a chance to re-take the Philippines.

The battles of the Coral Sea and Midway had changed the entire dynamic of the war in the Pacific. With its great offensive arm, its carrier fleet, destroyed at Midway, and US submarines sinking Japanese oil tankers, the US Navy had the Pacific, and the skies above it, largely to itself.

Though the US had decided to focus on building up its material assets before launching a major offensive against Japanese-held territory, the uprising in the Philippines offered the prospect of an easy victory and the chance to re-establish its air bases from where attacks on the other occupied countries could be launched. Ready or not, MacArthur knew he had to strike.

MACARTHUR'S RETURN

When the Japanese had invaded the Philippines, they had promised that the country would be liberated from US domination, though the Americans had already promised that they would give the country independence. With all but Manila and its environs in the hands of the Filipino resistance the Japanese could no longer pretend that they were still in control of the Philippines. So, on 8 July, General Tomoyuki Yamashita formally handed over the reins of power and the Republic of the Philippines was officially born. President Quezon, in a broadcast on US radio, denounced the new regime as illegitimate. He knew that the US Navy and Marines were on their way.

Knowing that no reinforcements could be sent to the Philippines Yamashita ordered all troops to be evacuated. MacArthur, who had vowed to return to the Philippines, found the islands undefended. The Filipino resistance had won back the country by its own endeavours – but at a cost. As the guerillas closed in upon Manilla, around 4,000 Japanese under the command of Rear Admiral Iwabuchi Sanji, took their anger out on the locals. Violent mutilations, rapes, and massacres occurred in schools, hospitals and convents. In what was later called 'the Manila Massacre', tens of thousands were mercilessly slaughtered. Just how many Filipinos were killed in Manila by the Japanese has never been definitively established, but most sources estimate that around 100,000 died in the battle for Manila, most of those deaths not being due to military action.

The US Navy and Air Force quickly moved back to the Philippines, and by the end of August, MacArthur was ready to take the war in the South Pacific to the enemy. Situated between Japan and its conquests to the west, US aircraft and warships were able to prevent the Japanese in Burma, Singapore, Malaya, Indochina, the Dutch East Indies and Cambodia receiving either reinforcements or resupplies of weapons and ammunition. Even more significantly, many Japanese cities were within the range of B-29 bombers based in the north of the Philippines. The attacks on Japan began on 25 November 1943 – Thanksgiving Day. Kyusyu was the first major city to be bombed in what became a sustained aerial assault upon the Japanese islands.

The first to succumb was the island of Okinawa, which suffered saturation bombing on an unprecedented scale. After a month of devastating attacks, US forces mounted an amphibious assault. Though it was thought that few of the enemy could have survived the bombing, the small number of Japanese soldiers that remained fought to the death.

Eventually, the island was taken and bases established for 3,000 B-29 bombers and 240 squadrons of B-17 bombers. From January 1944, the Battle of Tokyo began. Such was the devastation caused by the nine-month campaign, particularly the firebombing raid of 9–10 March 1944 against Tokyo in which about 100,000 people were killed in a massive conflagration that swept through the Japanese capital. With most cities destroyed and virtually no defensive forces capable of resistance, in September 1944, Emperor Hirohito surrendered unconditionally, to save his people from complete annihilation.

THE REALITY

President Laurel was indeed shot four times in the body on the 7th hole at Wack Wack Golf Course on 5 June 1943. The bullets missed his heart and liver and the surgeons at Philippine General Hospital saved his life. Laurel made a speedy recovery. Two suspects to the shooting were reportedly captured and swiftly executed by the Kempetai, the military police arm of the Imperial Japanese Army.

There was, somewhat intriguingly, another suspect, a former boxer named 'Little Joe' Feliciano Lizardo. It is said that Lizardo was presented for identification by the Japanese to Laurel at the latter's hospital bed, but Laurel said he could not remember what had happened, and therefore Liazrdo was released.

There now seems little doubt that Lizardo was involved in the attempted assassination, but the man who tried, and very nearly succeeded, in killing Laurel, became the President's bodyguard. Lizardo was so grateful that Laurel had not identified him as one of the would-be assassins and handed over to the Japanese, he then pledged to protect Laurel with his life. This was revealed in Laurel's memoirs written in 1953.

The mystery surrounding the attempted assassination continues to be a subject of interest in the Philippines, with the historian Teodoro Agoncillo in his book *The Fateful Years: Japan's Adventure in the Philippines* identifying a captain with a guerilla unit as the shooter.

Laurel continued in politics after the war even though MacArthur ordered Laurel to be arrested for collaborating with the Japanese. In 1946 he was charged with 132 counts of treason, but he was never brought to trial due to the general amnesty that brought peace and reconciliation to the islands. Laurel than ran for president again in 1949, but was defeated. He was later (in 1951) elected to the Senate, which he saw as a vindication of his efforts to help his people by moderating the effects of the Japanese occupation.

Wack Wack Golf & Country Club continues to be a world-class golf club, considered as one of the top 100 courses in the world. It was also on the golf course that during the US invasion of the Philippines in 1945 Japanese aircraft were dispersed into the golf course area to hide them from aerial observation and Allied bombing attacks. On the grounds of the golf course, a Japanese A6M5 Model 52 Zero was captured intact.

Having failed to hold Manila, and no doubt aware that he would face trial for war crimes after the war, Rear Admiral Iwabuchi Sanji committed suicide by detonating a hand grenade in his command post.

General MacArthur did lead US troops back to the Philippines, landing on 20 October 1944. The Americans needed to establish a major naval base at Manila Bay to support the expected invasion of Japan, planned to begin on 1 November 1945. But the Japanese fought on in the Philippines until the Emperor Hirohito surrendered on 15 August. The re-invasion of the Philippines saw the Americans suffer more than 79,000 casualties, and the loss of thirty-three ships and almost 500 aircraft.

Chapter 12

Target Tito: Operation Knight's Move

Killing the leader of the Yugoslav Partisans, January 1944

By John Grehan

The amalgamation of so many different ethnic groups after the First World War to form what was initially called the Kingdom of Serbs, Croats and Slovenes was never going to satisfy the disparate peoples of the perennially-troubled region of the Balkans. Re-named the Kingdom of Yugoslavia in October 1929, the country had already experienced political assassination in its National Assembly resulting in King Alexander suspending the country's constitution. The King himself was shot in 1934, to be replaced by his eleven-year-old son Peter, under the Regency of his cousin Prince Paul.

Yugoslavia remained neutral during the early months of the Second World War but, under pressure from Germany and Italy, Prince Paul joined the Axis on 25 March 1941. This was opposed by many senior military figures and they launched a coup which stripped Prince Paul of his authority and gave the young Peter II full royal powers.

This prompted Hitler to order the invasion of Yugoslavia, and on 6 April 1941, German, Italian and Hungarian troops marched across the border. After the bombing of the capital, Belgrade, and other major cities, representatives of Yugoslavia's various regions signed an armistice with Germany. It had taken the Axis just eleven days to conquer the country – or so it was thought.

Yugoslavia was broken up. Croatia became a German satellite state, whilst the other regions were occupied by German, Bulgarian, Hungarian and Italian forces. Almost immediately resistance movements sprang up, but like everything in Yugoslavia there were rival factions, each with their own aims. The resistance groups coalesced into two groups, the communist-led Yugoslav Partisans and the royalist (mainly Serbian) Chetniks. The group that emerged as the most effective, and the one that eventually received most of the aid sent from the UK through the SOE, were the Partisans led by Josip Broz Tito.

Tito's Partisans grew in strength and capability, but were continually hounded by the Germans and locally-raised pro-Axis forces and even the Chetniks. Hitler, whose attention was focused on the war on the Eastern Front, paid little attention to events in Yugoslavia. But by the end of 1942 it was apparent that the British and Americans were poised to open a second front in Europe and Hitler feared that the Allies would find an easy route through Yugoslavia, aided by Tito's rebels. In December 1942, Hitler issued Directive 47, which placed all the Axis forces in the region under a centralised command with the specific objective of wiping out the Partisans.

Five Italian divisions, three Croat brigades and 12,000 Chetniks (who now openly sided with the Germans against the Partisans) – 140,000 men in total – began operations on 3 January 1943 against Tito's 30,000 Communists. Tito's men were driven into the barren, and almost inaccessible mountains of Montenegro. Tito knew that he could not hold out in the mountains indefinitely and he attempted to fight his way back into Bosnia. On 7 June Tito broke out across the Neretva river. Though attacked from the air by Stukas and Dornier bombers, in which Tito was wounded in the arm by a bomb splinter, the Partisans reached Bosnia. Here they were broken up into small resistance groups and began to spread chaos around the country.

The Partisans received a further boost with the Allied invasion of Italy, followed by the Italian surrender in September 1943, which saw its ranks swelled by Italian resistors. By the end of that year, Tito's forces numbered 290,000 men and women, organised into eight mobile and twenty-six other divisions. The time had come to take Tito very seriously. The time had come to capture or assassinate the Partisan leader.

TRAPPING TITO

Before any attempt could be made on eliminating Tito, he first had to be found. The Abwehr's *Frontauflärungstruppe* 201 inserted agents into local communities in the hope of learning Tito's whereabouts and a team from the 1st Battalion of the Brandenburg Regiment led by

Oberleutnant Kirchner began operating with the Chetniks to try and track down the Communist leader. Draža Mihailović's Chetniks had reached the conclusion that they had more in common with the Nazis of Germany than the Communists of their own country. They sought to create a 'a Greater Serbia' after the war which would include all the territories to which they had a historical claim, not dissimilar to the Nazis' ideal of a Greater Germany. To this end, not only did they help the Germans in Yugoslavia, they even offered to send a division to help fight the Soviets, though Hitler declined the offer.

It was the Brandenburgers and Chetniks that discovered Tito was attending a conference in Jajce. Kirchner planned to send some of his men in Partisan uniforms accompanied by Chetniks to the conference, but this did not get official approval. Another scheme was devised in which two prisoners would be murdered and dressed up in British uniforms. They would then be fitted with defective parachutes and thrown out of an aircraft in the area where the bodies were likely to be found by Partisans. Inside the uniform of one of the men would be a package addressed personally to Tito. Inside would be a letter bomb. Again, this was not sanctioned. Then Hitler intervened. He gave SS Sturmbannführer Skorzeny orders to take Tito dead or alive.

Skorzeny discovered that Tito had his headquarters in the town of Drvar in what is today western Bosnia and Herzegovina. It was reported that there were some 6,000 Partisans in the area and 350 men acting as Tito's personal bodyguard battalion. Also based at Tito's headquarters were the American OSS and British SOE Missions to Yugoslavia. The latter included Winston Churchill's son, Randolph.

It would be no easy matter for the Germans to fight their way through the Partisans and by the time they had reached Tito's hideout he would have been long-gone. But there was an alternative method of attack – by airborne assault.

In September 1943, the 500th SS Parachute Battalion (*SS-Fallschirmjägerbataillon* 500) had been formed from mostly SS men who were in military prisons for minor disciplinary breeches. In true Hollywood style, these were a tough bunch of malcontents who were offered the chance to redeem themselves by volunteering for special services. Their ranks were filled out by volunteers from other SS units. Their leader was Sturmbannführer Herbert Gilhofer, an SS officer with experience of anti-partisan operations in Russia.

On 1 December 1943, the SS Parachute Battalion numbered more than 1,100 men, all trained in their new role and ready for action.

THE PLAN OF ATTACK

The senior German officer in the Balkans, Generalfeldmarschall Maximilian von Weich, who commanded Army Group B, committed an enormous force to the operation to eliminate Tito, codenamed *Rösselsprung*, or *Knight's Move*. This included the 7th SS Prinz Eugen Division, a Croat brigade, the 92nd Motorised Regiment, the 54th Mountain Reconnaissance Battalion, and the 202nd Panzer Company and the 4th Brandenburg Regiment from his operational reserve to operate in support of the SS Parachute Battalion. The combined force was named the XV Mountain Corps. The plan was that the enemy was to be attacked 'in an encircling operation using paratroops and our Air Force with the aim of destroying the enemy leadership, supply bases and headquarters in the area of Drvar-Petrovac and all enemy ground forces in the area.'[1]

The plan of attack was to deliver multiple thrusts towards Drvar from nine different directions and whilst the Partisans were tied down fighting off attacks from all sides, the Parachute Battalion would land directly on Tito's headquarters.

The offensive began at 05.00 hours on 10 January, with the advance of ground forces from their assembly points to their assigned operational areas in the bid to surround the Partisans in Drvar. At approximately 06.35, two Focke-Wulf Fw 190s, led the aerial assault. Behind them came a squadron of Ju 87s which dived-bombed selected targets whilst Italian-made Caproni 314 medium bombers and Fiat Cr 42 ground-attack aircraft struck other targets around Drvar and Petrovac.

After thirty minutes of bombing and strafing, twin-engine Junkers Ju 52 transport planes flew through the rising smoke and dust. Dropping to just 500 feet, the planes released their cargoes and the advance sections of *fallschirmjäger* of the SS 500 Battalion, led by Hauptsturmführer Kurt Rybka, dropped to the ground. Behind them came gliders with a further detachment of the Parachute Battalion. The gliders came under anti-aircraft fire as they descended. Some crashed into the hillside, others struck trees on landing, but most came safely to earth.

The Partisans were taken completely by surprise and by around 09.00 hours much of Drvar was in German hands, though there were still pockets of resistance. It was thought that Tito's headquarters was near a cemetery on high ground to the southwest of the centre of Drvar known as the 'Citadel' and the Germans concentrated their efforts on taking this position. Tito had indeed been in the town overnight but when the attack had begun, he had retreated to his headquarters when the attack had begun, which was in a cave more than a kilometre from the town.

The captured Partisans in Drvar were interrogated as were some Western journalists who were reporting from there. It was one of the latter who, inadvertently, revealed that Tito was in a cave in the nearby limestone cliffs.

The paratroopers now switched their attention to forcing the cave, which was defended by five guard-posts held by men with machine-pistols. Three of these posts were positioned directly in front of the cave's entrance. With Tito inside the cave were just twelve men and eight women of his immediate entourage.

Gradually, the German paratroopers closed upon the cave. But Tito's chief of staff, Jovanovic, and managed to rally around 100 men of the leader's escort battalion and they rushed against the German flank. Others positioned themselves in front of Tito's headquarters.

The battle outside the cave was fought out to the death – the Partisans were well aware of their ghastly fate if they were taken prisoner. The Germans lacked the aircraft to deliver the whole of the 500th Battalion and it was not until midday when the Ju 52s appeared overhead for a second time to drop the remaining 220 paratroopers.

Now reinforced, the SS battalion launched another attack upon the cave. The odds were simply too great for the defenders, and this time the paratroopers forced their way through the entrance, but were shot down as soon as the stepped inside the cave. Tito's resistance did not last much longer, as dozens of grenades were thrown angrily into the cave. When the dust settled, the paratroopers crept cautiously into the opening in the mountainside. The few Yugoslavs that had not been killed outright by the resultant explosions were shot. Tito, covered in blood and debris, was not immediately identified and there was momentary panic amongst the battle-hardened paratroopers who thought that their efforts and sacrifice had been in vain. But soon the Partisan leader was recognised and his body was dragged out to be taken to Belgrade for formal identification.

ROUNDING UP

Josip Tito was just one man and even though shorn of its inspirational leader, the Partisan movement would recover. Generalfeldmarschall von Weich was well aware of these facts, and his grand plan involved far more operations than the elimination of Tito. The other units of XV Mountain Corps had moved to encircle the entire area controlled by the Partisans. Though the SS Prinz Eugen Division found roads and bridges blocked and mined, they made steady, if slow progress.

The leader of the SOE Mission with the Partisans, Brigadier Fitzroy Maclean, was able to radio for help from the Allies, and over the course of the following four days the recently-formed Balkan Air Force, composed of units from the RAF and the South African Air Force attacked marshalling yards and airfields, flying more than 1,000 sorties from bases in Italy. Nevertheless, the back of the resistance movement was broken, as the Partisan groups, shorn of their leadership, were either rounded up or, having lost all hope of reassembling, disbanded. Backed by the Croats, the Chetniks took over the persecution of former Partisans, their ruthless methods providing a template for the ethnic cleansing the region would experience a generation later.

What was of more immediate significance was that there was no longer an enemy in Yugoslavia for the Germans to fight and, unusually, Hitler found that he had a considerable number of spare divisions. He now had the pleasant experience of being able to deploy tens of thousands of men to any threatened front. Troops were certainly needed in the East, but every division sent there disappeared into the depths of that vast country. Whilst to the West, Erwin Rommel was reporting that the defences of the Atlantic Wall were far from being the formidable barrier he had been led to believed they were. Normandy, in particular, with its flat open beaches, worried the Generalfeldmarschall. Hitler knew that the Allies were planning to invade northern Europe and his armies lacked the strength to fight on three fronts. So, Rommel would have the men he needed to defend France.

D-DAY DISASTER

The timing could not have been worse. Just how much Eisenhower knew about the seven divisions moving up through France has never been satisfactorily revealed. Along with questions concerning American pre-knowledge of the Japanese attack on Pearl Harbor, the decision to mount Operation *Overlord* in the first week of June 1944 remains one of the most hotly debated subjects of the Second World War.

It is hard to believe that, with the wide-reaching resistance networks and the large number of SOE and OSS agents in France that information about the movements of von Weich's columns, however imprecise it might have been, did not find its way to London. Equally, the Allied air forces had, by the summer of 1944, achieved supremacy in the air over western Europe. Are we really to believe that long convoys of trucks and armoured vehicles were never spotted as they spent more than a week traversing France?

The argument usually presented is that the invasion plans were too far advanced to be abandoned and that the Allied leaders calculated the risks and decided to continue with the operation. That decision led to the bloodbath on the Normandy beaches as von Weich's men, toughened by the bitter fighting in the Balkans, threw the US troops that had landed on the Cotentin Peninsular back into the sea. June 6, 1944, was the bloodiest day in US history. Only a small British and Dominion beachhead held on D-Day and had it not been for the non-stop bombing of the German positions by the Allied air forces *Overlord* would have been a complete failure.

THE REALITY

Hitler really did order Otto Skorzeny to eliminate Josip Tito. In April 1943 Skorzeny was taken from the Eastern Front to set up a school at Friedrichsthal near Oranienburg to train agents in conducting operations behind enemy lines. He was attached to the external intelligence service of the Reichssicherheitshauptamt and set about recruiting suitable men for special operations. The first task handed to Skorzeny and his new unit was the rescue of Mussolini from Italian partisans in September 1943. For this he was promoted to Sturmbannführer and was awarded the Knight's Cross. He was the ideal man to track down Tito. However, he learned that information on the planned raid on Tito's headquarters, had leaked out and, believing that the operation had been compromised, refused to have anything further to do with it. It is said that Skorzeny had known the exact location of Tito's new headquarters but when he withdrew from the operation he did not pass that absolutely vital piece of information on.

Skorzeny was also involved in another assassination attempt. On 20 July 1944, the day that Hitler was almost killed when Stauffenberg's bomb exploded in the Wolf's Lair, Skorzeny happened to be in Berlin, having travelled there by train from Vienna. Skorzeny did not believe that Hitler was dead and when the officers involved in the 'Valkyrie' plot tried to seize key ministry buildings he was instrumental in resisting them. He spent thirty-six hours in charge of the Wehrmacht's central command centre, helping suppress the coup. Hitler rewarded

Skorzeny with promotion to Obersturmführer and added oak leaves to his Knight's Cross.

The attempt to kill or capture Tito, Operation *Rösselsprung*, was undertaken on 25 May 1944, along the lines described above, with one important difference – Tito escaped. As Skorzeny had suspected, Tito was aware that an operation to assassinate or capture him was imminent and he moved his headquarters to the cave. The defences around his cave had been improved only days before the attack.

Nevertheless, Tito did find himself trapped in his cave headquarters with just twenty men and women and there is no doubt that he was in a desperate situation. It was only a matter of time before the weakened remnants of his escort battalion were overwhelmed – yet he escaped by cutting a hole in the floor of his office, which was situated by the mouth of the cave, and dropping down a rope into the bed of the stream that ran below. The stream was hidden by dense foliage and could not be seen by the German troops outside the cave. Once outside the cave Tito made his way to a cleft in the hillside where a rope-ladder had been prepared for just such an emergency. Tito described his escape: 'I left with the help of my escort and my dog, Tiger. After we climbed for a while, I had to take a rest. Tiger came with me. He started to whine. I grabbed him by the snout to keep him quiet. There were times that I thought we would have to shoot him with a pistol, because he would betray us, but I couldn't bring myself to do it.'

He reached the top of the mountain to find, much to his relief, a group of Partisans. It was at that moment the Germans spotted the band of escapers and began shooting at them. Shortly after this, the Axis aircraft returned to bomb Tito's headquarters again. It was said by those on the ground, that it felt as if the entire mountain shook under the impact of the bombs. Tito was fortunate not to have been hit and, without question, he had a very lucky escape.

The *SS-Fallschirmjägerbataillon* 500 failed in its bid to take Tito's headquarters. Hauptsturmführer Kurt Rybka's men were soon surrounded by Partisans and cut off from the rest of the German forces. The battalion hung on but Rybka was wounded. Ironically, Rybka was evacuated in the aircraft that was supposed to take away the captured Tito. After two days of almost constant fighting, the battalion was relieved. More than 800 of the 1,100 that started on *Rösselsprung* operation had been either killed or wounded.

Though Tito had escaped from the cave, he, and the Partisans, were still surrounded by the German forces which had not given up on their bid to capture the elusive Partisan leader. After evading the Germans for six days it was suggested that Tito should be air-lifted out of the danger area. Tito was reluctant to abandon his men but, eventually, on 3 June 1944, he agreed and he was evacuated, along with his entourage, that night from an RAF-operated airfield near the town of Kupres some ninety miles from Drvar. On seven Douglas C-47s Tito, the British SOE and American OSS Missions, and 118 wounded Partisans, were flown to Bari in Italy. Three days later Tito was taken by the Royal Navy destroyer HMS *Blackmore* to Vis, a small island off the southern Croatian coast, where he re-established his headquarters.

In September 1944, King Peter II called for all Yugoslavs to unite under Tito's leadership, and he became acknowledged by all the Allied nations as the country's Prime Minister and commander-in-chief of all the Yugoslav forces. That same month he agreed to allow Soviet troops into the country to help fight the Germans. With Soviet support, the Partisans launched a major offensive against the Germans, driving them out of the country.

With the German defeat in 1945, Tito, seen by most of the Yugoslavs as the man who had liberated the country, became the Prime Minister and then President of what, after a few changes of name, became the Socialist Federal Republic of Yugoslavia. His death on 4 May 1980, was the pre-cursor to the break-up of Yugoslavia and the terrible Balkan conflict of the 1990s.

In their bid to eliminate Tito and his Partisans, the Germans employed 200,00 German troops plus 160,000 Bulgarians and Croats. If, indeed, Tito had been captured and the Partisan leadership eliminated in early 1944, the suppression of the Yugoslav resistance movement could well have been left largely in the hands of the Chetniks and the Croats. This, in turn, would have released very large numbers of German troops for deployment on other fronts. If they had been sent to France just as the Allied troops were landing in Normandy, the story of D-Day might well have been one of slaughter rather than success.

NOTE:
1. Quoted in David Greentree, *Knight's Move, The Hunt for Marshal Tito 1944* (Osprey, Oxford, 2012), p.23.

Chapter 13

Death in The Wolf's Lair
The Plot is Successful, July 1944

By John Grehan

It was almost too good to be true. *Oberst* Claus Schenk von Stauffenberg had been made responsible for updating the official emergency mobilisation plans which were to be effected in the event of serious civil unrest. In this plan, codenamed *Valkyrie*, should there be an uprising by foreign labourers, a revolt by any armed group, or even an assault by enemy paratroopers, a signal would be transmitted from Supreme Army Command in Berlin to the various military forces across Germany which would trigger pre-determined action to secure key sites throughout the Reich. Such sites included government ministries and telecommunication centres, which would be taken over by the army – and the man given the task of reviewing the *Valkyrie* arrangements was at the heart of the secret military resistance to Hitler.[1]

Claus Schenk von Stauffenberg had been a staff officer in the 10th Panzer Army in North Africa when, on the morning of 7 April 1943, the vehicle he was in was attacked by US aircraft. Stauffenberg was badly wounded, losing his left eye, most of his right hand and two fingers of his left. For some time, his life hung in the balance, but he recovered from surgery and was transferred to a clinic in Munich. After further operations he was discharged, then returned to duty on the staff of the Reserve Army in Berlin. It is interesting to note that Stauffenberg told his uncle that he felt his survival from his terrible injuries was not mere good fortune, but that he had been saved for some special purpose. That purpose would soon be revealed not just to Stauffenberg, but to the world.

Stauffenberg had been an enthusiastic supporter of Hitler and his 'genius' for war, but as a staff officer in the organisational department of the General Staff he had witnessed many of Hitler's illogical decisions and unreasonable demands and by the August of 1942, he had become so disillusioned with the Führer's policies as to be openly stating that he believed Hitler stood in the way of victory and should be eliminated.[2]

That was very dangerous language yet, by 1943, many other officers not only felt as Stauffenberg did but also expressed those views to their comrades in arms. It seemed impossible that Hitler was unaware of the general mood of pessimism, despite the fact that he was only prepared to listen to positive opinion. But there was no denying that the military situation on the Eastern Front was deteriorating rapidly and, believing in his own infallibility, Hitler blamed his generals for the defeats the Heer was experiencing. Hitler had no love for the aristocratic Prussian officers, as he had demonstrated so ruthlessly in the past, and there was an aura of mounting tension amongst the officer ranks. Many feared another 'Night of the Long Knives', of mass arrests and executions, with the generals being accused of deliberately conspiring against the Führer.

When the German armies had rolled across Poland and overran France and the Low Countries, even the most sceptical military men had to concede that Hitler's seemingly reckless rush into war had achieved results far beyond anything the more conservative generals had imagined possible. At that time the atmosphere at the headquarters of the German Armed Forces, the Oberkommando der Wehrmacht (OKW), was one of great optimism. How things had changed in little more than three years. Defeat was in the air and no-one knew how Hitler would react. The growing opposition amongst officers to Hitler was prompted as much by fear of their own fate as much as that of Germany.

The all-intrusive Gestapo, well aware of the growing disenchantment with the Führer, had already begun to probe deeply into the affairs of some of those officers suspected of treasonable intentions. That there was a group of officers actively conspiring against Hitler was known even by Reich Minister Himmler, the second most powerful man in the Third Reich. He had told Admiral Canaris, the head of the German military intelligence service, the *Abwehr*, and a long-term opponent of Hitler, that 'he knew full well that leading circles in the army were considering plans for a coup. But it would never come to that. He would intervene.' Himmler also professed to know who was 'actually behind it', mentioning names that Canaris knew were key players in the developing resistance movement.[3] What Himmler was telling the

Admiral was that if the conspirators did not cease their plotting, they too would be arrested.

This had what Himmler must have regarded as the desired effect of disrupting the plans of the conspirators. To enforce his message a party led by senior judge advocate Manfred Roeder and *SS-Untersturmführer* Franz Sonderegger marched into Canaris' office to arrest one of the conspirators at *Abwehr* headquarters, special agent Hans von Dohnanyi, on the grounds of currency violations. Dohnanyi hurriedly attempted to dispose of any incriminating documents, warning his colleague, *Generalmajor* Hans Paul Oster, who was possibly the most active of the conspirators at that time, to remove 'the notes'. This was overheard by Roeder, who demanded to see these notes. Oster was placed under house arrest and a few days later dismissed from his post.

This was an immense shock to the resisters, as Oster was considered to be the 'managing director' of the movement. As might be expected, the officers of the *Abwehr* had covered their tracks well, and Roeder was unable to uncover anything other than questionable foreign currency dealings, poor financial accounting and a number of cases of bogus exemptions from military service (which was widespread across the upper echelons of the Nazi Party). Though suspected, the conspiracy went unproven. Nevertheless, the implications of the move against the conspirators were clear. Either they abandoned their efforts against Hitler or they acted quickly to remove him.

CIVIL WAR

The initial sentiment amongst the conspirators was one of despondency. Despite the reverses being suffered by the army in the East, Hitler's standing was still high amongst very many Germans and just how the people would react to his assassination could not be predicted. When four of the leading conspirators, businessman Erwin Planck, lawyer Carl Langbehn, former Ambassador to Rome Ulrich von Hassell, and *General der Infanterie* Georg Thomas, met, they accepted that 'Hitler's prestige is still solid enough that if he's left standing he'll be able to launch a counter-attack that will end in at least chaos or civil war'.

Hitler did indeed mount a counter-attack, but it was on the battlefield. Operation *Zitadelle* was launched in the summer of 1943 against the Soviets. It proved to be a disaster, with more than 200,000 men being killed, wounded or taken prisoner. In addition, the Germans lost around 1,400 tanks and artillery pieces whilst some 800 aircraft were destroyed or severely damaged. Any lingering belief in Germany emerging from the war victorious died along with its young men on the bloody fields of Kursk, 280 miles to the southwest of Moscow. Winter brought with it a Soviet counter-offensive which saw the German forces being pushed back for 500 miles.

Far to the south, British and US forces had invaded Italy, and Hitler's once-favourite ally, Mussolini, had been overthrown. German troops had been sent into Italy to halt the Western allies, and, with the very real prospect of an imminent invasion of northern Europe, Hitler was faced with fighting a war not on two, but three fronts. The conspirators knew that Hitler had to be removed, and quickly, before Germany was destroyed. As German fortunes declined the conspiracy had gained not only a renewed momentum but many new adherents.

It was one thing wishing to see the end of Hitler and his dysfunctional regime, but how to accomplish such an objective was something altogether different. The conspirators had devised schemes to take over the government of the country upon Hitler's death, but what they needed was both someone in Berlin who could activate these schemes under the guise of the official *Valkyrie* arrangements and a person to assassinate the Führer. This they found in one person – the now famous, or infamous, *Oberst* von Stauffenberg.

The summer of 1944 brought further setbacks for German forces. In the East the Soviets continued what appeared to be an unstoppable advance towards the Reich and, on 6 June, the expected invasion of France by British, US and Allied armies began. At this point, with the end of the war and a German defeat an inevitability, the conspirators questioned whether or not they had left it too late. The answer was provided by *Generalmajor* Hermann von Tresckow:

> The assassination must be attempted at all costs. Even if it should not succeed, an attempt to seize power in Berlin must be undertaken. What matters now is no longer the practical purpose of the coup, but to prove to the world and for the records of history that the men of the resistance movement dared to take the decisive step. Compared to this objective, nothing else is of consequence.[4]

There was, therefore, no time to lose. The sooner the attempt could be made, the greater the impact, and there was still hope that the death of Hitler would enable the new administration to renounce the policies of the Nazi Party to the world as an aberration and beg the Allies to save Germany – a new democratic and peace-loving Germany that had finally thrown off the shackles of a detested dictator. This could not happen if the leading Nazi's stepped into Hitler's shoes. There had to be a complete overthrow of the existing regime. The only chance, the only possible chance, of avoiding a complete calamity was to depose Hitler without delay, and with British and American troops storming ashore in Normandy the conspirators and von Stauffenberg knew they had nothing to lose.

Stauffenberg had proven to be a very capable organiser and, as Chief of Staff to the Commander-in-Chief of the Home Army, had gained Hitler's confidence. As a result, he had unfettered access to the Führer, and he would be the one who would kill the German leader.

For the plan to succeed, the coup must be enacted quickly to ensure the new regime was fully established before any counter-revolution could be mounted. The plan, therefore, required Hitler to be assassinated when out of Berlin. As Stauffenberg could not simply go up with a pistol and shoot Hitler, the only possible way to kill the Führer was by planting a bomb; and planting it so close to him that his death was a certainty.

When he was informed that Hitler wanted to see him at the Berghof to discuss the movement of fifteen newly-formed grenadier divisions to the Eastern Front to try and hold back the Russian advance he knew that his chance had come. On 11 July Stauffenberg flew down to Berchtesgaden with explosives in his briefcase, notifying his co-conspirators that he was about to act. Consequently, *General der Infanterie* Friedrich Olbricht, the principal coordinator of the resistance, summoned *Generalfeldmarschall* Job Wilhelm Georg Erdmann Erwin von Witzleben, the highest ranking member of the conspiracy, and *Generaloberst* Erich Hoepner to Berlin to be ready to undertake their roles in the coup. Twenty signals officers were also alerted that they would be required for 'special duty'.

Everything was set, all were prepared. Stauffenberg had taken explosives with him to the Berghof five days earlier, on 6 July, possibly to see how practical an assassination attempt might be. This time he fully intended to carry out the task he had been destined to perform. Nothing happened.

Stauffenberg, after discussions with some of the other conspirators, decided that Himmler and Göring must also be eliminated at the same time as Hitler so that there was no possibility of either of these characters being able to mount a successful claim to the leadership of the country. Neither were present and Stauffenberg, and his explosives, returned to Berlin.

Stauffenberg knew that he had become a trusted individual and that he could carry explosives in his briefcase without being searched. He also knew that another opportunity would present itself in time. Time, though, was what the conspirators did not have.

On 15 July, Stauffenberg flew to another meeting with Hitler, but this time at the *Wolfschanze*, the Wolf's Lair at Rastenburg. Once again he carried his briefcase in which were two 1kg slabs of plastic explosives hidden under a spare shirt.

After breakfast with *Generalfeldmarschall* Wilhelm Keitel he attended a succession of short meetings in Hitler's conference room but, as on 11 July, Stauffenberg was unable to carry out the assassination. The reason for this, it would seem, was the setting of the fuze. He had a British-made time fuze, taken from failed or misdirected RAF drops to the SOE or Resistance groups. Before setting the fuze, Stauffenberg had to ensure that not only would Hitler be present, but also that he would still be there when the bomb exploded. Part of this problem was that the fuze worked far more quickly in warmer weather than cold, making it difficult to determine exactly when the bomb was likely to be detonated.

Once again, neither Himmler nor Göring were present, so, when he had the chance Stauffenberg slipped away to call Berlin, where the conspirators were waiting to receive the call that Hitler was dead. His call was taken by Colonel Mertz von Quirnheim who asked Beck and Olbricht what Stauffenberg should do. Stauffenberg was told to stand down, but by this time the pressure of repeated aborted efforts was proving too great a strain on the brave officer and he asked von Quirnheim what he thought, and received the reply 'Do it'.[5]

Stauffenberg returned to the conference room determined at last to blow Hitler to Hell only to find his suitcase missing! As he frantically looked round the room fellow conspirator General *Generalmajor* Helmuth Stieff walked in with the briefcase. There was now no time to set the fuze, and Hitler left the room to live for another few days.

So certain had the conspirators been that this time the assassination would happen, orders for Phase One of *Valkyrie* had already been issued, and troops were on the move towards Berlin. These orders had to be quickly cancelled before any of Hitler's acolytes learnt of it.

The conspirators knew that they could not risk another such failure. Fortunately, on 19 July, Stauffenberg was ordered to meet Hitler the following day, this time to bring the the Führer up to date with the state of preparedness of the fifteen new divisions he had earlier been told to cobble together from the shrinking number of available troops. After the debacle of 15 July it had been agreed that the assassination would take place whether Himmler or Göring were present or not. Due to the short notice Stauffenberg had received, there was not the time to make the thorough preparations in Berlin that were needed for the coup to be effected smoothly. The consequences of this would prove fatal.

20 JULY 1944

Stauffenberg woke early, to prepare for what was to be a day that would live forever in history. Once washed, shaved and dressed, he was met by his driver, Corporal Karl Schweizer, who had delivered not one but two identical bomb-laden briefcases to Stauffenberg the previous afternoon from its place of safe-keeping in the hands of Colonel Fritz von der Lancken. This time there would be no mistake.

Stauffenberg landed at Rastenburg shortly after 10.00 hours, along with Stieff, Major Röll and Lieutenant Werner von Haeften, and taken by staff car to the Wolf's Lair. At 11.00 hours he attended his first meeting of the day which was with the Chief of the Oberkommando der Wehrmacht's Army Staff, *General der Infanterie* Walter Buhle, and others, before briefing *Generalfeldmarschall* Keitel on the state of the fifteen new divisions.

The next meeting was in the presence of the Führer at 12.30 hours. Stauffenberg now knew he could set his fuze with confidence. He asked to be excused momentarily to change his shirt, which he told Keitel was necessary due to seepage from his wounds. He went into the lounge in Keitel's bunker where he was joined by von Haeften who was carrying the second briefcase in which were hidden both bombs. Stauffenberg had decided to put both bombs into his briefcase to ensure a massive explosion that was certain to kill most, if not everyone inside. But before the transfer could be made, Platoon Sergeant Werner Vogel opened the door. Stauffenberg was wanted on the telephone.

General Fellgiebel demanded to speak to Stauffenberg on an urgent matter. With the sergeant stood at the door there was only time for Stauffenberg to break the capsule of the chemical timer on one of the bombs with the pair of plyiers he had become accustomed to using with the three fingers of his remaining arm. With the other bomb back in von Haeften's briefcase. Stauffenberg walked out in his fresh shirt to meet Hitler. A ten-minute timer had been used and in the warmth of late July there was nothing to stop the bomb from exploding. The German dictator had just ten minutes to live.

The much respected Stauffenberg, badly wounded in action but undeterred in his efforts against the enemy, looked, according to the deputy chief of the OKW *General der Artillerie* Walter Warlimont, the very model of a General Staff officer: 'The classic image of the warrior through all of history. I barely knew him, but as he stood there, one eye covered by a black patch, a maimed arm in an empty uniform sleeve, standing tall and straight, looking directly at Hitler.'[6]

The briefing was already underway when Stauffenberg entered the conference room. He had handed his briefcase to Major Ernst John von Freyend, one of Keitel's aides who had offered to carry it for the disabled Stauffenberg. He asked von Freyend to put him as near as possible to Hitler so that 'I catch everything the Führer says for my briefing afterwards'.

General Adolf Heusnger was giving an assessment of the Eastern Front, which cannot have been very positive, but Keitel announced that Stauffenberg was going to give a statement about the fifteen new divisions, on which Hitler placed so much hope. Freyend placed the briefcase by the thick leg, of the conference map table to the right of Heusnger who was standing next to Hitler. This was quite by chance the ideal spot as the 'massive' wooden table leg would help contain the blast which would be forced outwards directly towards where Hitler was standing in the eighteen-by-forty-foot room. Satisfied that he could do no more, Stauffenberg left the room, whispering something intentionally incoherent, as if he had an important task to perform.

He went straight to the signal officer's room in the *Wehrmacht* adjutant building where Haeften was waiting with the staff car. There he heard that Hitler was requesting Stauffenberg's briefing and already General Buhle had set out to find him. It was at that moment a deafening blast rent the air.

'In a flash the map room became a stampede and destruction,' remembered General Warlimont … there was nothing but wounded men groaning, the acrid smell of burning and charred fragments of maps and papers fluttering in the wind.'[7]

For a few moments all was chaos with debris that had been flung into the air falling and floating to the ground. Then there was the pungent smell of seared hair and burning flesh. Then the first semblance of order began to be reasserted, as Keitel cried out, 'Where is the Führer? Where is the Führer?' It was Heusinger, who had been closest to Hitler, who gave the chilling answer. 'He is dead. My god, Hitler is dead'.

THE MORNING AFTER

As soon as the bomb had done its deadly work, a relieved Stauffenberg set off with Haeften for Rastenburg airfield. Whilst the conspirators had flown into Rastenberg that morning on a Junkers Ju 52 transport, they flew back to Berlin in a much faster Heinkel He 111 which had been prepared for their hurried return trip. Speed was now of the essence.

In Berlin, Olbricht heard from Rastenburg that there had been an explosion at the *Wolfschanze* but that there were no further details. It was enough for him to go to *Generaloberst* Friedrich Fromm to ask for the *Valkyrie* orders to be taken out of the safe and signed. The army units designated to defend Berlin whilst the new administration seized power were therefore instructed to move towards the capital. At the same time Colonel Albrecht Mertz von Quirnheim gathered all the senior generals in Berlin together to inform them that Hitler was dead and that *Generaloberst* Beck would be assuming the position of head of state whilst *Generalfeldmarschall* von Witzleben would become commander-in-chief of the *Wehrmacht*. All the *Valkyrie* instructions were passed to the military districts and the army schools in and around Berlin.

Alarm Level One of the *Valkyrie* instructions demanded that all leave was cancelled amongst those army units around Berlin and all troops confined to base to await further orders, and tank commanders were to equip their machines with live ammunition and line them up for immediate deployment. When the various commanders confirmed that their units were ready for action, orders were sent for the defence of Berlin for the inevitable SS counter-action.

A communiqué was then issued to the Reserve Army, ordering the occupation of all important buildings and facilities, and that all *gauleiters*, government ministers, prefects of police and the heads of the propaganda offices were to be arrested. All concentration camps were also to be seized immediately, the new leaders of the country eager to show that the hated Nazi regime had been ended. 'The population must be made aware that we intend to desist from the arbitrary methods of the previous rulers.'[8]

The previous rulers, in the form of Himmler, were not about to surrender power. With communications between Rastenburg and Berlin cut, neither Himmler nor any of the SS commanders were aware of the coup until *Heer* troops stormed into Reich Security Main Office and SS Headquarters in Prinz-Albrecht-Strasse. Himmler was actually at home at 10 Dohnensteig and for some reason no provision was made to send troops round to his house. Needless to say the official *Valkyrie* orders did not allow for the arrest of the leading Nazis, only for their protection. This was to prove a fatal mistake.

Himmler received warning soon after the raid at Prinz-Albrecht-Strasse and, whilst unaware of what was really happening, was sufficiently alarmed to order round his driver and speed out of the city. He was stopped at a road block on the road south to Jüterbog where one of his panzer divisions was based but no-one dared arrest the Reich Minister and he was waved through. This was the last chance to prevent the civil war that Carl Langbehn had so accurately prophesied. But it could hardly be expected that a junior army officer, conditioned to unquestioned obedience to the Nazi leadership, would have thought of arresting the Deputy Führer. Himmler had been allowed to slip through the net.

Nevertheless, the new government was announced. Beck was President, with the economist Carl Friedrich Goerdeler as his Chancellor. Olbricht was Minister of War, with von Stauffenberg as State Secretary. As well as Commander-in-Chief of the *Wehrmacht*, von Witzleben was the Minister of Defence. Hans Oster was made President of the Military Supreme Court, the *Reichskriegsgericht* and *Generalmajor* von Tresckow became Chief of Police. In total seventeen senior positions were declared.

THE FIGHT BACK

The SS, the *Schutzstaffel*, was devoutly loyal to both Hitler and Himmler, and under no other authority. Numbering around 800,000 men, its divisions were well equipped compared to most of those of the *Heer*. Even though many of these divisions were serving in the armies in the East, instructions were sent to them to re-deploy immediately to Berlin. In many cases, there was no attempt to stop them, despite orders from von Witzleben. The army officers might be jealous and resentful of the SS, but they knew that if they tried to disarm them as von Witleben had instructed, there would be a bloodbath.

At Army Group Centre, however, von Kluge, now fully committed to the coup, did move rapidly to neutralise the SS 'Das Reich' Motor Division, with cataclysmic consequences. More than 3,000 men were killed in a savage battle which saw the entire SS division wiped out or taken prisoner. Many who had wished for a change in Berlin, including if necessary the removal of the once-beloved Führer, did not want to see Germans fighting Germans.

Equally across the Reich, when the news of the death of the Führer on 20 July 1944, those multitudes who celebrated can hardly have conceived of what was to follow. The German people might well have been under terrible strain, with their armies suffering repeated reverses on all fronts and the relentless aerial bombardment of their towns and cities, but still the state functioned. There was order in the streets and a recognised system of government at all levels. Germany was heading for defeat, but the country was still to a large degree unified in its fight for survival, in whatever form that might ultimately take. After 20 July there was only chaos.

From the very beginning, the conspirators encountered many who were unwilling to be involved in the overthrow of a regime that had been in power for more than a decade. General Kienitz, the commander of Military District II saw the implementation of the *Valkyrie* orders for the contradiction they were. The principle behind *Valkyrie* was to safeguard and defend the Reich, not to replace it. He saw the orders as 'clearly treacherous' and he refused to comply. 'I confess that, despite [fighting in] two world wars, these were the most difficult hours of my life …,' Kienitz later reflected. 'I remember that I said to my staff: "It is terrible to stand with your heart on one side and your reason and duty on the other." Without having made a decision I set off for my office, and on the way there it became clear to me that under the circumstances it was completely irresponsible as a military district commander to join the coup.'[9]

Soon every available SS division, most of which were heavily armoured Panzer divisions, began to converge on Berlin. With many of the military commanders in the Berlin area refusing to commit their troops to the coup, (but equally unwilling to depose the new government) there was little to stand in the way of the SS. There were some, a large proportion of who were citizens, who were fully behind the move to dispose of the Nazis. But it was inevitable that the SS Panzer divisions would be able to break through the weak cordon around Berlin. In a desperate bid to retrieve the situation von Witzleben attempted to call back troops from France and Italy to help defend the new administration. He was too late. In just a matter of days, news that Berlin was in turmoil and that Himmler had already publicly denounced the conspirators in damning terms, repeating the stab-in-the-back mantra so familiar to Germans, meant that not a single battalion was sent to Berlin.

Himmler was soon aware that the coup had little military support and he went on to the offensive with the single division at Jüterbog, knowing that other divisions were on their way. A weak effort to halt the panzers was brushed aside and the tanks and armoured vehicles of the

SS were to be seen on every street corner in the capital just five days after Hitler had been killed. Under Himmler's directions, the SS quickly and ruthlessly, began to round up the ringleaders of the coup.

BLOODY REVENGE

Generaloberst Fromm, when he realised that he had been premature in releasing the *Valkyrie* orders, was quick to turn on the conspirators. At the head of an armed retinue, he marched into Beck's office and told him that the coup was over. He arrested the six main conspirators. Dragging the thinly-built Beck to the window overlooking the Bendlerstrasse, he pushed the former Chief of the German General Staff's head forward. 'Look, look, what you have done. In the streets of Berlin our own country folk are at each other's throats. Do we not have enough enemies?' Fromm pulled Beck round and shoved him back into the centre of the room.

Beck asked Fromm if he could keep his pistol, 'for private purposes'. Knowing full well what those purposes would be, Fromm agreed. 'Go ahead, but be quick about it!'

Beck began to make a speech, but was cut short by Fromm, 'I told you, just do it!' Beck hesitated for a moment, then put the barrel to his head and pulled the trigger. But, as with the coup attempt, he failed to complete his objective, the bullet merely grazing his scalp. Fromm told two of his men to take Beck's gun off him.

Beck tried to resist, only managing to wound himself again, but this time fatally. He collapsed to the floor, writhing in his death throes, being put out of his misery by a sergeant who dragged him into an adjoining room.

Fromm told the others that they could write a statement if they wished, but that they were to hurry. He knew that his own position was likely to come into question and that Himmler was on his way. He had not hesitated in releasing the *Valkyrie* orders and so could be seen as being complicit in the coup. His best chance of survival was in killing off those that knew what he had done. On the news that an SS battalion had arrived in the courtyard below, Fromm told the conspirators that a Court Martial had been held and that they had all been found guilty of treason, and were to be summarily executed.

They were taken immediately downstairs and lined up in front of a small pile of sand. A squad of ten NCOs under the command of a Lieutenant Werner Schady, took aim and, one by one, Olbricht, Haeften, Stauffenberg, Hoepner and Metz were shot.

Fromm went straight round to see Goebbels who had been out of Berlin on 20 July, to tell him that he had crushed the coup. But as he was the man who was supposed to safeguard the Reich capital, and whom it was immediately assumed must have been aware of the conspiracy which was fermenting under his very nose, he was arrested.

Himmler ordered that no more executions were to take place. He wanted to know the full extent of the uprising and dead men do not talk.

Over the course of the following weeks anyone, and everyone, suspected of involvement in the coup, whether they actually participated or not, was arrested. Himmler's venom was even more lethal than anything Hitler had spewed forth – and now there was no longer the restraining hand of the Führer. Remarkable as it now seems, Hitler was, and still is, seen by most of the German people as being a strong and ruthless man, but also a brilliant leader. Himmler is considered by all to have been the devil incarnate, and a sadistic buffoon.

In total more than 7,000 people were arrested and around 4,980 of those were executed. Britain took advantage of the turmoil to create even more instability in Germany by issuing, via the BBC, the names of a number of senior figures who were not involved in the plot. These people were also arrested.

The officers implicated in the conspiracy were tried before the Court of Military Honour, where only one verdict was ever given, that of 'guilty'. The men were then handed over to the People's Court to await trial.

The first trials were held on 7 and 8 August 1944, with Himmler demanding that those found guilty should be 'hanged like cattle'.[10] Many, like Beck, took their own lives prior to either their trial or their execution. This included von Kluge, who had openly shown his hand directly after the assassination.

WESTERN FAILURE

Order, albeit one that was even more repressive that before, had been restored, but on the Eastern Front the loss of the tough SS divisions proved disastrous. Within a week of the assassination, Army Group Centre, which had been reduced to around 700,000 men was surrounded by 2,200,000 Soviet troops and before the end of August 1944 it had suffered the loss of 400,000 men dead, wounded, missing or sick, of whom 160,000 were captured.

The recently-appointed *Generalfeldmarschall* Otto Walter Model, who replaced von Kluge, also lost more than 2,000 tanks and 57,000 other vehicles. Army Group North was surrounded and forced to capitulate in its entirety just two weeks later and with no reserves available from civil-war-torn Germany, on 18 August, Model ordered his men to lay down their arms following armistice talks in Warsaw. It marked the effective end of the fighting in the East, and saw half a million men being marched into the gulags.

The advance across France and the Low Countries by the American and British forces was held at the Rhine, and the loss of the SS divisions made little practical difference to the fighting in Italy, with the Alps proving as equal a barrier at the Rhine. Severe criticism has been levelled at Montgomery and Eisenhower for their failure to break into Germany, and for failing the German people. By the beginning of September Berlin was in Soviet hands. The war in Europe was at an end and Germany belonged to Stalin.

THE REALITY

The thick oak leg of the table in the conference room at the *Wolfschanze* where Stauffenberg's briefcase had been placed, saved Hitler's life. Of the twenty-four people in the room at the time of the explosion only four subsequently died of their wounds, thanks to that wooden table leg, which actually would be better described as a solid wooden stand or support.

Though upon his arrival in Berlin von Stauffenberg told the conspirators that Hitler was dead, the truth – that the Führer was not even badly wounded – soon reached the German capital, and the coup began to rapidly unravel. In a number of places, such as Vienna and Prague, leading Nazi and SS officials were rounded up following the initial announcement that Hitler was dead. In Paris, *General der Infanterie* Carl-Heinrich von Stülpnagel, one of the key conspirators who was to have tried to negotiate a peace deal with the Americans and the British, ordered the arrest of the senior SS and Gestapo officials, but so as to cause as little alarm as possible, these arrests were not to take place until 23.00 hours that night. Long before that time, everyone knew that Hitler was alive but even after hearing Hitler's radio broadcast shortly after midnight, in which the Führer ranted about the 'very small clique of ambitious, wicked and stupidly criminal officers' who had tried to kill him, von Stülpnagel still believed the coup could succeed. When he finally had to conceded that the tide had turned against him, and he was ordered to return to Berlin, he tried to commit suicide with his pistol, but only succeeded in blinding himself. He did not need his eyes covered when he was marched to the gallows.

The coup might well have achieved its aims if Hitler had been killed, as a considerable number of high-ranking officers were prepared to support the conspirators had they succeed in removing the Führer. Many officers in Berlin, on the other hand, had refused to follow the *Valkyrie* orders, suspecting that they were illegitimate. The conspirators assumed that the traditionally obedient German soldiers would follow the instructions they had been given without question. It is surprising how many officers actually disobeyed a direct order issued from *Generaloberst* Fromm's headquarters. If Hitler had indeed been killed, such officers, there can be little doubt, would have then accepted the new government.

We can be equally certain that if Hitler had been killed, Himmler, Goring, Gobbels and other senior Reich officials would not have taken the coup lying down, and would have mounted a counter-attack, knowing as they did that defeat and capture by the Allies would see them facing war crimes charges. It is hard to see how civil war could have been avoided. The results of that would have been catastrophic for Germany and would have brought about its collapse even sooner than actually occurred. It is strangely ironic that little good would have come from the assassination of Adolf Hitler.

NOTES:
1. Roger Moorhouse, *Killing Hitler, The Third Reich and the Plots against the Führer* (Jonathan Cape, London, 2006), p.194.
2. Joachim Kramarz, *Stauffenberg: The Architect of the Famous July 20th Conspiracy to Assassinate Hitler* (Macmillan, New York, 1967), p.106.
3. Joachim Fest, *Plotting Hitler's Death, The German Resistance to Hitler 1933-1945* (Phoenix, London, 1997), p.202.
4. Fabian von Schlabrendorff, *The Secret War Against Hitler* (Hodder and Stoughton, London, 1966), p.277.
5. James P. Duffy and Vincent L. Ricci, *Target Hitler, the Plots to Kill Adolf Hitler* (Praeger, Connecticut, 1992), p.155.
6. Quoted in Moorhouse, p.203.
7. Walter Warlimont, *Inside Hitler's Headquarters* (Weidenfeld & Nicolson, London, 1964), p.440.
8. Quoted in Fest, p.266.
9. Quoted in Helena Schrader, *Codename Valkyrie*, (Hayes, Sparkville, 2009), p.253.
10. Fest, pp.289-90.

Chapter 14

The Emperor is Dead
The Killing of Hirohito, August 1945

By James Luto

The message was clear. If Japan did not surrender the Americans would drop more of their terrible new bombs. After the first attack on 6 August, President Harry Truman had told the Japanese that they could 'expect a rain of ruin from the air, the like of which has never been seen on this earth', unless the country surrendered. Of course Emperor Hirohito could not surrender, no emperor of Japan could ever surrender. For months the lovely towns and cities of the islands had endured a relentless campaign; more than 100 places had been bombed. Even Tokyo had been burnt to the ground in what was the single deadliest air raid in history, in March, yet still the proud Japanese people fought on with never the slightest thought of surrender. But now?

The second bomb had struck Nagasaki just three days after the first one. The Americans, it seemed, could strike at will, whenever and wherever they chose. The nuclear scientists who had visited Hiroshima had told the Emperor that the Americans had indeed perfected the technology and that Japan had suffered the first ever nuclear strike.

One bomb, however powerful, could not stop Imperial Japan. The Americans knew that they would have to invade the islands and it would cost them dear. Every Japanese would fight until the death. They would never surrender. So how could their Emperor? But now?

The American dogs had developed not one, but two, nuclear bombs. Was it true what the President had said? Was this just the beginning?

These bombs, the Emperor had been told, did not just kill with the explosion – even though tens of thousands of people had been killed. For many years afterwards people would die from radiation sickness, and the land would be contaminated – nothing that grew there could be eaten. It was no longer a case of man fighting man, which no Japanese feared. Now they faced something they could not fight against.

Hirohito therefore told the six-member Supreme Council for the Direction of the War on 14 August: 'If we continue the war, Japan will be totally annihilated. If even a small number of Japanese people's seed is allowed to remain … there is a glimmer of hope of an eventual Japanese recovery … 'I am not concerned with what may happen to me. I want to preserve the lives of my people. I do not want them subjected to any further destruction. It is indeed hard for me to see my loyal soldiers disarmed and my faithful Ministers punished as war criminals.'[1] Hirohito then stated that he was willing to make a live announcement, to tell his people that Japan will surrender unconditionally.

So destiny would mark him down forever as the emperor who had failed his people. His name would always be associated with defeat, and worse, humiliation. But at least he would save his people from the slaughter of these new weapons and the dreadful long-term consequences of nuclear war. That night, he would record his speech which would be broadcast to the world the next day, 15 August, at 12.00 hours.

SURRENDER

Four days earlier, on the morning of 10 August, more than fifty senior officers of the War Ministry had gathered at Army Headquarters on Tokyo's Ichigaya Heights. Somewhat ignominiously, the meeting to which they had been summoned had to take place in an adjacent air-raid shelter for fear of US bombers. At 09.30 hours War Minister General Korechika Anami arrived. He took his place on a low platform and as the officers crowded round him in a semi-circle, he told his audience that the decision had been taken to accept the 'Potsdam Proclamation' announced by President Truman on 26 July which had called for Japan's unconditional surrender. Gasps and incredulous cries of 'No!' erupted from the officers. These were men who had only ever heard the word 'surrender' on the lips of their enemies. This could never be allowed to happen.

Anami was no less distraught by this decision, but he had been outvoted. Anyway, the Emperor had agreed. The War Minister held up his hands to quieten the crowd. 'I do not know what excuse I can offer, but since it is the wish of his Majesty there is nothing that can be done.' The outcries softened to murmurings, but the officers were evidently far from willing to accept this state of affairs. 'Your individual feelings and those of the men under your command,' Anami continued, 'must be disregarded.'[2]

The nation, and its soldiers, sailors and airmen, would have to be told of the Emperor's decision but it was feared that such an announcement would result in a complete collapse of morale. With the Soviet Union already advancing in Manchuria, the last thing that the Japanese authorities wanted was their forces in China to stop fighting. So an official broadcast was composed by Kainan Shimomura, President of the Information Board, that would warn the people to be prepared for hard times, but with no mention of surrender. Not yet.

Many of those officers who had listened to Anami were already talking of taking action to prevent the ignominy of surrender and they knew that, in truth, Anami was on their side. The first thing to do was keep the troops fighting in Manchuria, and so Lieutenant Colonel Inaba of the Military Affairs Bureau spoke to Anami with a plan to encourage the Army to continue to resist. So, on the same day that Shimomura informed the Japanese people that 'we are now beset with the worst possible situation', the Japanese soldiers were told, 'We are determined to fight resolutely, although we may have to chew grass, eat dirt and sleep in the fields. It is our belief that there is life in death.' Already, the movement that would see the unfortunate murder of Emperor Hirohito was gathering momentum.

Anami had been ambushed at the Cabinet meeting, the decision to accept the Potsdam Proclamation having already been decided upon by Foreign Minister Togo in league with the Prime Minister's Secretary, Hisatsune Sakomizu. Admiral Yonai had also been drawn into the net, maybe the entire episode arranged by Prime Minister Suzuki. Anami's protests had been ignored, as had General Umezu's claim that his anti-aircraft defences could prevent another nuclear bombing attack. Be that as it may, the other concern was with that of the Soviets. 'If we delay,' explained Suzuki, 'the Russians may occupy Hokkaido as well as Manchuria, Korea and Sajhalin Island. That would deal this country a fatal blow. We must act now while the negotiations are primarily with the United States.'

But whatever the ministers said, the final decision was that of the Emperor, and it was former Prime Minister and now President of the Privy Council, Kiichiro Hiranuma, who delivered the telling stroke, advising Hirohito that, 'In accordance with the legacy of His Imperial Forefathers, His Imperial Majesty is responsible for preventing unrest in the nation. I should like to ask His Majesty to make his decision with this point in mind.'

The debate lasted for two hours, but Hiranuma's argument still troubled the Emperor. The burden of responsibility weighed heavily upon his shoulders. If he surrendered his country would soon recover, his people were resilient and strong, but if he fought on there would be no country, no people. This he could not allow. The final words were those of the 124th Emperor of Japan: 'I have given serious thought to the situation prevailing at home and abroad and have concluded that continuing the war means destruction for the nation and a prolongation of bloodshed and cruelty in the world.'[3] There was no more to be said.

Yet Anami believed that the Emperor had made the wrong decision, forced on him by the others, seeking to save their own positions. America could not bomb Japan into submission and no US politician would risk the enormous loss of life they knew would result if the Americans tried to invade Japan. Now, more than ever, was not the time to show weakness.

Whilst Anami nurtured such thoughts others were taking more positive action. Unbeknown to the War Minister, a secret meeting was taking place in his own Ministry building. Lieutenant Colonel Masahiko had brought together a number of officers to consider what could be done to stop the Emperor from announcing the surrender. As most of the more senior officers were too feeble to fight, it was left to the young bloods. They concluded that the old men must be pushed aside and the Emperor advised to change his mind. What they discussed was a coup, nothing less. As Masahiko warned his co-conspirators, what they were proposing, even suggesting, was punishable by death. Unworried, even uplifted, by the thought that they would sacrifice themselves, the determined little group began to plan the revolution that would save Japan.

THE DAY COMETH

The Emperor had said that he would tell the nation in person of his decision to accept President Truman's offer. There was not the slightest chance, however, that Hirohito would make a 'live' broadcast. The Emperor was regarded as being infallible and it would be 'unimaginable' if he stuttered or made a mistake. Instead, his announcement would be pre-recorded.

It was at 23.30 hours on the evening of the 14th, when Hirohito sat down in his bunker in the Palace grounds to record his acceptance of the

American and Chinese demands. It would be recorded twice, onto two records in case one should be damaged or prove defective. One of the six-man team from NHK (*Nippon Hōsō Kyōkai*), Japan's Broadcasting Corporation, ordered to make the recording, twenty-three-year-old Shizuto Haruna, remembered that fateful day well. A Palace car came to fetch him and the rest of the team at 14.00 hours. They set up their equipment in two rooms of the Imperial Household Ministry. In the room where the Emperor was to speak, they set up their heavy record-cutting machines. A playback machine was also brought over from the NHK building, so that the Emperor could hear his broadcast.

At the time scheduled for the recording to be made, there was no sign of Hirohito. The recording team waited and waited. At 18.00 hours they were given a meal; and still they waited. The delay, it transpired, was due to the wording of the Emperor's message. Over in the Prime Minister's office, ministers and aides argued over the phrase 'The war situation grows more unfavourable to us every day', as this contradicted the positive, though entirely inaccurate, bulletins issued by the Government. Instead, 'the war situation has not developed to Japan's advantage' was agreed upon as offering an explanation to the Japanese people for the surrender without specifically stating that Japan had been beaten.

Finally, the paper from which the Emperor would read was taken to the Imperial Household Ministry. Just in case Hirohito stumbled over his words, the NHK team had brought sixty uncut discs with them, but, as it happened the Emperor, in his first ever recording, read the message flawlessly. A second recording was made but the first one was judged the best and would be the one used to transmit to the world. On both occasions, two recording machines were used.

When this sad task had been completed, Chamberlain Yoshihiro Tokugawa placed the four 25-cm discs in metal containers and put into a cotton bag. When it was time for the recording team to leave the Imperial Household Ministry an air raid was in progress, so rather than run the risk of trying to transport the discs to the NHK building in the middle of a heavy bombardment, they were deposited in a small safe on the first floor of one of the Emperor's rooms, hidden behind a pile of papers – just in case. The decision to surrender had been opposed by many, particularly in the military, and there was no way of knowing what some of these fanatics might do.

Hirohito had only just settled down to a fitful sleep, when it happened.

HONOUR PRESERVED

Lieutenant Colonel Masataka Ida had presented himself to fifty-two-years-old Lieutenant General Takeshi Mori, commander of the First Imperial Guards Division which was responsible for the safety and security of the Palace, shortly after the Emperor had retired, at around 00.40 hours in a bid to encourage him to join a group of Army officers who were intent on stopping the Emperor from surrendering: 'Your excellency, if we obey the Emperor's order, the emperor system could be abolished … A plan has been devised to kill you, though it depends on your response,' Ida told Mori, 'I am prepared for the worst.' Mori replied, 'I will risk my life to defend the palace.'

Mori utterly rejected Masataka's arguments and refused to join any such a plot against the Emperor's wishes. Then, at approximately 01.40 hours, Major Kenji Hatanaka led a number of co-conspirators into Mori's headquarters demanding that the Lieutenant General order his 4,000-strong division to join the revolt, and to move against the government and seize the palace. Mori refused and was shot by Hatanaka and then hacked to death by Captain Shigetaro Uehara. Mori's wife's older brother, Lieutenant Colonel Michinori Shiraishi, staff officer of the Hiroshima-based Second General Army, who had come to Tokyo the previous day and called on Mori, before he was to fly back to Hiroshima, met the same fate. He was in the wrong place at the wrong time.

Using the dead Mori's official seal Major Hidemasa Koga, a staff officer of the Guards Division, and son-in-law of former Prime Minister General Hideki Tojo, issued an order for the division's soldiers to occupy the Imperial Palace, seize all gates and cut all telephone lines except one linking the Palace to the Guards headquarters.

The objective of the rebels was to cut all communication between the Palace and the outside world, therefore stopping the broadcast of the surrender. This move would also prevent the Emperor from calling for help from forces loyal to him that sought peace. No harm would be done to the Emperor but it would demonstrate to Hirohito that his shameful act would not be accepted by the people. Japan would fight on. The effeminate liberals in Washington, governed by their so-called 'free' press, would never accept the casualties an invasion of Japan would bring and they would have to come to terms with Tokyo.

Seeing Mori's seal on the orders, Colonel Toyojiro Haga, commander of the 1,000 Imperial Guards in the grounds, believed the document to be authentic and responded accordingly, taking control of the Palace, which was accomplished by 02.20 hours. At the same time as the rebels entered the Palace, a sixty-strong company of the Guards Division's First Regiment occupied the NHK building, then based in Tokyo's Uchisaiwaicho district around a mile from the Imperial Household Ministry, preventing all broadcasts.

The Emperor had heard the tumult, not knowing what it presaged. He had remained in his rooms. After accepting that Japan, under his direction, had been defeated, he cared little for what was to come, providing he could give his country a future.

He did not have long to wait before the door opened. The rebels, led by Hatanaka, approached the Emperor with all the due deference. 'Your Lord, my Emperor. There will be no surrender. Ever. Your announcement will not be made.' He already knew that he had widespread support, including that from the Naval Air Service and the Army Air Force. Over the course of the previous few days there had been calls for 'last ditch' resistance and for the murder of the 'traitors' who had given the Emperor 'bad advice.'

Hirohito smiled. Now he knew what his fate would be. Not the man who had surrendered his country, but the Emperor who died to save his people. For he understood that he would not be permitted to leave his palace alive if he opposed the men that stood before him.

'I have decided. We cannot win against the American bombs,' Hirohito explained to the rebels. 'Yes, we can make bold statements, but the sound of our voices will be drowned by the noise of the explosions, of the crashing of falling masonry, and the wailing of the wounded. No, I will not permit my people to die in this way.'

'Then you must be prepared to die,' snarled Uehara.

'Kill me, and see if the people will follow you.' The Emperor replied, his high-pitched voice unusually firm.

'The people will not surrender, and nor should you. You are the Emperor of Imperial Japan,' insisted Hatanaka.

'I will announce the surrender,' said Hirohito, 'and you must hand over you weapons. You will be forgiven your actions of this day, for they were well-intentioned. But it all ends now.'

At that moment a shot rang out and Hirohito collapsed to the floor. The shot came not from any of the officers, but one of the accompanying Guards.

The shocked conspirators turned to see the young Guardsman hold his bayonet up level with his eyes. He called out, 'the honour of the Emperor has been preserved', before thrusting it into his stomach as he fell forward to ensure the blade penetrated deep into his body. As the soldier squirmed in his death throes, the group rushed up to the Emperor. But at such close range the rifle shot had been all-too accurate. Blood flowed from the back of Hirohito's head.

His killer had spoken well. The surrender would not be broadcast, no-one would ever hear of its existence, and the Emperor Hirohito would always be remembered as having died rather than submit his country to humiliation. If the Emperor died in this fashion, then every one of his subjects must be prepared to do the same. America would bleed.

The die was now cast. It was now imperative that the coup was completed quickly before anyone was aware of the Emperor's death. The Guards moved rapidly, capturing General Shizuichi Tanaka, commander of the Eastern Defence Command, in his bed. The buildings of the Imperial Diet were seized before the sittings of the day. The discs were found, after the NHK team had been threatened with immediate beheading, and all four destroyed.

Then at noon, the exact time that Hirohito's declaration of unconditional surrender was to be played, it was announced that the government of Kantarō Suzuki had been dismissed and that a new administration had been formed under Anami. Japan would fight on. 'Let the American pigs come,' Anami declared, 'here they will find their graves'. The announcement was made in the name of the Emperor. No word was mentioned of the events in the Imperial Palace. The news that an insane Imperial Guardsman had killed the Emperor and then committed hari-kari would be allowed to be leaked over the course of the next few days.

FAT BOY

The news of the change of regime in Tokyo was met with resignation in Washington and London. The Japanese response was of no surprise. It would take a while before the Japanese authorities fully appreciated the devastation the 'A' bombs were causing; after all, there had never been anything like these weapons before. A third bomb was already close to completion at Tinian in the Mariana Islands and more were not far behind. Soon there would be few buildings standing in Japan, but, if past experience was anything to go by, it would make no difference to the people and they would fight and die for their beloved Emperor.

Inevitably this meant US and Allied ground forces would have to be used to take the country, island by island, just as they had across the

Pacific. All this meant more deaths, more destruction. Many in Washington voiced their thoughts that if only someone could assassinate Hirohito the oaths the Japanese armed forces had sworn to the Emperor would no longer be valid, and a face-saving peace might be possible. Little did the Americans realise how wrong they were.

Back in Tokyo, Hirohito's eleven-year-old son, Akihito, was informed of the murder of his father by a lone fanatic. He was told that the crazed Guardsman wanted to surrender to the Americans and killed the Emperor because he knew Hirohito would never surrender. Akihito was told it was his duty to follow his father's ambition of making Japan a giant among nations and for this to happen, America had to be prevented from dominating the Asia-Pacific region and strangling Japan's growth.

Isolated from outside influence, and surrounded by ardent military leaders, the young Emperor quietly assented to permit the Diet to continue as it saw fit. The bright youngster was kept in the dark and over the following days was fed false news of great Japanese victories fought under his name. Beyond the Palace walls, the assassination of Hirohito remained unknown.

For the next two days the new Government continued to issue defiant statements and with no further bombs, hopes began to rise that the US had only been able to manufacture two of the technically-difficult weapons. That was until 19 August.

At 02.45 hours, *Enola Gay* once more took to the skies from the North Pacific island of Tinian in the Marianas, 1,500 miles south of Japan, with a single bomb in the B-29 Superfortress's specifically-designed bomb bay. The target, of what had been given the name 'Fat Boy' following the naming of the two previous bombs 'Little Boy' and 'Fat Man'. The plutonium bomb was estimated to be as powerful as twenty kilotons of TNT. At 08.23 hours, 'Fat Boy' fell from the skies above the city of Kokura, the site of Japan's largest arsenal still standing.

Visibility was very good, and the twelve-man crew had an excellent view of the town, as *Enola Gay* circled the city for its return across the North Pacific. Moments later a mushroom cloud spread upwards and out over the Straits of Shimonoseki. Kokura all but disappeared from the map.

After an initial defiant outburst from Anami, there were no further broadcasts from Tokyo – and it was the Japanese capital that was to receive the next bomb on 9 September. In the earlier firebombing of Tokyo approximately sixteen square miles in and around the Japanese capital were incinerated, and between 80,000 and 130,000 Japanese were killed. After 9 September, there was little left of Tokyo other than the charred remains of its wooden houses.

The buildings of the Imperial Diet and Palace were flattened, their occupants never seen again. A third bomb six days later, also dropped on the capital, effectively ended all centralised control in Japan. The regions were left to their own resources.

As is now well-known, no further nuclear bombs were dropped on Japan. Air reconnaissance by US aircraft showed little or no military activity on the ground. The news that Tokyo had been destroyed along with the government and the Emperor seemed to crush the spirit of the people. This assessment proved sadly, and fatally, over-optimistic.

When US and British forces landed on Honshu they met widespread opposition. Whilst there was no coordinated resistance, individual commanders held their ground. The result was a protracted and bloody struggle, city by city, street by street, house by house. Anyone, boy, girl or woman, who appeared to offer the slightest threat was killed, with no questions being asked. The terrible Battle of Japan saw levels of brutality and savagery never before experienced by mankind.

As has so often been said, the nuclear bombing of Japan was halted more on humanitarian rather than on military grounds. But what followed was far worse. The kindest act would have been to continue bombing until a deputation from the Japanese cities would have approached the US with an appeal to stop the fighting on whatever terms the Allies sought. It would certainly have prevented the tens of thousands of US and British casualties and stopped the Soviets from seizing northern China.

There was never a formal surrender, nor indeed an official end of hostilities. Hatred still seethes beneath the surface in Japan, which remains garrisoned by US forces. It was an unsatisfactory conclusion to a war which, until the invasion of Japan, the United States had held the moral high ground.

THE REALITY

There was indeed an attempt just as described above by a group of Army officers, and Lieutenant General Mori was shot and butchered by the conspirators. Masahisa Enai, a former corporal in the Imperial Guards Division's Second Regiment and an eyewitness to the incident told the *Japan Times* of 12 August 2005, that 'My estimate is that the number of soldiers who entered the palace premises was more than 1,000 … Those who invaded the Imperial Household Ministry building to seize the recordings of the rescript numbered between 40 and 50.'

The rebels looked for the recordings for one and a half hours but did not discover their hiding place. Whilst they were searching for the discs the Chief of Staff of the Guards Division, Major General Tatsuhiko Takashima, began to doubt the authenticity of the orders and he rang General Tanaka, who was not, in fact, caught asleep by the plotters. Tanka quickly sent two of his trusted Eastern Army officers to the Palace to find out what was going on. When these officers went to see General Mori, they found only his body.

At 04.00 hours, Tanaka arrived at the barracks of the Guards Division just in time to stop Colonel Taro Watanabe, commander of its First Regiment, sending 1,000 reinforcements to the Palace. Tanaka then informed Colonel Haga, that Mori had been murdered and that the occupation order was false. Haga ordered his troops to stand down. At this point the conspirators should have accepted that the coup was at an end – but Hatanaka was not going to give up that easily.

But there were many in the military, at all levels, who were opposed to any form of surrender. A squad of Yokohama Guards went to Prime Minister Suzuki's official residence and opened fire with machine-guns, and when they discovered that he was not there, they tried to burn the building down. They then went on to his private house and burnt that also.

It was a close call. If the discs had been discovered by the rebels they would have been destroyed and Hirohito's broadcast, which ended the Second World War, would not have been made. A third nuclear bomb would, almost certainly, have then been dropped on Japan.

Captain Nobuo Kitabatake, commander of one of the three Guards Division battalions that took over the palace, considered that Japan would have fought on if the broadcast had been stopped. He wrote in his memoirs: 'If the Imperial Guards Division became the first to rise in revolt, it would embolden the entire military to rise, thus leading Japan to continue the war.'

Following the failure of what was called the Kyūjō incident (Kyūjō is the Imperial Palace) War Minister Korechika Anami committed suicide by *seppuka* (ritual disembowelment) early the next morning. His suicide note read: 'After tasting the profound benevolence of the Emperor, I have no words to speak. For my supreme crime, I beg forgiveness through this act of death. I believe in Japan's indestructibility.'

Major Kenji Hatanaka shot himself with the same pistol he had used on Mori. In his pocket was found his death poem: 'I have nothing to regret now that the dark clouds have disappeared from the reign of the Emperor.' Lieutenant Colonel Jiro Shiizaki, another of the conspirators, watched Hatanaka die and then drew out his ceremonial sword and drove it through his own belly.

Captain Shigetaro Uehara was arrested by the Kempeitai, the Japanese secret police, but released on the promise that he would commit suicide.

Lieutenant Colonel Masataka Ida, who had tried to warn Mori of the plot, did not commit suicide. As well as alerting Mori, Ida also told Hatanaka that the Eastern District Army was on its way to the Palace and that the plot had failed. He claimed that he actually tried to persuade Hatanaka that the only course of action available to him was to make an honourable end to it all and kill himself. Ida was court-martialled but managed to convince the court that he had done his best to stop the coup. Ida changed his name to Iwada, and eventually became the head of a department in Japan's largest advertising agency. He died in February 2004 at the ripe old age of ninety-one.

A book on the Kyūjō incident, titled *Japan's Longest Day* was made into a feature film in 1967.

The US did have a third bomb under assembly at Tinian in the Mariana Islands where the *Enola Gay* and *Bockscar*, the B29s that had dropped the first two bombs, had flown from. The main plutonium core for the bomb was about to be shipped from the USA when the Japanese surrender was announced. Although on its casing were the words 'Tokyo Joe', it was destined for Kokura, the original target for the Nagasaki bomb. It was scheduled for 19 August. Twelve other bombs were close to completion, with the aim of releasing them throughout September and October.

It may well have been the case that if the Emperor had been prevented from surrendering, Japan would have continued to fight on. Certainly Brigadier General Bonner Fellers, an adviser to General Douglas MacArthur, believed that Hirohito's surrender 'unquestionably shortened the war by many months and prevented an estimated 450,000 American battle casualties'.

Yet, it must be recalled that the Japanese fought for their Emperor and if Tokyo had been targeted by nuclear bombs and Hirohito and his family had been killed, it is difficult to accept that the ordinary Japanese would have had the will to continue the struggle. There had already been signs of a weakening of Japanese resolve in Burma, where Japanese troops had been abandoning their defensive positions before the advancing British Fourteenth Army and discarding equipment in hasty, almost panicked retreats. The great imperial dream of Japan was already fading before Hiroshima and Nagasaki.

Hirohito's surrender may have saved Japan from complete destruction but, remarkable as it may seem more than seventy years later, there are still US forces in garrison in Japan.

NOTES:
1. Edward Behr, *Hirohito, Behind the Myth* (Hamish Hamilton, London, 1989), p.361.
2. John Toland, *Rising Sun, The Decline and Fall of the Japanese Empire 1936-1945* (Pen & Sword, Barnsley, 2011), pp.814-5.
3. ibid, p.812.

Selected Bibliography and Sources

Chapter 1
Alexandrov, Victor, *The Tuchachevsky Affair* (Prentice-Hall, Englewood Cliffs, NJ, 1964).
Brackman, Roman, *The Secret File of Joseph Stalin: A Hidden Life* (Taylor & Francis, New York, 2003).
Brook-Shepard, Gordon, *The Storm Petrels: The Flight of the First Soviet Defectors* (Ballantine Books, New York, 1977).
Medvedev, Roy Aleksandrovich, and Shriver, George, *Let History Judge: The Origin and Consequences of Stalinism* (Columbia University Press, New York, 1989).
Montefiore, Simon Sebag, *Stalin: Court of the Red Tsar* (Vintage Books, New York, 2005).
Rogovin, Vadim, *1937: Stalin's Year of Terror* (Mehring Books, 1998).
Skoblin History Blog, http://skoblin.blogspot.com, accessed 4 October 2011. This source contains the records of the purge trials of Marshal Tukhachevsky and others and the rehabilitation measures taken after the Soviet XX Party Congress.
Stoecker, Sally W., *Forging Staling's Army: Marshal Tuckhachevsky and the Politics of Military Innovation* (Westview Press, Boulder, CO, 1998).
Tucker, Robert C., *Stalin in Power: The Revolution From Above, 1928-1941* (W.W. Norton & Co., New York, 1962).

Chapter 2
The National Archives:
MEPO 3/1713, George Andrew McMahon attempt on the life of H.M. King Edward VIII at Constitution Hill on 16 July 1936.
KV 2/1506, Security Service Personnel Files, Right Wing Extremists.

Chapter 3
Duggan, Christopher, *Fascist Voives, An Intimate History of Mussolini's Italy* (Bodley Head, London, 201).
Lamb, Richard, *War in Italy, 1943-1945: A Brutal Story* (St Martin's Press, 1994).

Chapter 4
Allingham, Margery, *The Oaken Heart* (Michael Joseph, 1941).
Charmley, John, *Churchill: The End of Glory* (Hodder & Stoughton, 1993).
Hastings, Max, *Finest Years* (Harper Press, 2009).
Knightley, Philip, *Philby: The Life and Views of the KGB Masterspy* (Andre Deutsch, 1988).
Reynolds, David, *In Command of History* (Penguin, 2004).
Roberts, Andrew, *The Holy Fox: A Biography of Lord Halifax* (Weidenfeld & Nicholson, 1991).

Stoner, Julia Camoys, *Sherman's Wife: A Wartime Childhood Among the English Catholic Aristocracy* (Bennett & Bloom, 2006).

Chapter 6
Payne, Robert, *The Life and Death of Gandhi* (The Bodley Head, London, 1969).

Chapter 7
Rigden, Denis, *Kill the Führer, Section X and Operation Foxley* (The History Press, 2009).
Seaman, Mark, *Operation Foxley, the British Plan to Kill Hitler* (PRO, 1998).

Chapter 8
Berthon, Simon, *Allies at War* (HarperCollins, London, 2001).
Clark, S.F., *The Man Who is France: The Story of Charles De Gaulle* (Harrup, 1960).
Danchev, Alex and Todman, Daniel, *War Diaries 1939-1945, Field Marshal Lord Alanbrooke,* (Weidenfeld & Nicholson, London, 2001).
General de Gaulle, *War Memoirs, The Call to Honour, 1940-1942, Documents* (Collins, London, 1955).
Grehan, John, *Churchill's Secret Invasion, Britain's First Large-Scale Combined Operations Offensive 1942* (Pen & Sword, Barnsley, 2013).

Chapter 9
Duffy, James P. and Ricci, Vincent L., *Target Hitler, The Plots to Kill Adolph Hitler* (Praeger, London, 1992).
Fest, Joachim, *Plotting Hitler's Death, The German Resistance to Hitler 1933-1945* (Phoenix, London, 1997).
Gill, Anton, *An Honourable Defeat, A History of German Resistance to Hitler, 1933-1945* (Henry Holt, New York, 1994).
Schlabrendorff, Fabian von, *The Secret War against Hitler* (Hodder & Stoughton, London, 1966).
Schrader, Helena, *Codename Valkyries, General Friedrich Olbricht and the Plot Against Hitler* (Haynes Publishing, Yeovil, 2009).

Chapter 10
Moran, Lord. *Winston Churchill – The struggle for survival 1940/65* (London. Constable, 1966).
Pelling, Henry, *Winston Churchill* (Ware, Wordsworth, 1999).

Chapter 12
Greentree, David, *Knight's Move, The Hunt for Marshal Tito 1944* (Osprey, Oxford, 2012).

Chapter 13
Kramarz, Joachim, *Stauffenberg: The Architect of the Famous July 20th Conspiracy to Assassinate Hitler* (Macmillan, New York, 1967).
Moorhouse, Roger, *Killing Hitler, The Third Reich and the Plots against the Führer* (Jonathan Cape, London, 2006).
Warlimont, Walter, *Inside Hitler's Headquarters* (Weidenfeld & Nicolson, London, 1964).

Chapter 14
Behr, Edward, *Hirohito, Behind the Myth* (Hamish Hamilton, London, 1989).
Toland, John, *Rising Sun, The Decline and Fall of the Japanese Empire 1936-1945* (Pen & Sword, Barnsley, 2011).